The Communicative Syllabus

Open Linguistics Series

The *Open Linguistics Series,* to which this book makes a significant contribution, is 'open' in two senses. First, it provides an open forum for works associated with any school of linguistics or with none. Linguistics has now emerged from a period in which many (but never all) of the most lively minds in the subject seemed to assume that transformational-generative grammar — or at least something fairly closely derived from it — would provide the main theoretical framework for linguistics for the foreseeable future. In Kuhn's terms, linguistics had appeared to some to have reached the 'paradigm' stage. Reality today is very different. More and more scholars are working to improve and expand theories that were formerly scorned for not accepting as central the particular set of concerns highlighted in the Chomskyan approach — such as Halliday's systemic theory (as exemplified in this book) Lamb's stratificational model and Pike's tagmemics — while others are developing new theories. The series is open to all approaches, then — including work in the generativist-formalist tradition.

The second sense in which the series is 'open' is that it encourages works that open out 'core' linguistics in various ways: to encompass discourse and the description of natural texts; to explore the relationship between linguistics and its neighbouring disciplines such as psychology, sociology, philosophy, artificial intelligence, and cultural and literary studies; and to apply it in fields such as education and language pathology.

Open Linguistics Series Editor
Robin F. Fawcett, University of Wales College of Cardiff

Modal Expressions in English, Michael R. Perkins
Text and Tagmeme, Kenneth L. Pike and Evelyn G. Pike
The Semiotics of Culture and Language, eds: Robin P. Fawcett, M.A.K. Halliday, Sydney M. Lamb and Adam Makkai
Into the Mother Tongue: A Case Study in Early Language Development, Clare Painter
Language and the Nuclear Arms Debate: Nukespeak Today, ed.: Barbara Couture
The Structure of Social Interaction: A Systemic Approach to the Semiotics of Service Encounters, Eija Ventola
Grammar in the Construction of Texts, ed.: James Monaghan
On Meaning, A.J. Griemas, trans. by Paul Perron and Frank Collins
Biological Metaphor and Cladistic Classification: An Interdisciplinary Approach, eds: Henry M. Hoenigswald and Linda F. Wiener
New Developments in Systemic Linguistics, Volume 1: Theory and Description, eds: M.A. Halliday and Robin P. Fawcett
Volume 2: Theory and Application, eds: Robin P. Fawcett and David Young
Eloquence and Power: The Rise of Language Standards and Standard Language, John Earl Joseph
Functions of Style, eds: David Birch and Michael O'Toole
Registers of Written English: Situational Factors and Linguistic Features, ed.: Mohsen Ghadessy
Pragmatics, Discourse and Text, ed.: Erich H. Steiner and Robert Veltman

THE COMMUNICATIVE SYLLABUS

A Systemic-Functional Approach to Language Teaching

ROBIN MELROSE

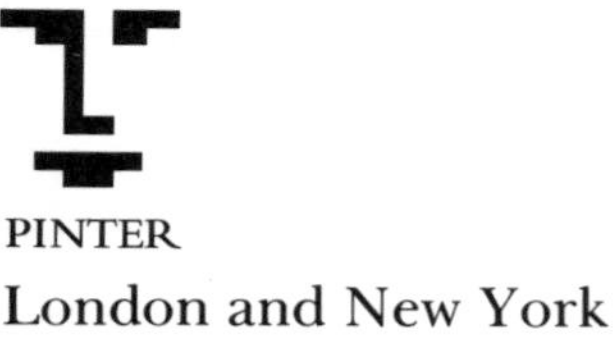

PINTER
London and New York

PINTER
A Cassell Imprint
Wellington House, 125 Strand, London WC2R 0BB
215 Park Avenue South, New York, New York 10003, USA

First published 1991
Paperback edition first published 1995

British Library Cataloguing-in-Publication Data
A catalogue record for this book is available from the British Library

ISBN 1 85567 341 X

Typeset by The Castlefield Press Ltd, Wellingborough, Northants
Printed and bound in Great Britain by Biddles Ltd, Guildford and King's Lynn

Contents

List of figures

List of tables

Foreword

I am particularly delighted that this book is being published in the *Open Linguistics Series* (of which I am the Editor) because I have been associated with the book, one way or another, from the time of its conception by the author — and indeed from well before that time. Let me explain.

In the 1960s I worked in the world of Teaching English as a Foreign Language (TEFL), in Kenya. After I returned to Britain, I worked on a PhD at University College London in which I sought to answer the question: 'What linguistic theory, or theories, holds out the best hope of capturing the psychological reality of language and its use, and so provides the best basis for planning language teaching courses?' This led me to Halliday's Systemic Functional Grammar (SFG) — a theory in which I continue to work happily and, I think, fruitfully — and my thesis (published as Fawcett 1980) expounds a version of SFG which adds to Halliday's social emphasis a specifically cognitive dimension. Since then my interests have been centred in theoretical and descriptive linguistics (and more recently in computational linguistics), but I have retained an interest in my original field of application. Thus it was that I contributed to the AILA/BAAL seminar organized by Chris Candlin (who now holds a Chair at Macquarie University, Sydney) entitled 'The Communicative Teaching of English'. This was among the first public uses of the term 'communicative' in relation to language teaching — indeed, perhaps it was *the* first. The 'communicative approach', in which Candlin and others at the conference such as Wilkins were to play a significant role, became the dominant force in language teaching throughout the 1970s and 1980s. Melrose provides, in the early part of this volume, an excellent overview of the movement.

Then in 1980 I was invited by the British Council to visit Nigeria and to lecture on the communicative approach to TEFL. As I read my way through the then recent books in the field (e.g. works by Brumfitt, Munby, Widdowson, Wilkins and others, as well as various text books that exemplified these principles) I was delighted to find the strength of the 'functional' influence — superimposed, as it were, on the preceding dominant concept, the 'situational' approach, which had in its turn replaced the 'grammatical' approach.

But there seemed to be a gap; by that time, there was a growing awareness that 'grammar' could not be thrown out completely, but no one was showing explicitly how to make the link that seemed to be demanded: that between the higher level functions and notions that language mediates, and the forms of syntax, lexis and intonation. To me, as to any systemic linguist, the way to make that connection is obvious: via (1) the *system networks* of choice in the 'meaning potential' of the language that are foregrounded in SFG, and (2) the concept of 'pre-selection' (with relative or absolute probabilities) from the higher components into the system networks of the lexico-grammar. In other words, if the material in the 'grammar' part of language teaching syllabuses were to consist of *a series of more and more complex system networks* for each of the various functional components into which a grammar may be divided, together, of course, with the rules that realize them in syntax, lexis and intonation, then we would have a helpful marriage of (1) the new emphasis on functional 'meaning' and (2) the re-emphasis on the centrality of grammar. And 'above' those would be various 'higher' semiotic systems, each again of increasing complexity as the syllabus developed.

I lectured along these lines in Nigeria, and on my return I published a short article in *Network* (Fawcett 1981), describing the visit and suggesting that we urgently needed someone to work on this. I even described the sort of qualifications needed for the task: '(1) at least seven years of experience of English language teaching; (2) probably a postgraduate TEFL qualification; and (3) familiarity with systemic linguistics'.

It was Robin Melrose, whose background fitted these specifications almost exactly, who responded. While he already held a PhD (on a literary topic), he proposed doing a second PhD, part time, with me, on the topic proposed. It is a revised version of that PhD thesis that you now have in your hands.

Melrose has brought to the work a wealth of practical experience of both teaching and working with teachers, and he has drawn on the work of Halliday, Martin, myself and others, as well as introducing significant new theoretical ideas of his own. The result is a book that should be used as a challenge to students everywhere who are taking postgraduate courses in language teaching. This book does not prescribe a full syllabus from beginner to advanced learner, but it shows by its detailed analyses of the syllabuses underlying recent communicatively oriented textbooks just what is needed in a full communicative syllabus. I anticipate that this invaluable book will prove a stimulus to a considerable amount of further work which, like the present book, offers an integrated approach to multi-level, multi-functional syllabus design.

This book will make challenging — indeed, exciting — reading for all who are involved in this important field: a field that probably employs more students of language than all of the rest of theoretical and applied linguistics put together.

Robin P. Fawcett
Cregrina, August 1991

REFERENCES

Fawcett, R.P., 1980. *Cognitive Linguistics and Social Interaction: Towards an Integrated Model of a Systemic Functional Grammar and the Other Components of an Interacting Mind.* Heidelberg, Julius Groos/Exeter University.

Fawcett, Robin P., 1981. 'Systemic linguistics and English Language Teaching: a proposal arising from a visit to Nigeria', in *Network No. 2,* pp. 32–4.

1. The principles (and practice) of communicative language teaching

1.0 INTRODUCTION

This book is directed at two readerships who, until a few years ago, used to be one (or virtually one): applied linguists and language teaching specialists. Indeed, about fifteen or twenty years ago we thought we had found the great overarching principle that would guide the development of the subject into the twenty-first century: the communicative approach. Yet today there is a deep and uncomfortable divide in our field. For while the communicative approach drew its initial inspiration from linguistics, it now looks increasingly to educational theory, psychology and ethnography to show it the way forward. Linguistics still, necessarily, has a part to play in communicative language teaching, but for many practitioners it has only a supporting role (the faithful retainer, perhaps?).

In this book I hope to show that linguistics does indeed have the potential to be a star, to match the performance of those players at present strutting the stage. But first we need to look at the linguistic origins of the communicative approach, then trace its drift away from its parent discipline.

1.1 THE ORIGINS OF COMMUNICATIVE LANGUAGE TEACHING

From the Second World War to the mid 1970's, language teaching was dominated by the oral–aural (audio-lingual) method. This assumed the approach to grammar of *immediate constituent analysis,* as developed by Leonard Bloomfield and his successors. The aim of immediate constituent analysis was to describe the structure of sentences without recourse to meaning (since, Bloomfield and his followers believed, descriptions of meaning were best left to anthropologists and sociologists). And since these sentences were all learnt as responses to particular stimuli, a model lesson for a proponent of the audio-lingual method might consist, in part at least, of uttering not very meaningful sentences in response to even less meaningful stimuli (cues), on the principle that learning a language meant learning its structures, that is, its syntactic patterns. Traditional immediate constituent analysis, of course, was largely swept aside, from 1957 on, by Chomsky's transformational-generative grammar, but the reluctance to deal with meaning lingered on for another few years. Finally, however, the outcast was readmitted to polite society: by the mid 1960's, at the urging of colleagues such as Katz and Fodor, Chomsky had introduced a meaning component into his model; and by the late 1960's the study of meaning had become a respectable area of study in mainstream linguistics.

With this change in the status of meaning in linguistics, it is perhaps not surprising that a new approach to language learning should emerge. The variously named 'functional', 'notional' or 'functional-notional' approach to language learning (for such were the names given to this early type of communicative syllabus) was first developed in the early 1970's, encouraged by the Council of Europe's research and development concerning the implementation of a European unit/credit system for modern language learning by adults. Its emergence dates from 1972 and the third International Congress of Applied Linguists in Copenhagen (see Wilkins 1972), but it came to the attention of a wider public with the works of van Ek (1975), Wilkins (1976), Widdowson (1978) and Munby (1978). And it began being used commonly in the classroom with the publication of the first functional-notional course books, such as Abbs and Freebairn's *Starting Strategies* (1977). It owes very little to transformational-generative grammar, but much to the interest in the study of meaning stimulated by Chomsky's *(Aspects of the Theory of Syntax* (1965) and by the work of the founder of systemic-functional grammar, M. A. K. Halliday. This study involved at least three areas of linguistics: (pure) linguistics, sociolinguistics and linguistic philosophy, which all had an influence on the functional-notional approach.

1.1.1. Pure linguistics

The only linguist working in a transformational-generative framework to have had any obvious influence on the new approach was Charles Fillmore. He developed a model called Case Grammar (see Fillmore 1968), which defines a level of deep structure more abstract and more 'semantic' than the standard deep structure level (see Chomsky 1957, 1965). Briefly, Fillmore proposed that in deep structure a sentence has two immediate constituents, Modality (tense, mood, aspect and negative elements), and Proposition (the verb plus the cases). The cases, or underlying semantic roles – which may or may not be marked in surface structure – proved difficult to determine, but the following list, taken from Fillmore (1971), is typical: Agent, Experiencer, Instrument, Source, Goal, Place, Time, Path and Object. These cases enabled Fillmore to show that elements with different surface forms could have the same underlying semantic role, as in these sentences:

1. John opened the door with the key.
2. The key opened the door.
3. The door opened.

Thus in Fillmore's analysis 'key' is Instrument in both 1 and 2, and 'door' is Object in both 2 and 3.

Much more influential in the new approach to language teaching was the British linguist M. A. K. Halliday, who, just at the time that Fillmore was putting forward his proposals for Case Grammar, was publishing similar but independently reached proposals, in the framework of what was to develop into systemic-functional grammar. Halliday, then as now, was concerned with a 'semantically significant' grammar, with that part of the grammar which is 'closest to' the semantics (see Halliday 1966); and this concern is embodied in his work on transitivity – whose participants and circumstances resemble Fillmore's cases – and theme (see Halliday 1967–8), and on modality and mood (Halliday 1970).

Like his teacher Firth and the anthropologist Malinowski (see Malinowski 1923), Halliday holds a functional view of language. In 1970 (see Kress 1976: 19–24) he argued that, although there are innumerable social purposes for which adults use language, these are reduced in the internal organization of the language system to a small set of functional components, or 'macro-functions' (later renamed 'metafunctions'). The experiential is the expression of experience – the phenomena of the external world and those of consciousness – and is realized by the processes, participants and circumstances of transitivity. The interpersonal component expresses the speaker's role in the speech situation, his/her personal commitment and his/her interaction with others; in the clause it is represented by mood and modality. The textual expresses the structure of information, and the relation of each part in the discourse to the whole and to the setting; it is realized in the grammar by theme and information focus. The message from Fillmore and Halliday was that grammar need no longer be analysed exclusively 'bottom up', as rules of combination, but could also be approached 'top down', as reflecting speakers' meanings – though Halliday went beyond Fillmore's cases (Halliday's participants and circumstances) to include, for example, modality (the grammar of probabilities and obligations, not to be confused with Fillmore's Modality), theme and information focus. In addition, Halliday showed how grammar reflects the broad functions which language is called upon to serve.

But Halliday also took a further step, one which was not available to Fillmore, and introduced context of situation into his model. This concept was first put forward by Malinowski (1923), and later taken up by Firth (1957). In Halliday *et al* (1964) context of situation was characterized in terms of field of discourse (social situation and subject matter), style of discourse (the relationship between the participants) and mode of discourse (the channel of communication). Halliday subsequently (1972) established a link between field and transitivity, tenor (formerly style) and modality/mood, and between mode and theme/information focus. This insight was of obvious value to those developing the new functional-notional approach, reinforced as it was by the contributions of sociolinguistics.

1.1.2 Sociolinguistics

The American sociolinguist Dell Hymes provided researchers into the functional-notional syllabus with the concept of *communicative competence*. In transformational-generative grammar, sentences were said to be *grammatical* with regard to competence and *acceptable* with regard to performance; but Hymes (1972b) maintained that a sentence must also be *appropriate* in relation to the context in which it is used, and that speakers of a language have communicative competence – a knowledge of appropriacy – just as they have (linguistic) competence – a knowledge of grammar. Appropriacy to context is related to a number of situational factors, summed up by Hymes (1972a) by the acronym SPEAKING: setting, participants, ends (aims and results of the communication), acts (the form and sequence of the message), key (the manner of delivery), instrumentalities (the channel of communication), norms (conduct of the participants) and genre. This approach to situation appeared to offer a more detailed model than the one presented by Halliday, without, however, indicating the ways in which situation could be reflected in grammar.

1.1.3. Linguistic philosophy

A fundamental influence on the development of the functional-notional approach was the British philosopher J. L. Austin and his work *How to do Things with Words* (1962). Austin, starting from a division of utterances into constatives (true or false statements) and performatives (utterances used to do things), ended up with the claim that all utterances simultaneously perform three kinds of acts: locutionary act (the propositional content), illocutionary act (the conventional force of an utterance, e.g. statement, offer, promise) and perlocutionary act (the effect of the utterance on the addressee). The most important of these for Austin was the illocutionary act (or speech act), of which Austin distinguished five general classes: verdictives (e.g. assess, estimate, describe, analyse); exercitives (e.g. order, warn, urge, advise); commissives (e.g. promise, intend, agree); behabitives (e.g. apologise, thank, congratulate); and expositives (e.g. affirm, deny, state, conclude, define).

The best known treatment of speech acts after Austin was that of Searle (1969). In discussing performatives, Austin had spoken of felicity conditions which performatives must meet if they are to succeed. Searle suggested that felicity conditions are jointly constitutive of speech acts, that is, they are rules in accordance with which speech acts are created and comprehended. Felicity conditions are of four types, depending on how they specify propositional content, preparatory preconditions, sincerity conditions and the essential condition, and can be used to compare different speech acts. Searle also offered a classification of speech acts supposedly based on felicity conditions: representatives (e.g. assert, conclude); directives (e.g. request, question); commissives (e.g. promise, threaten, offer); expressives (e.g. apologize, thank, congratulate); and declarations (e.g. excommunicate, declare war).

The concept that in uttering sentences one is also doing things is a cornerstone of the functional-notional syllabus, as we shall see in the next section.

1.2 THE FUNCTIONAL-NOTIONAL SYLLABUS

To understand the nature of that first manifestation of the communicative approach, the functional-notional syllabus, we should first examine David Wilkins's pioneering work *Notional Syllabuses* (1976). The work opens with a critique of the two types of syllabus then currently in use, the grammatical and the situational. The grammatical syllabus, says Wilkins (1976: 2), is 'one in which the different parts of language are taught separately and step-by-step so that acquisition is a process of gradual accumulation of the parts until the whole structure of the language has been built up'. His main criticism of the grammatical syllabuses seems to be that language learning is not complete when the content of a grammatical syllabus has been mastered: learning grammatical form does not guarantee the learning of grammatical meaning, and to describe the grammatical form of a sentence does not account for the way it is used as an utterance. (Wilkins is presumably saying that a formal description does not account for 'semantically significant' grammar or illocutionary force.)

Situational syllabuses, instead of being an inventory of grammatical forms, are a list of situations in which the learner may find him/herself, and a description of the linguistic content of each of these situations. The chief drawback of this approach, says Wilkins, is that situation does not necessarily predict language, and is unhelpful in the case of speech acts such as requesting or agreeing/disagreeing, which are used in a variety of situations.

After his critique of grammatical and situational syllabuses, Wilkins goes on to discuss the notional syllabus. Its starting point is 'the desired communicative capacity'; it does not ask how speakers of the language express themselves, but 'what it is they communicate through language'; it is organized 'in terms of the content rather than the form of the language' (Wilkins 1976: 18). In a notional syllabus it is assumed that speakers will need to express three kinds of meanings: semantico-grammatical categories (perceptions of events, processes, states and abstractions); modality (speaker attitude); and categories of communicative function (speech acts).

The semantico-grammatical categories (roughly corresponding to Fillmore's cases and Halliday's participants, processes and circumstances) consist of Time, Quantity, Space, Relational Meaning and Deixis. Modality includes scale of certainty (impersonalized and personalized) and scale of commitment (intention and obligation). The categories of communicative function include Judgement and evaluation (e.g. assess, excuse, approve, blame, disapprove); Suasion (e.g. advise, order, warn, threaten, permit); Argument (e.g. inform, request, refuse, agree, disagree); Rational enquiry and exposition (e.g. conclude, compare, define, explain); Personal emotions (e.g. pleasure, displeasure); and Emotional relations (e.g. greetings, sympathy, gratitude).

The first task of a notional syllabus designer, then, is to choose the types of meaning to be learned; once this has been accomplished, s/he must decide by what linguistic forms these meanings are to be expressed. Here, says Wilkins (1976: 57), the situational syllabus has a contribution to make: the 'choice between the different grammatical structures by which one function may be realized will be largely determined by the exact sociolinguistic (or stylistic) conditions under which communication is taking place'.

Thus the notional syllabus will present an inventory of concepts (semantico-grammatical categories) and functions (categories of communicative function) to be learned, together with linguistic forms by which each concept or function may be expressed, and a specification of the sociolinguistic conditions determining individual forms. Figure 1.1 is a representation of this model. Here concepts and functions are expressed in linguistic forms only after being filtered through sociolinguistic conditions. In fact Wilkins had very little to say about sociolinguistic conditions, limiting himself mainly to degrees of formality and channel (1976: 62–4), and he was vague about how sociolinguistic conditions might determine grammatical structures. For a fuller treatment of sociolinguistic conditions we need to turn to the work of another proponent of the functional-notional syllabus.

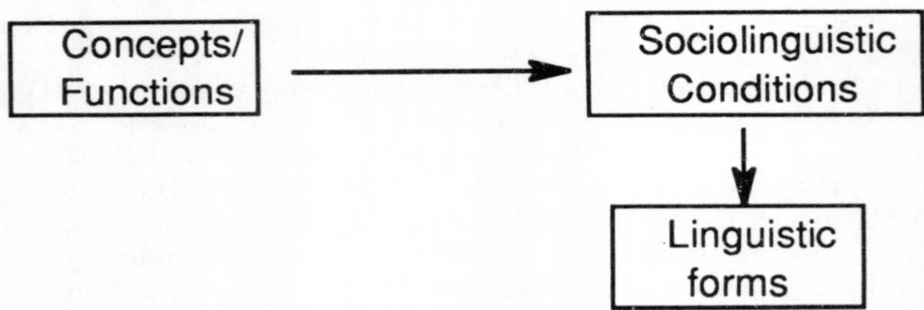

Figure 1.1 A notional syllabus model

1.3 DESIGNING A FUNCTIONAL-NOTIONAL SYLLABUS

Working within the same theoretical framework as Wilkins, Munby (1978: 31) presents a model for specifying communicative competence (see Figure 1.2). This model, it is claimed, enables a syllabus designer with all the relevant data at his/her disposal to produce a *communicative* syllabus (Munby's term) appropriate to the needs of a specific learner or group of learners. It works like this. Relevant information about the identity and language of the participant (learner) is first collected and referred to the Communicative Needs Processor. This takes account of the variables that affect communication needs (Wilkins's sociolinguistic conditions), by 'organising them as parameters in a dynamic relationship to each other' (Munby 1978: 32) – dynamic because, as the following list shows, parameters (e) to (h) depend on input from (a) to (d) before they can become operational:

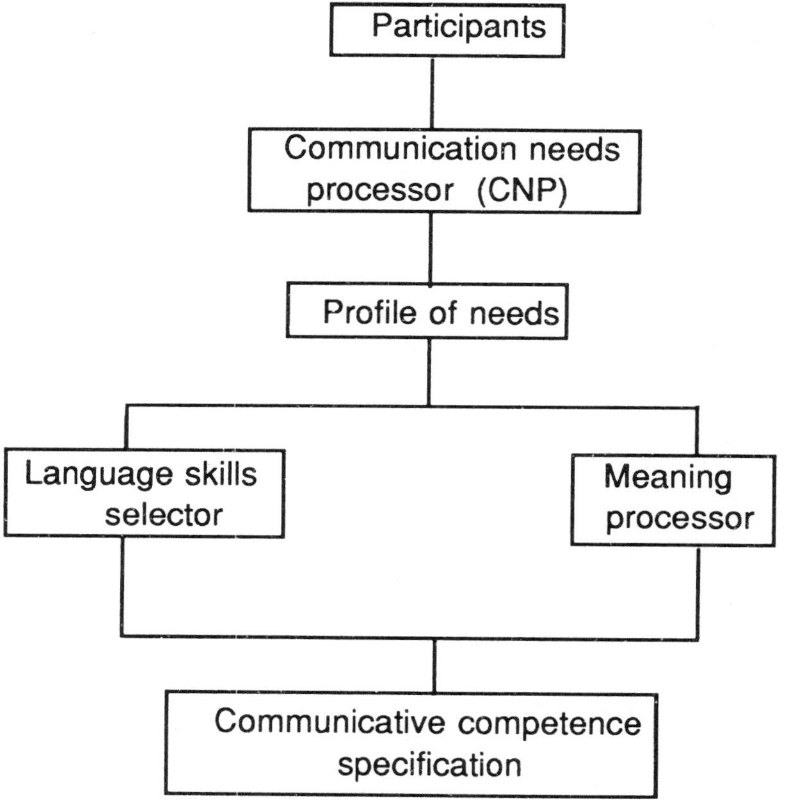

Figure 1.2 Model for specifying communicative competence (Munby 1978)

Variables of the Communication Needs Processor
(a) Purposive domain (the occupational or educational purpose for which the target language is required).
(b) Setting (physical and psychosocial).
(c) Interaction (position, role-set, social relationships).
(d) Instrumentality (medium, mode and channel of communication).
(e) Dialect.
(f) Target level.
(g) Communicative event (what the participant has to do).
(h) Communicative key (attitude).

Once the participants communication needs have been processed, a profile of needs emerges, which provides the input to the language skills selector and the meaning processor.

In the language skills selector, says Munby (1978: 40), 'the profile of needs is interpreted in terms of the specific language skills that are required to realise the events or activities that have been identified in the CNP'. In his taxonomy of language skills, both receptive and productive (1978: 123–31), Munby lists fifty-four skills. It is rather difficult to summarize the list: broadly speaking, it consists of Wilkin's concepts (semantico-grammatical categories); the cohesive relations discussed by Halliday and Hasan (1976); the rhetorical skills advocated by Widdowson (1978); discourse acts as outlined by Sinclair and Coulthard (1975); phonology (including stress and intonation) and graphology; skimming and scanning; and library skills.

In the meaning processor, communicative needs are converted into micro-functions (illocutionary acts, or, in Wilkins's terms, categories of communicative function plus modality). The micro-functions are as follows:

Categories of micro-functions

(a) Scale of certainty (impersonalized and personalized).
(b) Scale of commitment (intention and obligation).
(c) Judgement and evaluation (valuation, verdiction, approval, disapproval).
(d) Suasion (inducement, compulsion, prediction, tolerance).
(e) Argument (information, agreement, disagreement, concession).
(f) Rational enquiry and exposition.
(g) Formulaic communication.

A micro-function is then marked for attitudinal tone (using categories from the communicative key parameter of the CNP); at this point, selection of an appropriate linguistic form can proceed.

I shall now present a simplified version of Munby's model, reformulated in terms of Wilkins's categories (see Figure 1.3). In his model Munby has clearly filled a gap left by Wilkins in specifying sociolinguistic conditions (the variables of the Communicative Needs Processor). However, if it was Munby's intention to establish a firm link between sociolinguistic conditions, language skills, functions and linguistic forms, it cannot be said that he was any more successful than Wilkins – though his use of attitudinal-tone is an advance on Wilkins. In his language skills selector Munby has also introduced two important elements lacking in Wilkins's notional syllabus, discourse (that is, rhetorical skills and discourse acts), mentioned only fleetingly by Wilkins (1976: 49), and cohesion.

1.4 TOWARDS A MORE 'COMMUNICATIVE' CURRICULUM

1.4.1 The process approach

It seems that with Munby's work second language pedagogy had pushed the applications of linguistics to syllabus design as far as they could go, for shortly afterwards certain advocates of communicative language teaching abandoned the path of linguistics and set off in a new direction. One of the earliest

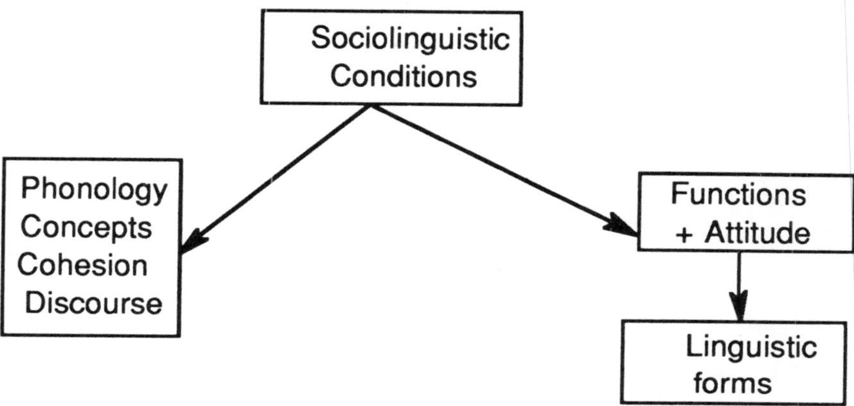

Figure 1.3 Munby's model simplified and reformulated

attempts to chart this new direction – and develop what might be called a *process approach* to language teaching – was a paper by Michael Breen and Christopher Candlin published in *Applied Linguistics* (1980). Their rejection of the role of linguistics is largely unspoken, stated only once, in a rather offhand way, in note 7 (1980: 109), which also indicates strong reservations about the functional-notional approach:

> The 'functional' aspect of language seems, at first sight, a . . . realistic basis for language teaching. However, it seems to us that recent efforts to incorporate 'Functions' into language teaching are based on inappropriate and quite misleading assumptions. First, that Functions are 'items' like categories of grammar or rules of syntax; second, that an utterance is likely to be associated with a single Function; and, third, that there is a predictable relationship between a Function and its syntactic or textual realisation. These assumptions seem to derive from the tendency to apply textual criteria alone to every aspect of language use.

So if communicative language teaching is not to be functional, what is it to be? What are the 'essentials' of a communicative curriculum? Obviously the answer to these questions is closely linked to the way Breen and Candlin envisage communication. Language learning, they say (1980: 90), is 'learning how to communicate as a member of a particular socio-cultural group'; therefore, the 'social conventions governing language form and behaviour within the group' are central to the process of language learning. But the social conventions are not fixed:

> these conventions are subject to variation while they are being used. In exploring shared knowledge, participants will be modifying that

knowledge. They typically exploit a tension between the conventions that are established and the opportunity to modify these conventions for their particular communicative purposes. Communicating is not merely a matter of following conventions but also of negotiating through and about the conventions themselves.

For this reason a communicative curriculum will specify its purposes not only in terms of a 'particular target repertoire' based on a 'sociolinguistic analysis of the target situation' (a nod in the direction of Munby, perhaps), but also in terms of the target competence which will underline and generate such a repertoire' (Breen and Candlin 1980: 91). Essential to this target competence are the 'communicative abilities of interpretation, expression, and negotiation' (1980: 92). This implies that the learner has an important contribution to make to the curriculum, and that we must rid ourselves of a 'partial and knowledge-based view of learner competence' and exploit the 'learner's communicative abilities underlying the initial repertoire' (1980: 93).

Within the framework of this view of communication and the purposes of the communicative curriculum, language learning 'may be seen as a process which grows out of the interaction between learners, teachers, texts and activities' (1980: 95). The learner's communicative abilities will develop in 'an arena of co-operative negotiation, joint interpretation, and the sharing of expression', and be activated by a range of different text types in different media which the participants 'can make use of to develop their competence through a variety of activities and tasks' (1980: 95). It is therefore not surprising that Breen and Candlin should claim that 'a communicative methodology will . . . exploit the classroom as a resource with its own communicative potential', for it is the 'meeting-place of all other resources – learners, teachers, and texts', each of which 'has sufficiently heterogeneous characteristics to make classroom-based negotiation a necessary undertaking' (1980: 98–9). The classroom is only artificial, they say (1980: 99), coming rather close to criticizing the functional-notional approach, if 'we treat it as a rehearsal studio where "actors" learn the lines from some pre-scripted target repertoire for a performance at some later time and place'.

What is the content of a communicative curriculum? Language teaching curricula typically specify a target repertoire consisting of a list of structures, functions and/or themes (topics), but the communicative curriculum does not do this, on the grounds that a static inventory of language items does nothing to foster an understanding of the 'dynamic conventions of communication', does not encourage the 'development and refinement of underlying competence', and hinders the activation and refinement of the process competences of different learners' (1980: 102). Instead, the communicative curriculum 'place[s] content within methodology and provide[s] it with the role of servant to the teaching–learning process': content is selected by learners and teachers so that the learner can 'use' the content of the curriculum as the "carrier" of his process competence and as the provider of opportunities for communicative experiences through which personal routes may be selected and explored as a means to the ultimate target competence' (1980: 102). Content, say Breen and Candlin, will focus on knowledge, both cognitive and affective, that is significant to the learner; it will be organized not as a simple sequence but cyclically; and it will be subdivided in terms of 'whole frameworks', so that the emphasis is not on 'units' of content but on 'units' of activity that generate communication and metacommunication (1980: 102–3).

This paper, with the exception of the very discreet note 7, maintains a studiously 'neutral' tone; by contrast, Candlin's paper 'Design as a Critical Process', published four years later (in Brumfit 1984c), is rather more polemical, and reveals some of the thinking that underlies the earlier paper. The criticism of the functional approach is now open and pointed. Functional syllabus designers, he says (1984: 39), based their plans for syllabus organization on a 'simple reading of early speech act theory . . . where acts were seen as discrete items to which . . . linguistic forms could be mapped on by *fiat,* or else in some unclear way associated by reference to "context"'. This reading of speech act theory then permitted the syllabus designers to 'adopt the "new" . . . functional units into traditional sequences' and present the change as a 'fundamental shift in syllabus conception . . . rather than mere relabelling' (1984: 38). But Candlin has a more serious charge to make against the designers of functional syllabuses (1984: 38):

> the selection of these functional items bore no evident relationship to any consideration of particular personal or culture-specific ideologies, despite the fact that to talk in terms of functions at all ought to have implied in the language teaching context an acknowledgement at least of the plurality of values. All learners, apparently, would value identically, and what is more implausible, in the same sequence and via the same linguistic forms. It is hard to imagine a greater travesty of language as a system for the exchange of meaning and value.

The seriousness of this charge can be better understood in the light of Candlin's earlier discussion of the role of ideology in syllabus design. Syllabuses, he says (1984: 30), come in two ideological forms: one which requires learners to 'bank received knowledge as a collection of "communiqués" or states of knowing', and another which encourages learners to 'explore ways of knowing, to interpret knowledge and to engage in dialogue with it and with themselves'. And he goes on to say:

> A syllabus of the former type is extrinsic, idealistic and presents a picture of static 'reality'; the latter type is personal, intrinsic and is one of 'reality' in process. Sociopolitically, we may say that the first acts to sustain some social order, the view of the world whence the syllabus came, through this unchallengeable selection and organization of content done on behalf of rather than by the learner, while the second acts to engage and challenge this world-view, through a praxis of action and reflection by all the participants to question its content and organization.

The functional syllabus is clearly of the first type and therefore ideologically suspect, since it is 'premised upon a pre-packaging of knowledge seen-as-items' and oriented to 'the institution or to the teacher as agent' (1984: 32). The communicative syllabus, on the other hand, is oriented to the learner; its 'function can only properly be one of facilitating the exploration precisely by that learner of his or her own values and ways of "cutting up the world"' (1984: 32); it is a 'dynamic and negotiated concept rather than one which is static and imposed' (1984: 33).

The ideology of communicative teaching naturally has implications for the content and implementation of the syllabus. Such a 'praxis-oriented model', says Candlin (1984: 34), would be 'appropriately realized through a series of problem-posing tasks . . . , a series of guided experiences, focusing on what is to be learned and on how and why it is to be learned'. The syllabus, then, would be organized on two levels: at one level, that of curriculum or *strategy*, would be found 'guidelines for purposes, content/experience, and evaluation', including 'banks of items and accounts of procedures for drawing upon them as open-ended examples of usable data and information' (1984: 35); the other level, that of classroom process or *tactical planning*, would 'address matters of what is to be done, what questions suggest themselves to be asked, what processes are most conducive to the exploration of the problem being addressed, what additional information is needed, what activities are worthwhile' (1984: 36). These ideals were later put into practice, with the task-based syllabus and the learner-centred curriculum (see, for example, Candlin and Murphy 1987, and Nunan 1988a, 1988b, 1989), discussed in Chapter 8 below.

It might seem from this – and here we return to our starting point – that Candlin sees no role for linguistics in communicative syllabus design. Yet he does offer the poor linguist a glimmer of hope, a foot in the communicative door when he conceeds (1984: 39) that it is not speech acts as such which pose problems for learners; rather it is:

> their particular occurrence and placing in culture-specific events and activity-types, their consequent realization in language-specific forms, and their role in conversational and written discourse which constitutes the learning problem. All such matters require an understanding of underlying principles of relation between form and function, extended contextual evidence and a process of interpersonal negotiation, themselves precisely the conditions excluded in principle or in practice by syllabuses of the first type

To which he adds encouragingly (1984: 40) that 'contemporary analyses of language in use not only insist upon meaning negotiation but have offered some procedures and practices whereby this negotiative practice can be informed by general and activity-type specific pragmatic principle'.

Any linguist who sees this as an invitation to the communicative party would do well to ponder the following view, put forward by the polemical Candlin. With reference to the disparity between what a syllabus specifies and what actually happens in the classroom, Candlin asserts (1984: 33):

accommodating these opposing forces of specification and actualization is a major problem of syllabus design and implementation. It is the view of this paper that this accommodation cannot be attained, as some of the other papers in this collection seem to suggest (see Widdowson, Brumfit, Allen and Yalden in this volume), merely by making a syllabus of the first type 'more sensitive', or by establishing a series of parallel syllabuses grounded in the same principles of design. The contradictions involved in such an approach are too deep for that.

1.4.2 The product/process approach

The process approach could not be ignored, but, as Candlin's uncompromising declaration makes clear, quite a few very respectable communicative syllabus designers were uneasy about cultivating anything more than a nodding acquaintance with this unruly new element in language teaching. Candlin singles out four applied linguists contributing to Brumfit (1984), so I shall consider their contributions, with an emphasis on their attempts to assimilate the notion of process in a basically product-oriented approach.

The least interesting of the four contributions – least interesting in being the only paper that refuses to take any explicit ideological position – is the one by Allen. His reservations about the process approach – which he refers to (1984: 65) as the 'non-analytic', experiential, or "natural growth" approach' – are apparently based on the view that, since it makes no selection of data, it is inefficient (1984: 66):

> In the interests of efficient learning, there must be some selection of data by the teacher, and various judgements about selection can be compared only if they are based on a set of descriptive categories which are capable of being interpreted systematically . . . I will continue to assume, then, that for language teaching in general we need to recognize a level of syllabus planning in which an inventory of items to be taught can be developed in a systematic and objectively verifiable way.

Selection of data entails grading, which Allen sees as a 'universal requirement in language teaching', such that even 'methods which place a high value on naturalistic, real-life input usually contain a hidden curriculum which enables the teacher to maintain control over the material, although in such cases the nature of the control is relatively unobtrusive and indirect' (1984: 66). Thus, he adds, 'the choice is not between close control, and no control at all, but between "finely tuned" (explicitly graded) and "roughly tuned" (implicitly graded) input for the learner' (1984: 66) – roughly tuned input being valuable, in Krashen's view, because (as Allen puts it) 'it reduces the anxiety level, provides more opportunities for recycling, and focuses attention on meaning rather than form' (1984: 66).

Hence a syllabus for Allen is based on an inventory of items (a product), to promote efficient learning (I hardly need insist on the ideology implied by the term *efficient*), with a dash of roughly tuned input to lessen anxiety and encourage a concern with meaning rather than form (process, but 'unobtrusively' controlled). Such a syllabus embodies what Allen calls a 'variable focus approach'. In this approach there are actually two syllabuses: a language syllabus, which includes a grammatical component and a discourse and sociolinguistic component, and a concurrent syllabus, defined in terms of cultural knowledge, other-subject content or general life experience (1984: 68). The language syllabus and the content syllabus:

> both feed into classroom methodology, which contains three interconnected activity components: structural practice . . . which is systematic and controlled on the grammatical level, functional practice . . . which is fluency-oriented and not subject to any kind of linguistic control, although we will expect it to be meaningful and organized in terms of the task being undertaken or the message being conveyed.
>
> [1984:69]

The paper by Yalden covers much the same ground as that of Allen, but is somewhat more open in proclaiming its ideology. Her starting point is that a syllabus is a public document which concerns 'the ends of the instruction, its social purpose' and also the means, though these are a 'secondary consideration' (1984: 13), implying that the syllabus 'should', in the first instance, be a specification of content, and only in a later stage of development, a statement about methodology and materials' (1984: 16). A syllabus may be either *directive* (as are structural or functional syllabuses), or *descriptive* (as in the case of the communicative syllabus advocated by Breen and Candlin), and not surprisingly Yalden opts for the directive type (1984: 15).

But what content and methodology is Yalden going to direct us to? That depends on what basis the syllabus is organized: if it is organized according to a view of how language is learned, then it will be a structural syllabus; if organized according to a view of how language is acquired, then a process approach is called for; if the basis of organization is a view of how language is used, then there will be an attempt to forecast the possible settings for use of the target language (1984: 16–17). Yalden favours an organization based on a view of how language is used, which will 'stress the connections between present study and future use' and will 'exploit the "inter-organism" rather than the "intra-organism": aspects of the second language development in the classroom' (1984: 17). This means, explains Yalden (1984: 18), that 'settings' will provide the content, and 'structures' and 'process' will supply materials and methodology.

The actual working of the syllabus is not entirely clear, though it is probably similar to Allen's variable focus approach. The organization, Yalden says (1984: 18), is 'semantic': the linguistic component is treated 'non-systematically', and is 'derived from functional areas of language use'; the component that provides continuity is the 'theme', which may be 'subject-matter related' or 'of general interest' and is chosen 'in terms of the needs and wishes of the learners' (1984: 19). Thus, despite her advocacy of a directive syllabus, Yalden directs with a light touch – the theme is chosen in accordance with the needs and wishes of the learners, the functions are treated non-systematically: product flirting with process.

Widdowson and Brumfit both oppose Candlin on explicitly ideological, almost 'political', grounds. Widdowson's paper starts with the observation that education makes provision both for future social role and for individual development, and that different education systems give different weightings to each of these general purposes (1984: 23). Now a syllabus that allows learners to negotiate their own progress through communicative activities in class with minimum intervention from the teacher (what Widdowson, after Bernstein, calls the person-oriented approach) may be acceptable in a system that favours individual development, he continues (1984: 24), but in a system oriented towards future social role such a syllabus will cause problems. In any case, he contends (1984: 25), proponents of the person-oriented approach are not motivated solely by pedagogic considerations, for they are also influenced by an educational ideology which 'proclaims the rights of individuals against the imposition of institutional control'. But the control imposed by a syllabus has a positive side – it provides for 'security', it serves as a 'convenient map'. To which he adds, in what might also be a cry against the excesses of Thatcherite Britain: 'Freedom of action . . . is anyway only meaningful when bounded by constraint of one kind or another; without such constraint, initiative tends to dissipate in anomie, a state of disorientation and normlessness.'

As for the nature of this 'convenient map', Widdowson has only some general remarks to offer. A syllabus, he ventures (1984: 26), might be defined as a 'stereotypic construct which provides a point of reference for procedural work in classrooms which converts the stereotypes into actuality'. Apparently it does not matter to Widdowson which stereotypes are used – structures, functions and notions, or Firthian situations – as long as they are regarded not as rules for determining what is to be learned but as points of reference: in short, a process approach to a product-based syllabus.

The position taken by Brumfit seems close to Widdowson's stance. He is in favour of 'using what can be systematized as the *basis* for . . . syllabus development, and allowing what cannot be systematized to spiral round a core' (process dancing around product); and he believes that 'since the syntactic system is generative and therefore economical, there are not yet compelling reasons to discard it as the most fundamental component of the language syllabus' (1984: 78). When it comes to systematization, there are three types of analysis available (1984: 77–8): linguistic analysis (e.g. analysis of syntax or of semantic categories); interactional analysis (e.g. of situational and functional categories); and analysis of what is talked or written about (e.g. of literature, culture or content subjects). Each analysis has produced different approaches to language teaching: the linguistic analysis has given rise to the grammar-translation and audiolingual methods, the interactional to certain types of ESP course, and the content analysis to Prabhu's Bangalore programme of problem-solving activities, or to the Canadian immersion programmes (1984: 78).

Although Brumfit does not mention Candlin by name, he makes no secret of his opposition to the approach that Candlin advocates. For Brumfit, classroom processes cannot be 'usefully' turned into a syllabus (1984: 78); and a syllabus that specifies learning content' may not be able to specify teachers' classroom procedural choices without limiting them so much that they are unable to respond to the immediate personal and interactional needs of individuals or groups in the class' (1984: 80). And he adds this warning (1984: 80):

> It is not helpful to suggest that the process of making necessarily improvized choices is the same as that of planning what can be planned; nor is it helpful to imply that we should not or cannot plan. The important question is how best to plan, and when to do it precisely and when vaguely because to do it precisely would be to destroy the interactive process we are trying to encourage. Paradoxically, the radical wish to incorporate methods into a syllabus may – if interpreted strongly – limit the freedom of teachers and students more than the traditionalists' refusal to specify in that area at all.

A syllabus, he concludes (1984: 81), 'may be used restrictively . . . but there is nothing intrinsic to a pre-planned syllabus to make it restrictive. Far more restrictive in practice will be a general view in the teaching profession that public specification of teaching plans is somehow reactionary'. For the essence of a syllabus is that it is a public document, and nothing is more inimical to public accountability than what Brumfit calls the 'demand for the subjectivity of individual interpretations of specific and separate classroom negotiations'.

1.5 CONCLUSION

Although not all syllabus designers followed the example of Breen and Candlin and turned their back on linguistics, it is nevertheless noticeable that few advocates of syntactic, semantic, functional or situational categories as the basis of a communicative syllabus actually sought to go beyond the insights of Wilkins and Munby and show how linguistics might help in the search for a means of 'specifying' process or incorporating process into a product-based syllabus. I cannot say whether this omission was due to the perceived impossibility of the task, or to a reluctance to embrace a discipline that some of their peers apparently considered irrelevant; whatever the case, in the next chapter I shall examine whether linguistics has a role to play in a process or product/process approach to language teaching and learning.

2. The future of communicative language teaching: can linguistics help?

2.0 INTRODUCTION

It will be recalled that in the first chapter I discussed the contribution of linguistics to communicative language teaching in general terms, focusing on linguists like Fillmore and Halliday, sociolinguists such as Hymes and linguistic philosophers like Austin and Searle. I then sketched the role that linguistics played in syllabus design in the 1970s, concentrating on Wilkins and Munby. Wilkins, I said, saw the notional syllabus as an inventory of concepts (semantico-grammatical categories) and functions (speech acts), together with the linguistic forms by which each concept or function might be expressed, and a specification of the sociolinguistic conditions determining individual forms (see Figure 1.1). Wilkins said little about sociolinguistic conditions, and this gap was filled by Munby and his communication needs processor: in his model, specification of the Communication Needs Processor, of the sociolinguistic conditions, determined the inventory of language skills (phonology, concepts, cohesion and discourse), on the one hand, and the list of functions and attitudinal tones, together with their linguistic realizations, on the other (see Figure 1.3).

Wilkins and Munby, of course, are looking at the language syllabus as a product. Thus what they are describing is, depending on your point of view, at worst irrelevant and at best partial. I would prefer to think of it as partial, and to consider how it might be made more complete.

2.1 PRODUCT LINGUISTICS AND PROCESS LINGUISTICS

Linguistics deals with hard-edged categories, so it is scarcely surprising that Wilkins and Munby came up with hard-edged products. To take account of the fluidity of process, linguistics itself must change, at least 'at the edges'. Some of these changes are hinted at by applied linguists working in the field of communicative syllabus design, among them Littlewood, Candlin and Cook, whose work I shall now consider.

For Littlewood (1981: 6) there are four broad domains of skill that make up a person's communicative competence. The first is 'skill in manipulating the linguistic system'; the second is an ability to 'distinguish between the forms which he has mastered as part of his linguistic competence, and the communicative function that they perform'; the third domain (actually fourth on Littlewood's list) is an 'aware[ness] of the social meaning of language forms'; and the fourth (Littlewood's third), the most interesting in the context of the present discussion, and therefore quoted in full, is this: 'The learner must develop skills and strategies for using language to communicate meanings as effectively as possible in concrete situations. He must learn to use feedback to judge his success, and if necessary, remedy failure by using different language.'

The ability to manipulate the linguistic system, and awareness of the social meaning of language forms, need no further comment, but the other two skills require some elaboration. Understanding functional meanings, says Littlewood (1981: 3), is not straightforward, for there are three aspects to the skill: the ability to understand structures and vocabulary; knowledge of the potential communicative function of linguistic forms; and, finally, 'the ability to relate the linguistic forms to appropriate non-linguistic knowledge, in order to interpret the specific functional meaning intended by the speaker'. And he adds:

> An important implication of the third aspect is that the foreign language learner needs more than a 'fixed repertoire' of linguistic forms corresponding to communicative functions. Since the relationship between forms and functions is variable, and cannot be definitely predicted outside specific situations, the learner must also be given opportunities to develop *strategies* for interpreting language in actual use.

Likewise, declares Littlewood (1981: 4), in order to express functional meanings, the learner 'needs to acquire not only a repertoire of linguistic meanings, but also a repertoire of strategies for using them in concrete situations'. After all:

> The most efficient communicator in a foreign language is not always the person who is best at manipulating its structures. It is often the person who is most skilled at processing the complete situation involving himself and his hearer, taking account of what knowledge is already shared between them (e.g. from the situation or from the preceding conversation), and selecting items which will communicate his message effectively.

It is interesting to compare the model of syllabus design implied by Littlewood's account of communicative competence with the models of Wilkins and Munby. Certain aspects of the earlier models remain unchanged: linguistic forms still realize functions, and functions are still influenced by sociolinguistic conditions. What has changed is the status of functions. It is now recognized that there is no simple one-to-one fit between form and function, and that the learner must therefore be equipped with *strategies* for recognizing the communicative function of utterances-in-context — the ability to take into account the current state of knowledge shared between speaker and hearer being one such strategy. Littlewood has thus moved from the purely product view of linguistics embraced by syllabus designers like Wilkins and Munby to a somewhat more process-oriented approach.

Such a process-oriented approach to linguistics is not dissimilar to the approach adopted by Candlin in his discussion of speech acts (Brumfit 1984: 39, and Chapter 1.3 above). In that discussion Candlin said that it was not speech acts as such that raised problems for learners, but their 'particular occurrence and placing in culture-specific events and activity-types, their consequent realization in language-specific forms, and their role in conversational and written discourse'. Such matters, he continued, require an 'understanding of underlying principles of relation between form and function, extended contextual evidence and a process of interpersonal negotiation'. With these requirements Candlin goes somewhat further than Littlewood in the direction of a process-oriented linguistics. An 'understanding of underlying principles of relation between form and function' is more ambitious than mere strategies for interpreting the communicative function of linguistic forms in particular contexts; 'extended contextual evidence' seems more demanding than Littlewood's appeal to shared knowledge and degrees of formality (see 1981: 5); and 'process of interpersonal negotiation', though implicit in an ability to make use of feedback and shared knowledge, does appear to suggest more sophisticated skills.

Candlin's three requirements represent a rather uneven movement away from a product-oriented and towards a process-oriented linguistics. It is not clear whether a linguistics that attempted to understand the 'underlying principles of relation between form and function' would be oriented towards product or process, though it does suggest the kind of exhaustive taxonomy much loved of traditional linguists, or perhaps the type of transformational-generative grammar practised by the Chomskyan revolutionaries, rather than some sort of fluid process. The notion of 'extended contextual evidence' is similarly unclear, although again there is the implication of an exhaustive taxonomy. The only point at which Candlin makes an unambiguous movement towards a process linguistics is in his allusion to a 'process of interpersonal negotiation'. The phenomenon of interpersonal negotiation covers a multitude of linguistic and non-linguistic behaviours, but in this instance it plausibly relates to the role played by speech acts in conversational and written discourse, which Candlin had just mentioned as a problem for learners. In that case, it may be that Candlin sees the relation between form and function (and possibly also 'extended contextual evidence') as best explored within the framework of a discourse model focusing on interpersonal negotiation. This would take the relation between form and function out of the realm of taxonomy or transformational-generative grammar, free it from the influence of 'speaker intention' (see below for a discussion of intentionality) and make it part of a new process linguistics.

It seems from the discussion so far that a discourse model focusing on interpersonal negotiation could provide one of the keys to a process linguistics capable of contributing to the design of a communicative language teaching syllabus. But how would such a discourse model work? There is, of course, no simple answer to this question, but the beginning of an answer is provided in a paper by the applied linguist Vivian Cook (1985) on social factors and language functions in second language teaching and learning. The most original observation of this paper is that choice of functions and realizations is constrained not only by situation but also by what he calls *interaction sequence*. At a given moment in a conversation:

> the speaker or hearer has a choice of what to do next, a meaning potential from which to select the most appropriate next move to suit his or her goals . . . The language function has to fit not just within a structure of conversation in syntagmatic terms but into a sequence of moments of paradigmatic choice.
>
> [1985: 178]

In the light of this observation, Cook (1985: 190–1) believes that a second language learner needs to acquire (a) a set of language functions for use in the second language; (b) a set of ways of realizing and interpreting language functions; and (c) a set of sequential and situational factors influencing the choice of function and realization. And he goes on to note that, although all communicative courses provide learners with a set of language functions and a set of ways of realizing and interpreting these functions, few specify situational factors influencing the choice of functions and realizations, and even fewer try to deal with sequences of functions in interactions lasting more than two turns.

It seems possible that Cook's notion of interaction sequences with 'moments of paradigmatic choice' opens the way to a discourse model focusing on interpersonal negotiation of the type Candlin may have been envisaging (though Cook's reference to a 'set' of sequential factors influencing the choice of function and realization does rather smack of the old linguistics). Cook's observations, unlike those of Littlemore or Candlin, permit us to construct a model for syllabus design (Figure 2.1). In this representation of the syllabus design model implied by Cook's observations on the needs of language learners, choice of functions is influenced by both sociolinguistic conditions (situational factors) and interaction sequence; choice of linguistic forms (realizations) is influenced not only by functions but also by situation.

But how does the notion of interaction sequence open the way to a discourse model focusing on interpersonal negotiation? The answer is that if the 'speaker or hearer has a choice of what to do next, a meaning potential from which to select the most appropriate next move to suit his or her goals', then the possibility always exists that a move, or the realization of a move, chosen by a speaker may leave the hearer in some uncertainty as to what the speaker is 'getting at', thereby forcing the hearer to negotiate with the speaker the meaning of the move. Which brings us quite naturally to one of the sticking points of speech act theory, namely speaker intentionality.

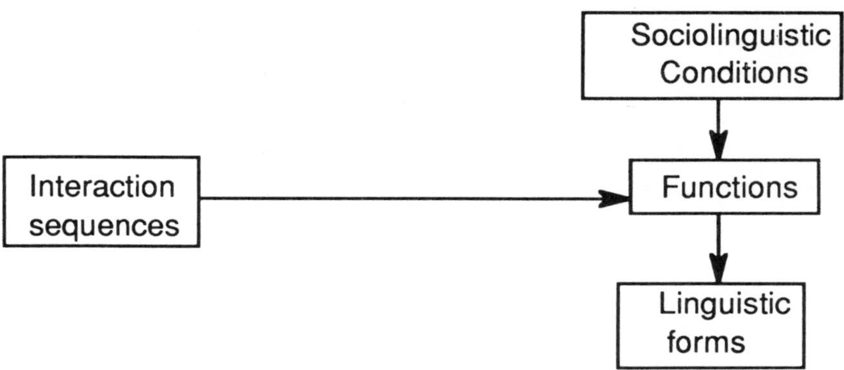

Figure 2.1 A representation of Cook's model of syllabus design

2.2 THE PROBLEM OF INTENTIONALITY

Speaker intentionality obviously refers in general to the belief that, if we are unsure as to the meaning of an utterance, we need only ask the utterer what s/he 'intended' by the utterance; more specifically, it refers to the so-called 'sincerity conditions' that attach to speech acts; thus an utterance can be counted as a promise only if the utterer intends to perform the act mentioned in the utterance. The importance of intention was first asserted by J. L. Austin, the founder of speech act theory (see Austin 1962), but was given a far greater emphasis by John Searle, the popularizer of the theory (Searle 1969).

Interestingly, Austin himself was aware of the problems posed by speaker intention, noting in a paper entitled 'Three Ways of Spilling Ink' that intention was like a 'a miner's lamp on our forehead which illuminates always just so far ahead as we go along', but whose 'illumination is always *limited*' (1979: 284).

One of the most influential critiques of speech act theory and speaker intentionality has been that of the French theorist Jacques Derrida, in two papers published in English in 1977, 'Signature Event Context' (Derrida 1982), which examines some of the problems of (Austin's) speech act theory, and 'Limited Inc abc . . . ' (Derrida 1977), written in response to a reply by Searle (1977) to Derrida's first paper. In 'Signature Event Context' Derrida discusses one of the central tenets of speech act theory, namely that, although a performative cannot be true or false, it may still be 'happy' (felicitous) or 'unhappy' (infelicitous), and that the 'happiness' of a performative depends on the total context of the utterance, one element of which is the intention of the speaker. What is significant here for Derrida is that Austin, while recognizing that the failure of a performative is a structural possibility, an 'essential risk', still excludes this risk as 'an accidental, exterior one that teaches us nothing about the language phenomenon under consideration' (Derrida 1982: 323), just as later he (Austin) excludes a performative 'if said by an actor on the stage, or if introduced in a poem, or spoken in a soliloquy', that is, used 'in ways parasitic upon its normal use' (Austin 1962: 22).

Derrida's argument for problematizing context and speaker intention, and for focusing on 'unhappy' or 'parasitic' performatives, is a complex one, but of considerable interest to anyone exploring ways to develop a process linguistics and a discourse model that takes account of interpersonal negotiation. The argument goes something like this. Speech acts are, as Austin and Searle make clear, conventional in the sense that a successful performative must be executed according to a conventional procedure, by appropriate persons in appropriate circumstances, and both correctly and completely. All very well, says Derrida (1982: 323), but Austin ignores the fact that language is also conventional in the sense that signs are arbitrary, as Saussure pointed out. As he had argued earlier in the paper (Derrida 1982: 318), all signs, whether spoken or written, are 'graphemes' ('writing', in Derrida's specialized use of the term), since any sign may be 'repeated in the absence not only of its referent, which goes without saying, but of a determined signified or current intention of signification, as of every present intention of communication'. And as he had already proposed in two papers on Saussure, 'Linguistics and Grammatology' (Derrida 1976) and 'Semiology and Grammatology' (Derrida 1981), taking as his starting point the principle of difference (the most precise characteristic of a sign is in being what the others are not), the meaning of a sign is constantly DIVIDED, for each sign carries within it the 'trace' of those signs which it is not, on the paradigmatic axis, and constantly DEFERRED, since it signifies only by referring to a past or future element, on the syntagmatic axis (see, for example, Derrida 1976: 63–5, 1981: 28–9). This division/deferral of a sign's meaning Derrida calls *différance,* after the French verb *différer* (present participle *différant*), which means both 'differ' and 'defer'.

Thus, says Derrida (1982: 325), speech acts are, from both a social and a linguistic point of view, ITERABLE: indeed, without this iterability there would be no such thing as a successful performative. That being so, speech acts spoken by an actor on stage or by a priest performing a wedding ceremony could be regarded as different forms of citation. But Derrida prefers to put it another way (1982: 326): 'one must less oppose citation or iteration to the non-iteration of an event than construct a differential typology of forms of iteration'.

And what about speaker intention? Derrida is quite firm about this (1982: 326): 'given the structure of iteration, the intention which animates utterance will never be completely present in itself and in its content. The iteration which structures it *a priori* introduces an essential dehiscence.' The term 'dehiscence' ('the bursting open of capsules, fruits, etc., in order to discharge their mature contents') is borrowed from botany, and is explained in Derrida's response to Searle (1977: 197):

> As in the realm of botany from which it draws its metaphorical value, this word marks emphatically that the divided opening, in the growth of

a plant, is also what, in a *positive* sense, makes production, reproduction, development possible.

Dehiscence (like iterability) limits what it makes possible, while rendering its rigor and purity impossible. What is at work here is something like a law of undecidable contamination.

2.3 CONCLUSION

Up to a point there is nothing new in what Derrida is saying – that language is conventional, is made up of repeatable (iterable) words, structures and speech acts. But the conclusion that he draws from this – that it is precisely the iterability of language that drains away any fully realized intentionality, denies the possibility of any single fixed meaning, and makes 'misunderstanding' an integral part of any linguistic or (in the broadest sense) semiotic transaction – is rather more novel. The implications for a process-oriented linguistics are clear: we may continue to look at the iterable – lexis, grammatical structures and conventional speech acts – but we must also find a way to account for what Derrida calls différence or dehiscence – that is, utterances whose 'intention' is disputed, polysemic utterances, 'misunderstandings'.

A process-oriented linguistics cannot come from nowhere, and in the next chapter I shall examine systemic-functional linguistics, and show that it has the elements necessary for the development of a process linguistics with a discourse model that can account for Candlin's 'interpersonal negotiation' and Cook's 'interaction sequence'.

3. Systemic-functional grammar: a 'communicative' model of language?

3.0 INTRODUCTION

The process-oriented model of language I am seeking is one which can match form to function, incorporate 'extended contextual evidence', find a place for interaction sequences, account for interpersonal negotiation, and recognize that meanings are not fixed and 'misunderstandings' are an integral part of communication. For these reasons, borrowing terms from Halliday (1978: 10), the model must adopt an 'inter-organism' (social) rather than an 'intra-organism' (cognitive) perspective. Models such as transformational-generative grammar, which see language as knowledge, take an intra-organism approach, and are inappropriate for the present purpose. Systemic-functional grammar, which sees language as behaviour, takes an inter-organism approach, and it is to this model that I now turn.

3.1 SYSTEMIC-FUNCTIONAL GRAMMAR

3.1.0 Introduction

The model developed by Michael Halliday over the past twenty-five years meets some of the requirements of a process-oriented model, particularly with regard to the matching of form to function and the incorporation of contextual evidence. In order to show what Halliday's model can and cannot do, I now present the main aspects of systemic-functional grammar.

3.1.1 Situation and language

A fundamental principle of the model is, as previously noted, to regard language as social behaviour. The relationship between language and social behaviour is set forth in a paper published in *Language as Social Semiotic* (Halliday 1978: 39):

> If we take the grammatical . . . system, this is the system of what the speaker *can say* . . . What the speaker can say, i.e., the lexicogrammatical system as a whole, operates as the realization of the semantic system, which is what the speaker *can mean* – what I refer to as the 'meaning potential' . . . Now, once we go outside the language, then we see that this semantic system is itself the realization of something beyond, which is what the speaker *can do* – I have referred to that as the 'behaviour potential'.

Figure 3.1 is a diagrammatic representation of Halliday's explanation. The diagram indicates that context of situation is manifested in language by semantics; which assumes shape in the lexicogrammar, which in turn is expressed by phonology. This explanation may sound rather cryptic, but before I clarify it any further I need to discuss the twin pillars of systemic-functional grammar (henceforth SFG), systems and the metafunctions.

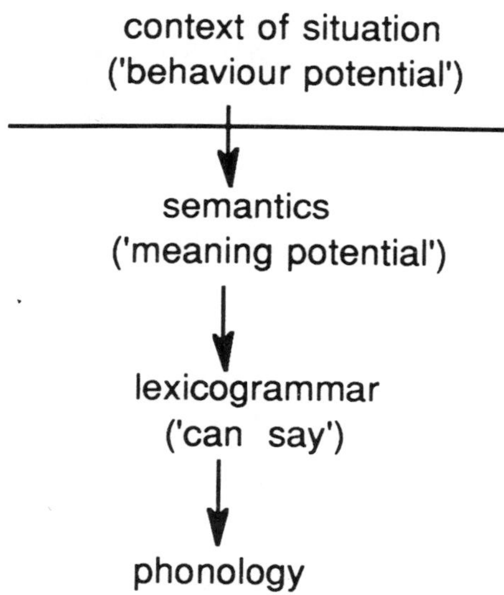

Figure 3.1 Context of situation and language

3.1.2 Systems

As the terms 'can say' and 'can mean' imply, at each level there are sets of options (systems) representing the speaker's potential at that level. Thus at the level of lexicogrammar a number of systems have been described, including transitivity, mood, modality/modulation, theme and information. I explore these more fully below, but at this point an example might be helpful. Consider the system of mood in Figure 3.2. If a major clause (that is, a clause

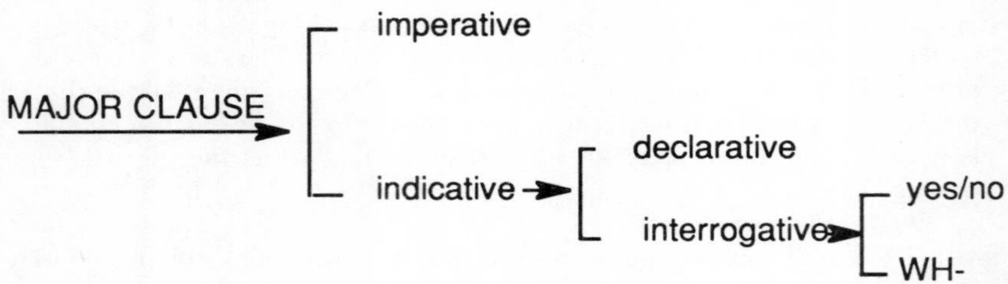

Figure 3.2 They system of mood

with a verb, excluding present or past participles without any auxiliary – 'walking' or 'surprised', for instance) is being formulated, then imperative or indicative must be chosen. If indicative is selected, then declarative or interrogative must be chosen. If interrogative is the option selected, then a further choice must be made between yes/no question or *wh-* question. (And if *wh-* question is chosen, then further choices remain to be made . . . but the principle is already clear enough.)

3.1.3 The metafunctions

The second pillar of SFG is the metafunctions, referred to in Chapter 1 as 'macro-functions', where they were also described as the functional components of the grammar. Halliday has characterized them (1973: 99) as 'relatively discrete areas of formalized meaning potential': the experiential is 'that part of the grammar concerned with the expression of experience'; the interpersonal metafunction is the 'grammar of personal participation'; and the textual is 'concerned with the creation of text'. In the clause the experiential component is represented by the participants, processes and circumstances of transitivity; the interpersonal by mood and modality (i.e. assessment of probabilities); and the textual by the message-structuring systems of theme and information.

I will discuss at length the metafunctions and their systems below (3.1.5), but first a few words about semantics.

3.1.4 Semantics

In the paper called 'Towards a sociological semantics' semantics is characterized (Halliday 1973: 72) as '"what the speaker can mean". It is the strategy that is available for entering the language system. It is one form of, or rather one form of the realization of, behaviour potential.' The characterization of semantics as a 'strategy' is intriguing to anyone searching for a process linguistics, as is this description (1973: 96) of semantic networks, which are said to:

> constitute a stratum that is intermediate between the social system and the grammatical system. The former is wholly outside language, the latter is wholly within language; the semantic networks, which describe the range of alternative meanings available to the speaker in given social contexts and settings, form a bridge between the two.

To illustrate this Halliday, starting from the situation type 'parent exercising verbal control over child', drew a semantic network for 'threat' and 'warning' (1973: 89). This network underlines Halliday's point: an option such as 'restraint on behaviour' is at the 'social' end of the bridge, while 'condition explicit: "if" type' is at the 'grammatical' end of the bridge.

It is in relation to semantics that we find two of Halliday's rare allusions to speech acts. In a paper entitled 'Language as code and language as behaviour' (1984) he is discussing the nature and ontogenesis of dialogue, with dialogue viewed as a process of exchange. At the level of social content (the 'move') the speaker (as initiator) can choose between giving and demanding, and between goods-and-services or information. At the level of semantics (the 'speech function'), giving or demanding goods-and-services is realized as offer or command, giving or demanding information as statement or question. Finally, at the level of lexicogrammar (the 'mood'), these options are realized as imperative, declarative or interrogative.

In the semantic network sketched above, the speech acts offer or command, statement or question – referred to by Halliday (1985: 70–1) as 'proposal' and 'proposition' respectively – form a bridge between social context and the grammar, with offer close to social context (an offer can be realized non-linguistically, by a gesture, for example), and statement close to the grammar. But it is only a sketch, as is apparent in Halliday's brief discussion of speech acts as metaphors of mood (1985: 342–3). Speech acts are seen here as a 'particular complex of semantic features; each feature being one out of a contrasting set'. So, to take an example, 'threat' and 'promise' represent the speech function 'offer' plus other semantic features: 'undesirable' and 'oriented-to-addressee' in the case of 'threat', 'desirable' and 'oriented-to-speaker' in the case of 'promise'. Seen from this perspective, speech acts are extremely complex, but they are still part of a semantic network with one pylon in the social and one pylon in the grammatical.

Semantics as a strategy, as a bridge between the social and the grammatical, wavering indeterminately between the two, is an attractive notion to which I shall return in Chapter 4. Meanwhile it is time to examine in some detail the link between the social system and language.

3.1.5 Context of situation, the metafunctions and discourse

In a paper published in *Language as Social Semiotic* Halliday describes situation (1978: 110) in these terms:

> The semiotic structure of a situation type can be represented as a complex of three dimensions: the ongoing social activity, the role relationships involved, and the symbolic or rhetorical channel. We refer to these respectively as 'field', 'tenor' and 'mode'.

Field, tenor and mode are defined more extensively in another paper, 'The sociosemantic nature of discourse' (Halliday 1978), and a strong claim is made about their relationship to the metafunctions and the grammatical systems. The quotation that I am about to present (1978: 143–5) is a long one, but I will break it up into four segments in order to comment on it and explain the grammatical systems mentioned in each segment. The first segment concerns field.

> The selection of options in experiential systems – that is, in transitivity, in the classes of things . . . , in quality, quantity, time, place, and so on – tends to be determined by [field]. This includes everything from, at one end, types of action defined without reference to language . . . ; through intermediate types in which language has some necessary but still ancillary function . . . ; to types of interaction defined solely in linguistic terms . . . At the latter end of the continuum the concept of 'subject-matter' intervenes . . . In a discussion about a game of football . . . the game constitutes a second order of 'field', one that is brought into being by the first order, the discussion . . . *It is to this second-order field of discourse that we give the name 'subject-matter'.*

Before I indicate how field might determine experiential options, I need to say something about the system of transitivity. Below is a summary of the different types of processes (verbs) and circumstances (adverbs and prepositional phrases) of transitivity:

Process types	*Circumstance types*
material	Extent and Location
mental	Manner
behavioural	Cause
verbal	Accompaniment
relational	Matter
existential	Role

Material processes are processes of doing or happening, and include two main types, one-participant (intransitive) and two-participant (transitive), as exemplified by sentences 1 and 2:

1.

The cat	crouched	in the grass
Actor	P:material	Location

2.

The cat	caught	the bird	with great ease
Actor	P:material	Goal	Manner

In sentence 1 the cat's action is confined to itself, affects nobody but itself; in sentence 2 the cat's action extends to another entity, affects another entity.

Mental processes are processes of thinking, perceiving and feeling, as sentences 3 to 5 show:

3.

My wife	didn't believe	my story
Senser	P:mental	Phenomenon

4.

She	saw	me	with my girlfriend
Senser	P:mental	Phenomenon	Accompaniment

5.

She	loves	me	for my money
Senser	P:mental	Phenomenon	Cause

In these processes the Senser doesn't act on the world as an Actor 'acts on' a Goal; rather the opposite is true, as sentence 6 indicates:

6.

My story	didn't convince	my wife
Phenomenon	P:mental	Senser

Here it is the Phenomenon that is 'acting on' (or, rather, failing to 'act on') the Senser.

Behavioural processes are midway between material and mental processes, being the outward manifestation of a (presumed) internal state. Consider sentence 7:

7.

I	've been yawning	all day
Behaver	P:behavioural	Extent

The action is plainly physical, but it presumably betrays some inner state such as fatigue or boredom.

Verbal processes are processes of saying, as sentence 8 demonstrates:

8.

He	said	some hurtful things	to me
Sayer	P:verbal	Verbiage	Receiver

Relational processes are processes of being, and are of two types, attributive (*x* belongs to the class of *y*) and identifying (*x* can be identified by the label *y*):

9.

This winter	has been	extremely mild
Carrier	P:relational	Attribute

10.

The author of this book	is	Robin Melrose
Identified	P:relational	Identifier

Identifying processes can be recognized by one peculiar feature: they are reversible (so that sentence 10 could equally well, in the right context, be 'Robin Melrose is the author of this book').

Existential processes are a type of relational process, as exemplified in sentence 11:

11.

There	are	too many Australians	in London
	P:existential	Existent	Location

It is now possible to indicate how field – in particular subject matter – might influence the choice of options in systems of the experiential metafunction. It is obvious that subject matter will generally determine choice of lexical items – as reader of this book you would, on seeing the title, have been able to predict at least a dozen words that were highly likely to occur in these pages – but it is probably less obvious that field also influences the types of processes that predominate in a text. Thus a fast-moving narrative is likely to be associated with material processes and, to a lesser extent, behavioural processes and mental processes of perception; a literary theory text tends to be characterized by a predominance of relational processes, together with another ideational feature, an abundance of nominalizations ('a predominance of relational processes' instead of 'relational processes predominate', an 'abundance of nominalizations' instead of 'nominalizations abound', 'nominalization' instead of 'we make something a noun'). Michael Halliday has himself illustrated the link between field and transitivity in a study of William Golding's *The Inheritors* (1973: 103–38): the Neanderthal people of the novel are generally described in terms of one-participant (intransitive) material processes, while the more advanced 'inheritors' are described in terms of two-participant (transitive) material processes, contrasting the powerlessness of the Neanderthal with the relative power of the more advanced tribe.

I now turn to the second part of this lengthy quote from *Language as Social Semiotic*, where tenor is dealt with:

> The selection of interpersonal options, those in the systems of mood, modality, person, key, intensity, evaluation, comment and the like, tends to be determined by the role relationships in the situation [i.e. tenor]. Again there is a distinction to be drawn between a first and second order

of such role relationships. Social roles of the first order are defined without reference to language . . . Second order social roles are those which are defined by the linguistic system: . . . the discourse roles of questioner, informer, responder, doubter, contradicter and the like. (Other types of symbolic action, warning, threatening, greeting and so on, which may be realized verbally or non-verbally, or both, define roles which are in some way intermediate between the two.)

I shall explore presently the ways in which tenor (the role relationships in the situation) may determine interpersonal options, but first an explanation of some of the systems listed in the quote. Mood has already been touched on above, so I will content myself with showing a sentence analysed for Mood:

12.

I	have	beaten	my wife	for 30 years
Subject	Finite	Predicator	Complement	Adjunct
Mood		Residue		

It can be seen from this analysis that the function of Mood is to make some entity responsible for the event, and to anchor the event to a specific time.

Modality is the network of meanings that lie between positive and negative, yes and no; it consists of four sub-systems, as Table 3.1 (taken from Halliday 1985: 337) shows. Table 3.1 indicates that there are four types of judgement we can make: we can estimate the probability or the frequency of an event, the obligation or the inclination of a person to perform an action. These judgements can be expressed by modal verbs such as *may* or *must,* adjectives like *probable* or *required,* and Modal Adjuncts such as *maybe* or *always.*

Table 3.1 The system of modality

Probability	Usuality	Obligation	Inclination
certain probable possible	always usually sometimes	required supposed allowed	determined keen willing

The system of person relates to personal pronouns like *you* or *s/he*, and needs no further comment. Key refers to intonation, a system which offers five main options:

Tone 1 (falling), which is used for making neutral statements.
Tone 2 (high rise), which is used for yes/no questions (e.g. 'Have you finished breakfast?').
Tone 3 (low rise), which indicates that an utterance is unfinished, as in the case of a dependent clause that precedes a main clause ('If you see Jane . . . ').
Tone 4 (falling–rising), which often expresses a reservation ('He's very hard-working ((but he's not very bright))).
Tone 5 rising–falling), which is used for strong emphasis ('That's *wonderful* news!).

Intensity refers to adjuncts such as *only* and *really*, and is of limited interest.

The system of comment permits the speaker/writer to comment on what s/he is saying, through Comment Adjuncts like *frankly, apparently* or *(un)fortunately*. The meaning of the term 'evaluation' is not entirely clear, but it is probably what Halliday elsewhere calls attitudinal lexis. This can be seen in terms of the traditional distinction between denotation and connotation – that is, between the 'core meaning' of a word (its denotation or, in our terms, its experiential meaning) and its 'association' (its connotation, or interpersonal meaning). Thus *slim* and *skinny* have roughly the same experiential meaning, but the former implies a positive evaluation, while the latter implies a negative one; *beat* and *trounce* also have the same experiential meaning, but while the former is more or less netural the latter seems to be extremely favourable to the victors.

It is not as easy to show the link between tenor and interpersonal options as it is to demonstrate the relationship between field and transitivity, but some examples should at least give an idea of how the role relationships in the situation influence choices in interpersonal systems. Take an employee giving advice to his/her employer. S/he may use frequent tag questions, expressions of 'low' or 'medium' modality like *might, perhaps, would* or *should,* tone 4 at strategic points to indicate reservation, 'neutral' lexis, and comment adjuncts like *apparently*. Or consider an argument between two spouses. Declaratives and interrogatives (especially interrogatives that express so-called rhetorical questions) are likely to predominate, with the modality generally 'high' (e.g. *must, certainly, always/never*), a liberal use of tone 5 to indicate definiteness, intensifiers such as *really* or *utterly,* Comment Adjuncts like *frankly* or *to tell you the truth,* and a range of lexical items betraying a negative attitude to the partner. It is clear that there would also be a variety of somatic features on display – a phenomenon I return to in Chapte 4. But even the linguistic features I have listed prove how complex and hard to analyse the link is between tenor and interpersonal options.

I now present the third part of the quote from *Language as Social Semiotic,* this time dealing with mode:

> The selection of options in the textual systems, such as those of theme, information and voice, and also the selection of cohesive patterns . . . tends to be determined by the symbolic forms taken by the interaction . . . This includes the distinction of medium, written or spoken . . . But it extends to much more than this, to the particular semiotic function or range of functions the text is serving . . . The rhetorical concepts of expository, didactic, persuasive, descriptive and the like are examples of such semiotic functions

Theme is the point of departure (at clause level) for the speaker or writer's message. The most common (unmarked) Theme is the first person pronoun:

13.

I	saw him in the pub last night
Theme	Rheme

Less common and therefore more marked as Theme is an adverb or prepositional phrase:

14.

Yesterday	I was in Newcastle
Theme	Rheme

The least common (most marked) Theme is what in a Mood analysis (see above) is called Complement:

15.

Trouble like that	I do not want
Theme	Rheme

Information is primarily a system of spoken language, since the focus of information in a clause is indicated by tonic prominence (intonation). Whereas Theme is oriented towards the speaker/writer, the system of information is directed towards the addressee – more specifically, towards what the addressee is thought to know (old information, or Given), or not know (New information). The unmarked position for New information is at the end of the clause:

16.

I'm going on holidays	TOMORROW
Given	New

But it may appear anywhere, even at the beginning of the clause:

17.

POLITICIANS	seem to enjoy elections
New	Given

Cohesive patterns have been studied exhaustively in Halliday and Hasan (1976), but I shall give only the very briefest of sketches. There are five main types of cohesive patterns:

1. *Reference.* This includes personal pronouns like *she, he* and *it,* and demonstrative pronouns like *this* and *that,* which can only be understood by referring to a previously mentioned entity
2. *Substitution.* The verbal substitute *do* and the nominal substitute *one* set up a cohesive link because they can be identified only by referring to a previous verb or noun:

   'Did you leave the window open?'
   'I might have done.'
   'Did you bring the brown shirt?'
   'No, I brought the grey one.'

3. *Ellipsis.* This is substitution by zero:

   'Did you leave the window open?'
   'I might have.'

Did you bring the green shirt?
No, the grey.

4. *Conjunction*. Sentences are linked by four major conjunctive relations:

   (a) *Additive:* the 'and' relation.
   (b) *Concessive:* the 'but' relation.
   (c) *Causal:* the 'so' relation.
   (d) *Temporal:* the 'then' relation.

   Note that in later work (see Halliday 1985: 302–9, for example) this analysis changes quite radically.
5. *Lexical cohesion*. This includes the lexical patterns of repetition, synonymy, atonymy, hyponymy (specific–general), meronymy (part–whole) and collocation (e.g. *pipe* and *smoke*, *cold* and *ice*)

As was the case with tenor and the interpersonal component, the influence of mode on the textual metafunction is complex and only partly understood, and all I can do here is give some examples. Thus, when the medium is spoken face-to-face, speakers can readily use exophoric reference items such as *that* and *there* whose meaning is clear in the situation but which could not be used in the written medium. Or when the semiotic function of a text is descriptive, we might expect to find a considerable number of Location circumstantials in Theme position (assuming, of course, that a place is being described), just as in a persuasive text modal and comment adjuncts might tend to be thematized.

I conclude this long quote from *Language as Social Semiotic* with some reflections on genre:

> The concept of genre . . . is an aspect of what we are calling the 'mode'. The various genres of discourse . . . are the specific semiotic functions of text that have social value in the culture. A genre may have implications for other components of meaning: there are often associations between a particular genre and particular semantic features of an ideational or interpersonal kind.

The term 'genre' is generally used to describe literary forms such as sonnets, short stories and essays, but here it is widened to include everyday spoken constructs like casual conversations, service encounters and narratives. The systemic linguist Martin says of genre (1985: 251) that it 'represents at an abstract level the verbal strategies used to accomplish social purposes of many kinds. These strategies can be thought of in terms of stages through which one moves in order to realise a genre'. Thus a service encounter consists of the following moves (simplified from Ventola 1984 and Martin 1985): Greeting, Service Bid, Service, Pay, Goods Hand-over, Closing and Goodbye; a spoken narrative consists of Abstract, Orientation, Complication, Resolution and Coda (see Labov 1972). I shall examine genre more closely in Chapter 4, but the brief illustrations I have given should give some idea of how genre works.

3.2 SYSTEMIC-FUNCTIONAL GRAMMAR AND PROCESS LINGUISTICS

This chapter began by asking, in its title, whether systemic-functional grammar is a 'communicative' model of language – in other words, since communication is being viewed as a process, whether systemic-functional grammar is process-oriented. As noted in the introduction (3.0 above), the process-oriented model of language I am seeking is one which can match form to function, incorporate 'extended contextual evidence', find a place for interaction sequences, account for interpersonal negotiation, and recognize that meanings are not fixed and 'misunderstandings' are an integral part of communication. Now the model developed by Michael Halliday certainly matches form to function, undoubtedly incorporates 'extended contextual evidence' and arguably, through the notion of genre, finds a place for interaction sequences. But apart from Martin's intriguing reference to genre as 'verbal strategies used to accomplish social purposes of many kinds' (I shall return to this in Chapter 4), systemic-functional grammar does not appear to account for interpersonal negotiation, or to recognize that meanings are not fixed and 'misunderstandings' are an integral part of communication. Or does it? In the same paper in *Language as Social Semiotic* from which I have just quoted at length, Halliday (1978: 139) is meditating on the nature of reality:

> reality consists of meanings, and the fact that meanings are essentially indeterminate and unbounded is what gives rise to that strand in human thought . . . in which the emphasis is on the dynamic, wavelike aspect of reality, its constant restructuring, its periodicity without recurrence, its continuity in time and space. Here there is no distinction between relations among symbols and relations among the 'things' that they symbolize – because both are of the same order; both the things and the symbols are meanings. The fact that aspects of reality can be digitalized and reduced to ordered operations on symbols is still consistent with the view of reality as meaning: certain aspects of meaning are also captured in this way. Pike . . . expressed this property of the linguistic system . . . by viewing language as particle, wave and field; each of these perspectives reveals a different kind of truth about it.

At this point Halliday does not elaborate on his interpretation of Pike's view of language as particle, wave and field, and one might be forgiven for thinking that it is nothing more than an attractive metaphor. But in a later work Halliday makes it clear that particle, wave and field have a quite precise linguistic meaning for him. In a discussion of interpersonal and textual contributions to the nominal group (noun phrase) Halliday says (1985: 169):

> The textual meaning of the clause is expressed by what is put first (the Theme); by what is phonologically prominent (and tends to be put last – the New, signalled by information focus); and by conjunctions and relatives which if present must occur in initial position. Thus it forms a wave-like pattern of periodicity that is set up by peaks of prominence and

> boundary markers. The interpersonal meanings are expressed by the intonation contour; by the 'Mood' block, which may be repeated as a tag at the end; and by expressions of modality which may recur throughout the clause. The pattern here is prosodic, 'field'-like rather than wave-like. To complete the triad . . . of 'language as particle, wave and field', the kind of meaning that is expressed in a particle-like manner is the experiential; it is this that gives us our sense of the building blocks of language.

Before I comment on this passage, which specifically links particle, wave and field to the experiential, textual and interpersonal metafunctions respectively, I must return to Halliday's meditation on reality. After alluding to Pike's view of language as particle, wave and field, Halliday contrasts this view with that of mainstream linguistics:

> Linguistic theory has remained at a stage at which particulateness is treated as the norm, and a number of different and not very clearly related concepts are invoked to handle its non-particulate aspects. As far as text studies, and text meaning, is concerned, however, we cannot relegate the indeterminacy to an appendix. The text is a continuous process. There is a constantly shifting relation between a text and its environment . . . : the syntagmatic environment, the 'context of situation' . . . can be treated as a constant for the text as a whole, but is in fact constantly changing, each part serving in turn as environment for the next . . . Hence the dynamic, indeterminate nature of meaning . . .
>
> The essential feature of text, therefore, is that it is interaction.

It emerges from the previous quotations that Halliday at least recognizes the process of interpersonal negotiation in communication, and is aware that meanings are not fixed. When he says that the text is a continuous process, and that the context of situation is constantly changing, with each part serving in turn as environment for the next part, he is acknowledging that texts and meanings are negotiated. And when he views language as particle, wave and field he is admitting the slipperiness of meaning. This slipperiness is not so obvious in the particulate aspect of language, represented by the processes, participants and circumstances of transitivity, but can be glimpsed in the wavelike textual and the fieldlike interpersonal metafunctions. Consider a text in which a particular individual is frequently thematized, either by name or by some other designation such as professional or familial status. This thematization forms a succession of waves (as in ocean, light or sound) whose peak is the individual in question. This wave presumably has a meaning, but the meaning is not clear-cut, nor is it even certain that the person(s) interacting with the text will even perceive the 'wave'.

This uncertainty is increased when we come to examine field – a confusing term of Halliday to use, which here has nothing to do with context of situation. As I understand it, 'field' is a term borrowed from physics, where the best-known example is an electromagnetic field; as a metaphor of interpersonal meanings it describes a kind of electrical charge of attitudes, judgements or comments that runs through a text. Thus *reluctance* might be signalled by a string of modals realizing possibility together with lexical items connoting unenthusiasm; anger might be expressed by lexical items with a strong negative or abusive connotation, by regular use of tone 5, by comment adjuncts such as *frankly* or *to tell the truth*, and by intensifiers like *utterly* and *incredibly*. There is, of course, no likelihood of anyone 'misunderstanding' a strongly charged field, but many fields are rather weak, and the possibility always exists that a listener (for I am now talking about spoken interactions) may charge the speaker's discourse with a field of which the speaker would deny all knowledge. A possibility all the stronger in face-to-face interactions, where the field is charged not only by modals and attitudinal lexis but also by the body (e.g. tone of voice, gestures, facial expressions and bodily posture).

3.3 CONCLUSION

The view of language as particle, wave and field, and the concept of a constantly changing context of situation, point the way towards a process linguistics, but still leave some crucial questions unanswered. The most important of these questions is: how do we model the process of interpersonal negotiation? Around it cluster other related questions. What is the best way to model a constantly changing context of situation? How do we represent what is conventional and iterable in language, and show the fluidity of meaning that flows from this? How can we model the non-particulate aspects of language, especially the linguistic charge that Halliday calls field? And, given the fact that this charge has a somatic dimension, should we bring the body into the act? Such are the questions that will be addressed in the next chapter.

4. A meaning negotiation model of language

4.0 INTRODUCTION

At the end of the previous chapter several questions were posed, beginning with the two linked questions: how do we model the process of interpersonal negotiation? And what is the best way to model a constantly changing context of situation? Setting aside for the moment the succeeding questions, I turn to a systemic-functional model that offers an approach to the problems raised by the process of interpersonal negotiation and a constantly changing context of situation.

4.1 PROCESS AND GENRE

The model I am referring to was developed by the systemic linguists Martin and Ventola, and set forth in Martin (1985). Martin's model, like Halliday's, has the two levels of lexicogrammer and phonology, but Martin differs from Halliday in that he replaces the level of semantics by a level he calls DISCOURSE. This discourse level is concerned with inter-clause relations, and its key systems are reference, conjunction, lexical cohesion (discussed in Chapter 3) and conversational structure (broadly speaking, the structure of conversational exchanges, generally seen, since Sinclair and Coulthard 1975, as a rather mechanical exchange of speech acts).

But language, of course, represents only part of the model, and the extra-linguistic dimension must be accounted for. Here again Martin departs slightly from the traditional Hallidayan model, as Figure 4.1 indicates. This model, which is in fact taken from Martin (1984) – Martin (1985), actually written in 1982, does not include Ideology – can be interpreted as follows: language is the 'expression' of register (that is, field, tenor and mode), language and register are the 'expression' of genre, and language, register and genre are the 'expression' of ideology (see 1984: 2).

There is no need at this point to examine just what might be meant by the term 'ideology', but the full meaning of 'genre' certainly needs to be clarified. In Chapter 3.1.5 I quoted Martin (1985: 251) as saying that genre 'represents at an abstract level the verbal strategies used to accomplish social purposes of many kinds'. But that is only half the story, for, as Martin had noted earlier

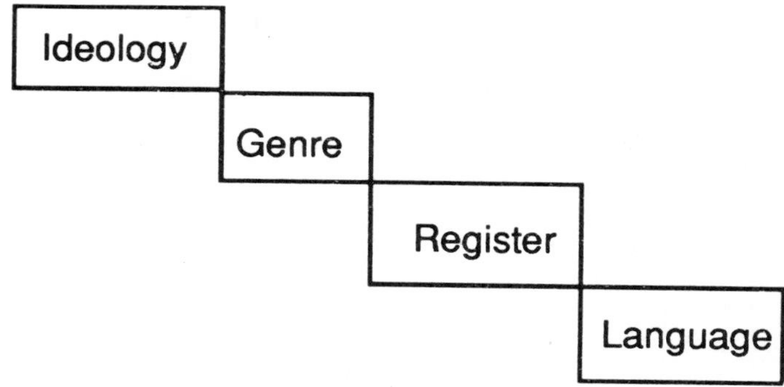

Figure 4.1 Martin's model

(1985: 250), 'one of the principle descriptive responsibilities of genre is to constrain the possible combinations of field, mode and tenor variables used by a given culture'. This is genre as producer of culturally appropriate contexts, what I shall call, even before defining the term, the 'ideological' side of genre. What, then, is genre-as-verbal-strategies? The answer to this question lies in another aspect of the model developed by Martin.

Referring to the Danish linguist Hjelmslev (whose work had a considerable influence on Halliday), Martin observes (1985: 248) that Hjelmslev distinguishes between PROCESS (the realization of a semiotic's meaning potential) and TEXT (the realization of a language's meaning potential). Process, says Martin, connotes an 'interactive dynamic perspective on manifestation', while text is 'static', and 'calls to mind a product, whole, complete'. Further on Martin (1985: 259) elaborates this idea in the form of a diagram (Figure 4.2). From a static perspective, potential is termed a synoptic system, while from an active perspective it is termed a dynamic system, while from an active perspective it is termed a dynamic system. Actual when viewed statically is termed text; when viewed dynamically it is referred to as process. Synoptic systems generate texts, whereas dynamic systems generate process.

static	synoptic system	text
active	dynamic system	process

Figure 4.2 Process in Martin's model

An example of a synoptic system is a system such as transitivity or mood; but what is an example of a dynamic system? When Martin uses the term 'semiotic' (sign system), he is thinking of ideology, genre and register, and the chief example he gives of a dynamic system is the decision tree or flow chart used by Ventola (1984) to generate a well formed schematic structure for the genre service encounter. This flow chart is virtually impossible to reproduce and difficult to describe: it is enough to say that at each point in the encounter the flow chart represents the possibilities open to customer and server, and the paths to be followed if different decisions are taken (see Martin 1985 and Ventola 1984 for further elaboration).

Genre-as-verbal-strategies, then, is a dynamic system, a process, a decision tree – in short, a locus of interaction, a point at which interpersonal negotiation may take place, at which changes in the context of situation may be observed. Since interaction seems to me the key to genre-as-verbal-strategies, I will henceforth refer to this interactive side of genre (borrowing Cook's useful term – see Chapter 1) as *interaction sequence*. I discuss interaction sequence more fully below, but before any such discussion is possible I need to examine genre and ideology.

4.2 GENRE AND IDEOLOGY

Martin, as noted above, believes that genre constrains the possible combinations of field, mode and tenor variables used by a given culture. This, I remarked, is the ideological side of genre, so it is obviously time to examine what might be meant by 'ideology', and how it might relate to genre. Martin, in Threadgold (1986), defines ideologies as the 'fashions of speaking' or the patterns of language that are consistently taken up by groups of speakers in specific situation types. Thus says Threadgold (1986: 48) – and here we return to Martin's model – 'the use to which the text is being put (ideology) constrains genre (institutionalised purpose) and this controls the choice in register which will involve "fashions of speaking"'. For Threadgold (1986: 35), this account of ideology is unsatisfactory, being 'too narrowly linguistic in focus and too specifically production oriented'.

These two criticisms are of considerable interest. The first is explained earlier in the paragraph when Threadgold is summarizing the views on ideology of three other systemic-functional linguists, Kress, Lemke and Thibault: their accounts, she says, 'avoid identifying ideology with language but also avoid seeing ideology as essentially outside language, imposed from above'. The explanation of the second criticism is not so much stated as implied: Kress, Lemke and Thibault's accounts of ideology, says Threadgold approvingly, focus not only on production but also on reception, and therefore allow for differing subject positions – in other words, they allow participants in an interaction to bring to the interaction different sociocultural baggage, whether the differences are relatively slight (British white working-class male conversing with British white middle-class male) or relatively large (female middle-class white teacher from urban Britain talking to male learner of

English from rural Thailand).

Ideology, then, must be viewed as the set of discursive and non-discursive practices that pervail in a given culture or sub-culture at a given moment. As this definition implies, the practices are constantly changing (sometime slowly and imperceptibly, sometimes rapidly and noticeably), and, while certain practices may be common to a whole society, others may be restricted to a certain class, occupational group or generation. It can therefore never be assumed that any two participants in an interaction will be positioned by exactly the same discursive and non-discursive practices, so a model that claims (as Martin's does) to give pride of place to ideology had better take this into account.

But first I must attempt to specify at least some of these discursive and non-discursive practices. One type of discursive and non-discursive practice, first formulated and explored in some detail by the French theorist Michel Foucault, is the DISCURSIVE FORMATION (see, for example, Foucault 1972). This is the discourse of an established 'institutionalized' discipline such as medicine, psychoanalysis, economics or education, which conforms to a specific 'regime of truth' and is characterized by systems of relations among discursive objects (subject matter, presumably, in terms of Halliday's model), speaker roles and subject positions (tenor, plausibly), and principles of organization of its statements (mode, perhaps).

By way of explanation, let us consider one of the disciplines most relevant to the present work – that is, *education*. Two of the discursive objects of this discipline, at least in so far as it applies to second language education, are arguably AUTHENTICITY and LEARNABILITY, which stand in a specific relationship to each other and to other discursive objects (LINGUISTIC DIFFICULTY, for example), a relationship which varies over time (compare the audio-lingual approach of 1955 and the communicative approach of 1985) and is not even stable at a given time. Equally variable are the speaker roles and subject positions of the discipline: the teacher as giver of information and as (a representative of) infallible authority, a role which may have been current in Victorian times and is still so in many societies, has given way in some Western countries to the teacher as facilitator of learning and caring (but fallible) counsellor. As for the principles of organization of the discipline's statements, Halliday's conception of genre (seen by him as an aspect of mode) seems to play a role here: educational psychology is likely to be taught in a standard textbook, while classroom management procedures or teaching practice procedures are likely to appear in a 'practical' handbook or manual. (The gulf between theory and practice that is here implied represents another discursive object of this and many other disciplines, but discussion of the topic is beyond the scope of this book.)

Also included in a discursive formation are the non-discursive practices that are brought into being by the discourse of the discipline. As far as education is concerned, one such non-discursive practice would be the arranging of chairs and desks in a classroom. Thus the traditional placing of chairs and desks in rows facing the front, with the teacher's chair and desk at the front, belongs to the discourse in which the teacher is the all-knowing giver of information; on the other hand, the placing of a number of chairs and desks together, so that there are several groups of students facing not the teacher but each other, is consistent with a discourse which positions the teacher as a facilitator and adviser.

The concept of discursive formation, however, applies only to institutionalized discourses and practices, and therefore has nothing to say about a mass of non-institutionalized discourses and practices. One person to have attempted to fill the gap left by this silence is the American physics educationist/social theorist/linguist Jay Lemke, with his twin concepts of INTERTEXTUAL THEMATIC SYSTEMS and SOCIAL ACTION SEMIOTIC. A thematic system, says Lemke (1985b: 24), is defined as 'the typical ideational–semantic meaning relations constructed in some set of texts . . . which are thematically relevant for one another's meaning constructions'. Now the term 'ideational' refers to one of Halliday's three metafunctions and, as I indicate below, concerns the transitivity and lexical relations into which a particular thematic item enters. It does leave us with the expectation that thematic systems will also be definable in terms of the interpersonal and textual meaning relations constructed in some set of texts, and indeed Lemke 1983 implies that other relations should be considered, including interpersonal-grammatical, rhetorical and discourse structure relations. So in the present work a thematic system will be a network of ideational-semantic, interpersonal-grammatical, rhetorical and discourse structure relations.

Ideational-semantic relations, as I have already hinted, are the participant roles and process types with which an entity (thematic items) is associated typically in a particular set of texts, together with the other entities that enter into some lexical or grammatical (cohesive) relationship with that entity. Thus, assuming a thematic system entitled 'traditional gender roles', it might be speculated that in a specific set of texts the thematic item *man* would be Actor in material processes belonging to a number of fairly well definable lexical sets (occupational and sporting activities, for example), and Carrier in relational processes whose Attribute would belong to other equally clear – even stereotyped – lexical sets (nouns or adjectives associated with strength or toughness, for instance). By the same token the thematic item *woman* would be Actor in a totally different set of material processes (domestic and child-rearing activities, say), and Carrier in relational processes with Attribute from entirely different lexical sets (nouns or adjectives describing fragility or softness are obvious candidates); and might in addition appear more frequently as Senser in mental processes, or Sayer in verbal processes, or even Goal in material processes. (I realize that I am looking at the thematic system from the point of view of its most traditional adherents, and that it has changed radically over the last twenty years, but the ideational-semantic relations that I describe are easily recognizable and still enjoy considerable currency.)

I can briefly discuss the other thematic system relations by imagining a thematic system entitled 'academic objectivity'. Thus in addition to the ideational-semantic meaning relations (a tendency to encode the relevant 'objects' of one's discipline as participants in relational processes) there are interpersonal-grammatical relations (a preference for unmodalized statements, indicating an unquestionable fact or truth, or the use of rhetorical questions, positioning the writer as a seeker after knowledge) and discourse structure relations (an example of such a relation is nominalization, a process in which an action or event is turned into a thing – for example, the clause 'he arrived early' becomes 'his early arrival' – and thereby made more 'objective').

Two final points need to be made about thematic systems. The first, minor, point is that thematic systems are not systems in the sense that systemic-functional linguists use the term – they are, as I shall demonstrate in Chapter 6, relational networks. The second, more important, point is that, although thematic systems are constructed in terms of grammatical categories such as transitivity, they are not grammatical or even semantic but 'ideological' constructs that reflect and shape the social system. It might be better to use different labels in the thematic systems, but no suitable labels exist – and, in any case, one of the main tenets of systemic-functional grammer is that language ultimately reflects behaviour, implying that a grammatical label is also, indirectly, a social label.

If thematic systems organize the non-institutionalized discourses of a culture, then the social action semiotic organizes its non-discursive practices. Lemke (1985a: 283) characterizes it as 'a semiotic system defining the meaning relations within and between the various recognised kinds of social practice in a community'. This explanation is rather opaque, and I find it helpful to see the social action semiotic as the non-discursive counterpart of thematic system, with its own ideational, interpersonal and textual meaning relations. Consider once more 'traditional gender roles', this time as a social action semiotic. There are the ideational meaning relations: the activities performed by men versus the activities performed by women, the clothes worn by men versus the clothes worn by women. There are the interpersonal meaning relations: the way men and women behave towards each other in a range of contexts. There are the textual meaning relations: *flirting* is as much a rhetorical function in this social action semiotic as nominalization is a discourse structure in the thematic system 'academic objectivity'.

I conclude this section by asking: is genre, as conceived by Martin, necessary to the model that is slowly being unfolded here, or can it be dispensed with? The answer, I suggest, is that genre has been superseded. The verbal strategy component of genre has been re-baptized *interaction sequence* – though its place in the model is yet to be discussed; and the responsibility of genre to constrain possible combinations of field, tenor and mode can be assigned to the discursive formation–thematic system–social action semiotic triad that can be loosely called ideology. So the term – if not the concept – genre will not be used in the model that I am developing.

4.3 INTERACTION SEQUENCE

Before I can outline this model I need to explore genre's child, interaction sequence, the 'verbal strategies used to accomplish social purposes of many kinds'. The concept I have of interaction sequence is shaped by the study of spoken genres, the approach to discourse analysis adopted by scholars such as Sinclair and Coulthard, and certain insights emerging from the conversation analysis practised by ethnomethodologists like Sachs and Schlegloff, and I will now briefly review these.

The study of spoken genres may be exemplified by the work of Ventola (see Ventola 1979, 1984; Martin 1985) on casual conversation and service encounters. In her research into casual conversation Ventola has proposed that the elements of schematic structure for this genre are, in their unmarked order, as follows:

1. Greeting.
2. Address.
3. Approach, either Direct, relating to health, appearance, family members, everyday or professional life; or Indirect, relating to weather, current news, etc.
4. Centring, an optional element in which one or more cognitive or informative topics is discussed.
5. Leave-taking.
6. Goodbye.

Also studied by Ventola are service encounters – here are the elements of schematic structure for this genre, listed in their unmarked order of appearance:

1. Greeting.
2. Turn Allocation (select next customer).
3. Service Bid (offer of service).
4. Service (statement of needs).
5. Resolution (decision to buy or not to buy).
6. Pay.
7. Goods Hand-over.
8. Closing.
9. Goodbye.

The structures of casual conversations and service encounters clearly represent the stages through which speakers move to accomplish particular social purposes, or, to put it another way, verbal strategies that speakers use to accomplish particular transactions. When we come to the discourse analysis of Sinclair and Coulthard, and their colleagues, however, such verbal strategies are less clearly in evidence. These researchers take a different tack, seeing conversation in terms of large units made up of smaller units. Thus the largest unit is the *lesson* (Sinclair and Coulthard 1975) or the *interaction* (Burton, in Coulthard and Montgomery 1981) – this largest unit is made up of *transactions*, which are made up of *exchanges*, which in turn consist of *moves*, which in their turn are composed of *acts*. But acts are not stages through which one moves to realize a lesson or interaction, they are speech acts – up to twenty-four, of which the most basic initiations and responses are:

informative–acknowledge
elicitation–reply
directive–accept/react
accusation–excuse

The three acts — informative, elicitation and directive — correspond to Halliday's statement, question and command, on the semantic level, and declarative, interrogative and imperative on the grammatical level; the fourth act, accusation, does not correspond to any clear semantic or grammatical category – perhaps it is what Halliday (1985: 340) calls a metaphor of mood, which means that it is only indirectly related to the first three, relying as it does on perlocutionary rather than illocutionary force (that is, on the force of the reaction rather than on the force of the utterance).

It would be tempting to dismiss this model of discourse analysis as a series of exchanges of goods-and-services, which adds little to an understanding of interaction sequences, but for this anomalous act *accusation*, and other acts not yet referred to, such as *metastatement* and *conclusion* (for an explanation of these acts see Coulthard and Montgomery 1981: 76–7), where something more complex seems to be at work. So rather than dismiss the model, I will examine the work of the ethno-methodologists for the light it can throw on the model's anomalies.

In their analyses of conversation the ethnomethodologists have introduced the notion of pre-sequence, to refer to a certain kind of turn or to the sequence containing that type of turn (see Levinson 1983: 345 ff.). There are various types of pre-sequences that have been noted, including pre-invitations, pre-requests, pre-arrangements, pre-announcements and pre-closings. All seem designed to orient the addressee towards what is to follow; and some like pre-requests also seemed designed to avoid what are called 'dispreferred' second turns in an adjacency pair (in the case of a request, a refusal would be 'dispreferred'). This concept of pre-sequence seems to add a new dimension to the exchange-of-speech-acts model of discourse analysis as practised by Sinclair and Coulthard. It is now possible to see exchanges like informative/acknowledge, elicitation/reply, directive/accept and accusation/excuse as elements in more complex transactions. In the case of directives, or any other act which has a fairly transparent grammatical realization, the directive might well be the central element – if a pre-request fails ('It's cold in here'), then the next step is a directive ('Shut the window, will you!'). In the case of acts such as accusations or excuses, which may have rather opaque grammatical realizations, that act could well be part of a pre-sequence that requires a more explicit sequence to follow it. In the following sequence of exchanges:

'You're late!'
'Oh, so I am.'
'Well, you shouldn't be.'
'Sorry. You know how bad the traffic is'.

the first utterance, which is presumably meant as an accusation, is turned into a kind of informative by the bland acknowledgement, forcing the 'accuser' to add a second utterance to bring out the accusatory force of the first utterance.

From this review of genre, Sinclair and Coulthard-style discourse analysis, and insights offered by the conversation analysis of the ethnomethodologists, it emerges that interaction sequence is something slightly more than the sum of all these models. Interaction sequence is genre as conceived of by Martin, Ventola and other systemic linguists, *plus* something that combines the discourse analysts' exchange and the ethnomethodologists' pre-sequence to create what I can only call an interaction sequence (as a count noun it describes a particular example, as an uncountable noun it describes the phenomenon). The confrontation between the late arrival and the accuser is part of just such an exchange-with-pre-sequence interaction sequence – it could not really be described as a genre in the way that a casual conversation or a service encounter is a genre, yet it certainly involves verbal strategies, the sense of passing through stages to accomplish a social purpose. I could as easily call this type of sequence a genre, but to avoid confusion I prefer to think of Martin and Ventola's genre as a more extended interaction sequence.

This, then, is a basic explanation of interaction sequence. Earlier I said that interaction sequence suggests a locus of interaction, a point at which interpersonal negotiation may take place, at which changes in the context of situation may be observed – yet this aspect of interaction sequence has not been touched on. But of course the nature and dynamic of interaction sequence can be understood only by seeing the model in action, so I now proceed to outline the model and show how it works.

4.4 LANGUAGE AS PROCESS

4.4.1 The model

Let me begin by presenting in outline form the process model of language I am going to develop (Figure 4.3). The term 'social discourses and practices' refers to what Martin calls 'ideology', and includes discursive formations, thematic systems and the social action semiotic as discussed above; 'situation types' is context of situation, with a slight modification of the familiar field, tenor and mode (see below); 'interactional processes' (further explained below) is interaction sequence plus some other elements. The solid downward-pointing arrows indicate some sort of influence or determination, and represent the act of producing a communicative event (not necessarily language); the broken upward-pointing arrows do *not* indicate the process of going automatically from the communicative event to its determinants – rather they represent the act of interpreting the determinants, implying the possibility of a mismatch between producer and interpreter. The communicative event is not necessarily language, because it can be expressed by paralinguistic features such as tone of voice, gesture and facial expression. (Usually, of course, paralinguistic features are accompanied by language.)

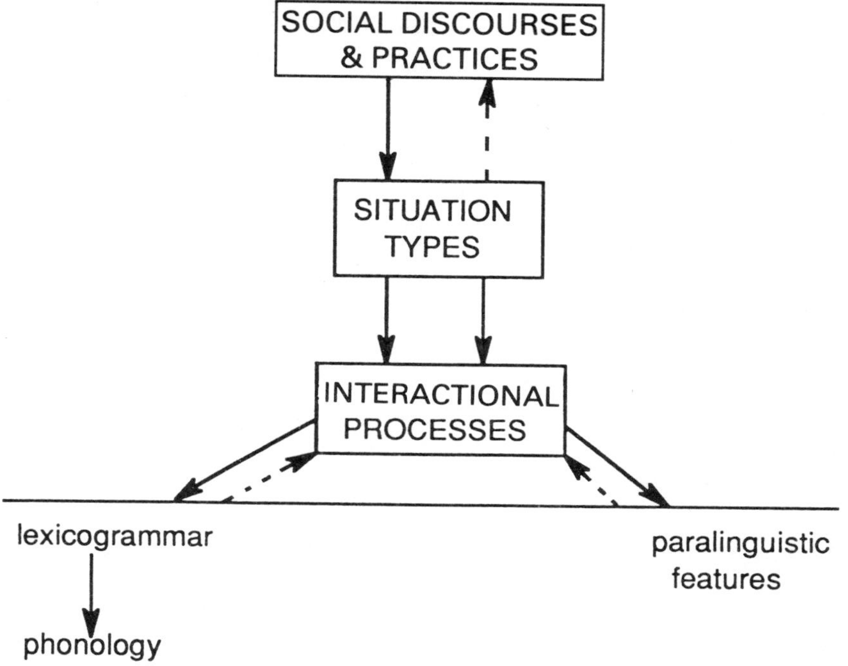

Figure 4.3 Outline of a process model of language

4.4.2 Situation type

To show how the model works, I begin by examining the 'downward' relationship between social discourses and practices (henceforth abbreviated to SocDP) and situation types. Situation, as I shall call it from now on, is discussed by Halliday in his essay *Language as Social Semiotic* (1978: 109):

> It will be necessary to represent the situation . . . not as situation but as situation *type*, in the sense of what Bernstein refers to as a 'social context'. This is, essentially, a semiotic structure. It is a constellation of meanings deriving from the semiotic system that constitutes the culture.

and in another essay (1978: 198):

> The linguistic system . . . is organised in such a way that the social context is predictive of the text. This is what makes it possible for a member to to make the necessary predictions about the meanings that are being exchanged in any situation which he encounters. If we drop in on a gathering we are able to tune in very quickly because we size up the

> field, tenor and mode of the situation and at once form an idea of what is likely to be being meant. In this way we know what semantic configurations . . . will probably be required if we are to take part. If we did not do this there would be no communication, since only a part of the meanings we have to understand are explicitly realized in the wordings. The rest are unrealized; they are left out – or rather . . . they are out of focus.

Situation thus has two characteristics: (1) it is a social phenomenon, deriving from the 'semiotic system that constitutes the culture' (that is, from the discursive formations, thematic systems and social action semiotic of social discourses and practices); (2) it forms part of a speaker–hearer's knowledge — assuming that subjects are positioned identically, they can 'size up' the field, tenor and mode of a situation, even though some of the meanings are 'unrealized' or 'out of focus' (the implication being that knowledge of situation types permits these meanings to be filled in).

The components of situation will therefore be viewed in terms of these two characteristics, situation-as-social-phenomenon and situation-as-knowledge. I'll begin with social situation and subject matter.

4.4.2.1 Social situation/subject matter

Social situation is here seen – following Martin 1984 – as an activity which is recognized (and therefore named) by a given society, and which consists of an ordered series of acts. The activity may be largely non-verbal (e.g. 'preparing a meal'), in which case the acts are physical; or it may be largely verbal (e.g. 'socializing'), in which case the acts are for the most part abstract (see section 4.4.3 on interactional processes); or it may be a mixture of the non-verbal and verbal ('renting accommodation' is an example of this category). The non-verbal acts are chosen from *objects* in the social action semiotic – I use the word 'chosen' though the degree of choice varies considerably, so that in the social situation 'preparing a meal' the activity 'bringing-to-the-boil-then-simmering-on-a-low-heat' may not be in the least optional, whereas the activity 'wearing an apron' may be perfectly optional. The verbal acts are chosen from ideational-semantic relations in one or more thematic systems (see Chapter 6 for clarification of this); there is more choice here, perhaps, than in the case of non-verbal acts – there is probably no verbal equivalent to the act 'bringing-to-the-boil-then-simmering-on-a-low-heat' in the sequence 'preparing a meal' – yet there are very real constraints, as I hope eventually to demonstrate.

This is a partial account of the first perspective on social situation – situation-as-social-phenomenon. When we come to describe the second perspective – the knowledge that users of a language have of social situation – we can choose between three different, though related, hypotheses. Knowledge of social situation may be organized into FRAMES – first proposed by Minsky and defined by Metzing (1979: 28–9) as:

> packets of knowledge that provide descriptions of typical objects or

events. These descriptions contain both an abstract template providing a skeleton for describing any instance and a set of defaults for typical members of the class. The defaults allow the information system to supply missing detail, maintain expectations, and notice anomalies.

Or knowledge of social situation may be organized into SCRIPTS, equally proposed by Minsky and described by Metzing (1979: 85) as follows:

> In each culture there are a number of sterotypic situations in which human behaviour is highly predictable and narrowly defined. Behaviour in these situations is often described in terms of cultural conventions. These conventions are learned in childhood, adhered to throughout one's life and rarely questioned or analyzed. Scripts describe these conventional situations that are defined by a highly stereotypic sequence of events.

Alternatively, knowledge of social situation may be organized into SCHEMAS. The concept of schema is derived from the work of F. C. Bartlett, a British psychologist researching into memory in the early 1930's. According to Brown and Yule (1983: 349):

> Bartlett believed that our memory for discourse was not based on straight reproduction but was constructive. This constructive process uses information from the encountered discourse, together with knowledge from past experience related to the discourse at hand, to build a mental representation. That past experience . . . must be organised and made manageable – 'the past operates as an organised mass . . .'. What gives structure to that organised mass is the schema, which Bartlett did not propose as a form of arrangement, but as something which remained 'active' and 'developing'.

In a model which claims a process orientation the concept of an 'active' and 'developing' schema seems rather more attractive than that of a 'stereotypic' script or a presumably rigid frame.

One aspect of social situation, as Halliday said, is subject matter. Once a recognized social situation becomes a topic of conversation, then it is transformed into a subject matter: preparing a meal is a social situation, but if I discuss it then it becomes a subject matter. Social situation and subject matter may be completely unconnected – I can be preparing a meal and discussing a film (in which case, of course, the discussion is a second, concurrent, social situation).

Is there knowledge of subject matter in the same way that there is knowledge of social situation? If knowledge of social situation is organized into schemas, each choosing objects (activities) from the social action semiotic and ideational-semantic relations from one or more thematic systems, then presumably knowledge of subject matter is organized into similar schemas, selecting only from the transitivity relations and lexical sets of the thematic system(s) in play.

I turn now to the second dimension of the situation, not Halliday's tenor, but one compenent of tenor, SOCIAL RELATIONSHIP.

4.4.2.2 Social relationship

Social relationship is that component of tenor that Halliday refers to as social roles of the first order (for second-order social roles see below). It is likely that social roles of the first order are best defined relationally, in terms of symmetrical pairs such as 'colleague–colleague' or asymmetrical pairs like 'employer–employee'. These social relationships are mutually determining, and carry with them certain behaviour patterns, rights, duties and obligations, all of them chosen from interpersonal meaning relations in the relevant social action semiotic network(s), and form interpersonal-grammatical relations in the relevant thematic system(s). Again choices are more or less free – in an 'employer–employee' relationship in Britain few types of behaviour, short of refusal to work in a normal situation, are actually forbidden to an employee, though many types of behaviour are fairly unlikely – and it is possible to mix social action semiotic networks and thematic systems, as may well happen when an employer and employee are also friends, or belong to some sort of club or organization away from the workplace.

I hypothesized before that knowledge of social situation is organized into schemas, and I would imagine that the same is true of social relationship – that we order the myriad differing social relationships in which we participate according to what I will call *social role schemas*.

And what are these social roles? Since the subject of this present work is the teaching and learning of English, I will use a set of social roles well known to ELT teachers – the inventory of social relationships drawn up by John Munby (1978: 72).

4.4.2.3 Purpose

Purpose is a category that I have borrowed from the systemic linguist R. P. Fawcett. There is no precise eqivalent to be found in Halliday's description of field, tenor or mode, and it could perhaps be best thought of as a cross between that other component of tenor, the second-order social roles – that is, those defined by the linguistic system, what Halliday calls discourse roles – and the rhetorical functions of mode such as persuasive or descriptive. Purpose can be best understood if we consider Martin's (1984) definition of field as a 'set of activity sequences oriented to some global institutional purpose', and Fawcett's network called SOCIO-PSYCHOLOGICAL PURPOSES (Figure 4.4). In this network there are two types of purpose. The first, pragmatic, includes control (the discourse role 'command' and the rhetorical function 'persuasive' would be examples of this), informational (compare this with the discourse role 'statement' and the rhetorical function 'descriptive') and heuristic (exemplified, perhaps, by the discourse role 'question' and one stream in the rhetorical function 'didactic'). The second type, relationship

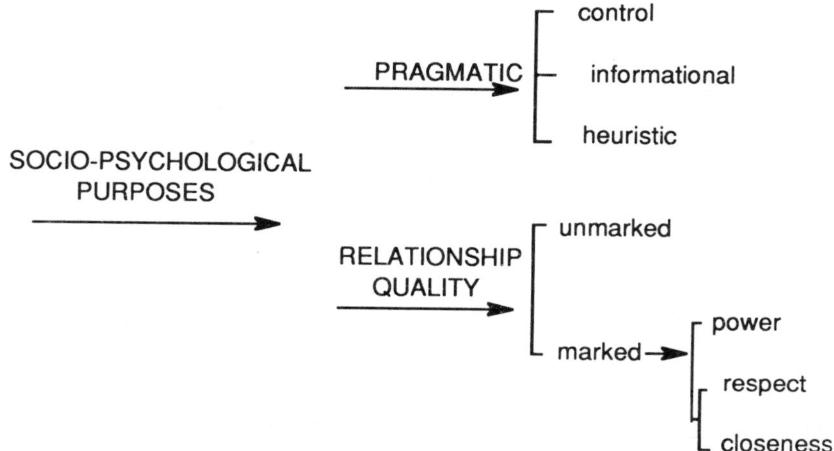

Figure 4.4 Fawcett's sociopsychological network

quality, includes unmarked (neutral), and the marked options power, respect and closeness, most conveniently illustrated not by any semantic system in English but by the subtle uses in French of the pronouns *tu* and *vous* (mirrored, of course, in other languages with a similar system of pronouns). Unlike pragmatic purpose, relationship quality seems to belong squarely to tenor, though it does not slot in very neatly – it might seem to be closely linked with first-order social roles, yet it can function independently of them, and therefore cannot be defined without reference to language, though it is not (like discourse roles) brought into being by the linguistic system.

Pragmatic purpose options derive from choices in the interpersonal-grammatical and rhetorical/discourse structure relations of the relevant thematic system(s), while relationship quality options derive from these same choices plus selections in the appropriate interpersonal and rhetorical/discourse structure relations of the social action semiotic.

4.4.2.4 Channel and symbolic function

These are both aspects of Halliday's mode. Channel covers the division spoken and written (which includes sub-types like spoken-to-be-written and written-to-be-spoken) on the one hand, and the distinction between face-to-face and mediated (e.g. through the medium of telephone) on the other. Symbolic function is the role played by language in the total situation: language may be almost fully constitutive of the situation — as in the case of a textbook on language teaching, for example — or it may only partly constitute the situation, and shared knowledge (of the immediate environment, personal history, local geography and events, etc.) may also play an important part in constituting the situation.

There is a link between the channel and symbolic function chosen, and the types of grammatical options and paralinguistic features selected. (In face-to-face conversation, to give a simple example, the demonstrative pronoun *that*, accompanied by a gesture, would be perfectly understood by anyone present and able to see the entity referred to; whereas if the same conversation were held on the telephone, *that* would have to be identified by name.) It is likely that channel and symbolic function derive from rhetorical and discourse structure relations in the relevant thematic system(s) and social action semiotic.

4.4.3 Interactional processes

Interactional processes are processes which permit the articulation of a situation and its distribution between an emitter and a receiver in a form which can be readily re-articulated in language (or other codes). I had initially intended to call this part of the model 'discourse strategies', but 'discourse' suggests that I am interested only in language, which is not the case, and 'strategies' suggests that interactants at all times know exactly what they are doing, which does not seem to be a tenable hypothesis.

The main component of interactional processes is interaction sequence. Interaction sequence, I have said, involves verbal strategies (with the proviso now that an interactant may not be aware of using a particular strategy), the sense of passing through stages to accomplish a social purpose; and the elements of situation that it articulates are above all social situation and purpose. This claim is borne out by Hasan (Halliday and Hasan 1985: 108), who discusses the relationship between field, tenor and mode (here called contextual configuration, or CC) and genre (that is, interaction sequence):

> Genre bears a logical relation to CC, being its verbal expression. If CC is a class of situation type, then genre is language doing the job appropriate to that class of social happenings.

At another point (Halliday and Hasan 1985: 56) Hasan is even more specific:

> . . . the features of the CC can be used for making certain kinds of predictions about text structure . . . More succinctly we would say that a CC can predict the OBLIGATORY . . . and the OPTIONAL . . . elements of a text's structure as well as their SEQUENCE . . . and the possibility of their INTERACTION.

With the qualification that interaction sequence (i.e. genre, text structure) is behavioural rather than verbal (since an interaction sequence may be realized non-verbally), I would see this position as close to mine.

Interaction sequence can therefore be seen (at least in the spoken channel) as an activity sequence shared between an emitter and a receiver, and realized both verbally and non-verbally. With this definition, we are now in a position to examine more closely the different components (genre, exchange plus pre-sequence) that go to make up interaction sequence, to determine whether they indeed conform to the definition. First I consider genre. It will be recalled that in examining the study of genre by Ventola and Martin I referred to two genres, casual conversation and service encounter. The first of these has the schematic structure Greeting ^ Address ^ Approach (Direct or Indirect) ^ Centring ^ Leave-taking ^ Goodbye, while the second has the structure Greeting ^ Turn Allocation ^ Service Bid ^ Service ^ Resolution ^ Pay ^ Goods Hand-over ^ Closing ^ Goodbye. Now a service encounter is clearly an interaction sequence, in that it is a well recognized activity sequence shared between an emitter and a receiver, but the case of casual conversation is less clear. Casual conversation is not an observable activity sequence the way making a purchase is, but perhaps it articulates a less observable activity sequence like 'maintaining social contact', whose activities are as much verbal as physical. This suggests that there are at least two types of interaction sequences: those like service encounter which derive from the schema of the ongoing social activity (i.e. shopping), and can therefore be seen as SCHEMATIC; and those like casual conversation which, since they do in fact constitute the ongoing social activity (i.e. socializing), derive from social discourses and practices, and can therefore be seen as DISCURSIVE.

I turn now to the exchange and pre-sequence. As previously implied, the exchange, as conceptualized by Sinclair, Coulthard and Burton, is not an activity sequence shared between two or more participants, and does not qualify as an interaction sequence. However, if the exchange is combined with the ethnomethodologists' pre-sequence, then it is possible to see exchanges as either the central part or the orientation in *discursive* interaction sequences, which derive, as I have just pointed out, from social discourses and processes. Once the exchange plus pre-sequence has been admitted to the ranks, we now have a list of interaction sequences that includes not only the (schematic) service encounter and the (discursive) casual conversation but also what we might call extended exchanges such as request sequences or invitation sequences.

In addition to interaction sequence, there are two other interactional processes at work in a communicative event, ATTITUDE and SHARED KNOWLEDGE. Attitude is a way of bringing into our model one of the non-particulate aspects of language, the linguistic charge that Halliday calls *field* (as in electromagnetic field, and not to be confused with the identically named dimension of situation). It is likely that attitude articulates social relationship or purpose, or a mixture of both, and that it is not necessarily co-terminous with a given interaction sequence, since two or more attitudes may be found in one interaction sequence, or one attitude may spread over two or more interaction sequences. Finally attitudes, which may well be unconscious, can best be thought of in terms of a set of features such as Munby's 'attitudinal-tone index' (1978: 104–10) rather than as a system.

Shared knowledge, however, is a system, illustrated in Figure 4.5. First, an explanation of the system. Context of co-text is the immediate or remote textual environment of a move in the ongoing interaction; maximum

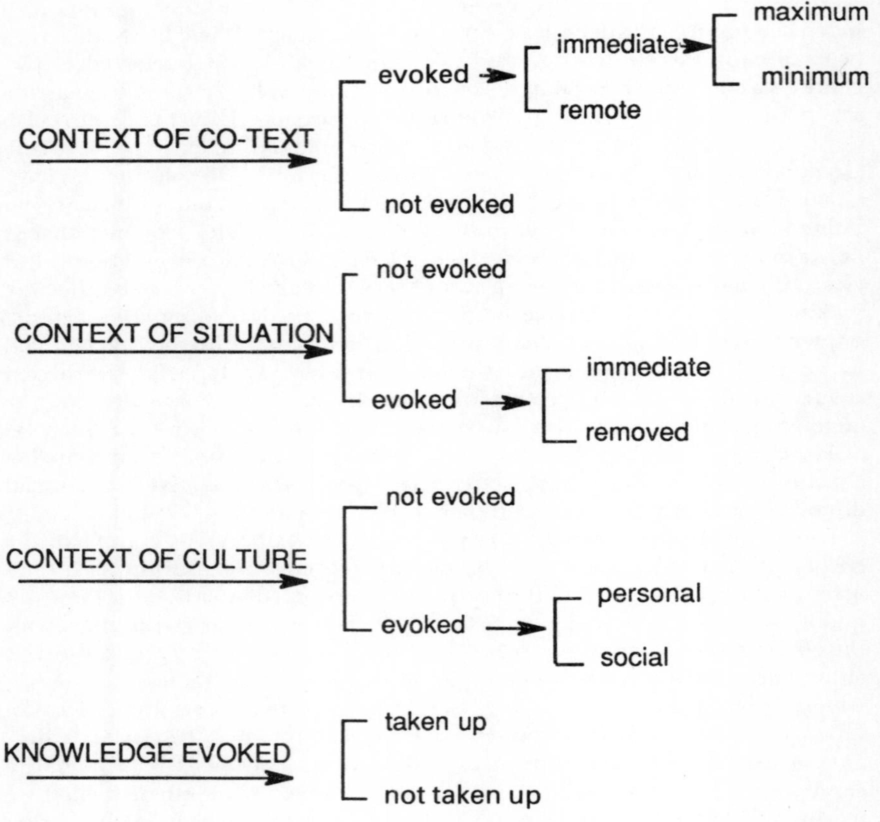

Figure 4.5 The system of shared knowledge

represents a choice such as ellipsis, minimum a choice such as lexical collocation. (Maximum and minimum are actually two extremes on a continuum rather than two opposing choices.) Context of situation is the relevant non-verbal environment of the text, whether visible (immediate) or invisible (removed). Context of culture is social (relevant discursive formations, thematic systems and social action semiotic) or personal (the idiosyncratic discourses, practices and experiences of small units such as families or groups of friends).

The choice of a particular option in shared knowledge – including the choice of whether or not to take up a particular piece of shared knowledge – derives from social relationship, purpose and symbolic function, in the sense that the relative status of interactants, their pragmatic and relationship quality purposes, and the part assigned to language in the interaction, all determine the extent to which shared knowledge can or will be evoked and taken up in the course of an interaction (as usual, this may not be a conscious choice on the part of interactants). Not surprisingly, then, shared knowledge, like attitude, represents an intrusion of the non-particulate into our model, both field (shared knowledge as index of feeling) and wave (shared knowledge as distributor of information).

4.4.4 Language and other codes

The situation type, mediated by the interactional processes of interaction sequence, attitude and shared knowledge, is realized not only by lexicogrammer but also (or alternatively) by non-verbal codes such as kinesics (gesture, posture, facial expression), proxemics (the relative closeness or distance of participants in a communicative event) and tone of voice. The relationship between the mediating interactional processes and the metafunctions is complex, but there is a tendency for interaction sequence to be linked to the experimental metafunction, attitude to the interpersonal, and shared knowledge to the textual.

The link between interactional processes and non-verbal codes is even more complex: for example, a smile may, given the appropriate context, realize a move in an interaction sequence, attitude to subject matter or addressee, or evocation of shared knowledge. This no doubt stems from the fact that codes such as gesture or facial expression do not appear to have a 'grammar'. Although researchers like Birdwhistell (1970) or Hall (1966) have attempted to analyse kinesic or proxemic codes (see Pennycook 1985 for an accessible account of the work of these and other scholars), their descriptions are often extremely technical. I shall limit myself here to a simple and impressionistic account of the most salient non-verbal features accompanying a verbal utterance or realizing a non-verbal utterance.

A final note: the lexicogrammatical analysis will use the terminology of Halliday (1985), since this book is the clearest and most accessible exposition of functional grammer. Where the terminology differs from earlier works (I am thinking in particular of clause complexes and conjunction), I will add a note of explanation.

4.4.5 The model in operation

I have been stressing the ability of this model to account for interpersonal negotiation, a constantly changing context of situation, and fluidity of meaning, so it is now time to demonstrate this ability. The model, as I indicated at the beginning of section 4.4, is two-way, in the sense that it represents not only the act of producing a communicative event, starting from the relevant social discourses and practices, and passing through situation type and interactional processes to language and other codes, but also an interpretation of the communicative event, starting from language and other codes, and passing through interactional processes and situation type to social discourses and practices. Now there may well be a mismatch between producer and interpreter: nothing guarantees that the interpreter will 'read' the interactional processes, situation type and social discourses and practices in the way the producer 'meant' them. (I am not saying that producer and interpreter consciously analyse all these variables – merely that the way they understand a given utterance is underpinned by an unconscious awareness of all the relevant variables that are in play at a particular moment.) And it is precisely in this mismatch that we can chart a changing context of situation, fluid meaning, and the process of interpersonal negotiation.

To show what I mean, I am going to analyse a short dialogue from Unit 10 of the ELT textbook *Starting Strategies* (Abbs and Freebairn 1977: 54), from the point of view first of the encoder (producer) and then of the decoder (interpreter). This will be a fairly crude analysis (I am not at this point presenting any thematic system networks, for example), intended largely to underline the importance of the twin perspectives to a process model of language. I will produce the dialogue in full – it is accompanied by drawings which will be represented here by 'stage directions' in parentheses.

1. (a) *Neville:* (i) Jackie! (ii) It's coffee time! (*Head Peeping Round Door.*)
   (b) *Jackie:* Coming! (*Seated at Typewriter.*)
2. (c) *Neville:* Well, this is the cafeteria. (*They Enter.*)
   (d) *Jackie:* It's nice and modern!
3. (e) *Neville:* Would you like a cup of coffee? (*Hand Reaching for Cup.*)
   (f) *Jackie:* Yes, please.
   (g) *Neville:* And a biscuit? (*Hand Reaching to Biscuit.*)
   (h) *Jackie:* (i) No thanks. (ii) Just a coffee.

It is also pertinent to note that the dialogue takes place in a workplace (the office of a company that makes films), and that the two speakers (both young, good-looking and probably single) are colleagues, 'Neville' being a cameraman, and 'Jackie' a secretary only recently recruited.

4.4.5.1 The encoder's perspective

Any text articulates the social discourses and practices that enable it, so I will begin by looking at the discursive formations, thematic systems and social action semiotic which inform this dialogue.

4.4.5.1.1 Social discourses and practices

Discursive formation: the discourse and non-discursive practices of (capitalist) economics and industrial relations. (Recall that discourse here is the sum of the discursive objects, subject positions, and the principles of organization of the statements.)

Thematic systems: the lexical item 'coffee' belongs to an extensive thematic system in which it typically realizes certain participant roles (such as Phenomenon and Range) in a set of mental or material processes (including 'like', 'need', 'have', 'drink') accompanied by certain types of circumstances (Location, Time). This is the main thematic system, but conceivably there is also another one, discreetly articulated by the pronoun 'you' (i.e. 'Jackie') functioning as Senser in a mental process ('like'), and contrasting with the speaker ('Neville'), functioning as a kind of non-verbal 'Actor' (when he reaches for the coffee). This contrast suggests the thematic system 'male–female relations'.

Social action semiotic: relations between colleagues (e.g. showing a new colleague the staff cafeteria); gender roles (e.g. man buys woman coffee); and cafeteria behaviour (e.g. serving oneself).

4.4.5.1.2 Situation

Social situation: socializing: coffee break/purchasing.

Subject matter: coffee, biscuits.

Social situation and subject matter both articulate the discourse and practices of industrial relations (which allow and even encourage socializing at certain fixed times), the thematic system of which the lexical item 'coffee' is a member, and the systems of the social action semiotic mentioned above. Discourse, non-discursive practices, thematic systems and social action semiotic systems are available to both participants in the speech event in the form of schemas – provided, of course, that both participants have the same cultural positioning. (Presumably the fictional participants do, but I'll consider below whether the same can be said of the authors of the textbook, on the one hand, and the learners using it on the other.)

Social relationship: colleague–colleague; male–female.

These social relationships are taken from Munby's inventory (1978: 72) – the former is a symmetrical relationship, while the latter is an asymmetrical relationship. The relationships articulate systems in the social action semiotic, though the influence of the discursive formation of industrial relations, particularly as it concerns the subject positions of hierarchically unequal colleagues, cannot be ruled out.

Purpose: [regulatory]; [closeness].

These pragmatic and relationship quality options articulate interpersonal and rhetorical relations of the thematic systems/social action semiotic 'work' and 'male–female relations', and possibly industrial relations discourse and practices (regarding behaviour towards a new member of staff).

Channel: spontaneous spoken; face-to-face (but for the learner: written-to-be-spoken-and-learnt; printed word).

The first channel articulates discourse structure relations in the social action semiotic; the second articulates the discourse of education, in particular of language teaching.

Symbolic function: ancillary.

For the participants the verbal action is ancillary, since actions such as leaning through the door or reaching for a cup also carry significant meaning. Here we can speculate that the relationship between language and paralinguistic codes derives from discourse structure relations in a given system of the social action semiotic (which perhaps provide options for posture, gestures, facial expressions, etc., to accompany various social practices in the system).

For the learner, too, the verbal action is ancillary, but in a different way: the dialogue itself is only part of the teaching/learning process; the relationship between the dialogue and the teaching/learning process derives from the objects and the principle of their organization of the relevant discursive formation (i.e. language education).

4.4.5.1.3 Interactional processes

Interaction sequence: Summons^Orient^Accept Invitation^Socialize Offer^ Accept^Offer^Refuse.

Interaction sequence here articulates social situation ('socializing: coffee break'), purpose ('regulatory; closeness') and, perhaps, the asymmetrical social relationship 'male–female'. This is clearly an activity sequence ('going to the cafeteria') shared between two people, though it could be argued that it is actually three separate sequences (if we ignore Summons): Invite (in fact a pre-invitation, here termed Orient) followed by Accept; Socialize; and Offer^Accept/Refuse. Classifying the first sequence as Orient^Accept Invitation raises an important question, one that will be addressed in discussion of the decoder's perspective.

Attitude: friendly/tentative; casual/enthusiastic.

Note that here, and in future analyses, the first set of attitudinal adjectives refers to the first speaker (in this dialogue, Neville), and the second set refers to the second speaker (in this case, Jackie).

Attitude to addressee and to social situation/subject matter articulate social relationship ('colleague–colleague'; 'male–female') and relationship quality ('closeness'), as well as social situation ('socializing').

Shared knowledge: (1) [social]^[immediate], (2) [immediate]^[minimum], (3) [social]^[maximum]^[maximum]^[maximum].

The shared knowledge evoked (and taken up) differs in each micro-sequence. In the first micro-sequence the initiator evokes social knowledge (a coffee break is an accepted institutional practice which often takes place in an area specially set aside for the purpose), while the responder evokes environmental knowledge (as shown by the Mood ellipsis in the utterance 'Coming!'). In the second micro-sequence the initiator evokes environmental knowledge (indicated by the exophoric demonstrative 'this'), while the responder evokes minimum knowledge of co-text (through the anaphoric pronoun 'It'). In the third micro-sequence 'Neville' at first evokes social shared knowledge (a thematic system related to 'offers' intersecting with the thematic system to which 'coffee' belongs, plus choices in the relevant system of the social action semiotic), then maximum knowledge of co-text (ellipsis of Mood and Predictor 'would you like'), while 'Jackie' evokes maximum knowledge of co-text (clausal ellipsis of 'I'd like a cup of coffee', then ellipsis of Mood and Predictor, namely 'I'd like').

4.4.5.1.4 Language and other codes

Micro-sequence 1:

(a) (i) [vocative]; [tone 5]
(ii) [relational:identifying]; [declarative]; unmarked theme and information focus; [tone 1]; [key:high]; STANDING AT DOOR LEANING IN

(b) [material]; [declarative] with Mood ellipsis; unmarked theme and information focus; [tone 1]; SEATED - - - ➤RISING FROM SEAT

The grammatical options are all taken from the experiential, interpersonal and textual systems previously described, except for [key:high], which is taken from Coulthard and Brazil (in Coulthard and Montgomery, 1981). Paralinguistic options are represented in capital letters. These grammatical and paralinguistic options articulate a combination of interaction sequence (Orient^Accept Invitation), shared knowledge (coffee break is an accepted practice that takes place in a separate area) and attitude (friendly; casual). Lexis is drawn from the 'coffee break' schema and so, indirectly, from the thematic system to which 'coffee' belongs; and postural options from the relevant system of the social action semiotic ('relations between colleagues'? 'gender roles'?).

Micro-sequence 2:

(c) [relational: identifying]; [declarative]; unmarked theme and information focus; exophoric demonstrative.
(d) [relational:attributive]; [declarative]; [tone 5]; unmarked theme and information focus; anaphoric pronoun; WARM.

The intiation articulates the Socialize element of 'going to the cafeteria (for the first time)' and shared knowledge of the immediate environment; the response articulates the Socialize element, the attitude to subject matter 'enthusiastic', and minimum knowledge of co-text. Lexis is drawn from the 'coffee' thematic system. Note that WARM indicates a tone of voice that here articulates the attitude 'enthusiastic'.

Micro-sequence 3:

(e) [mental:affect]; [interrogative: modalized]; modal and topical theme, unmarked information focus; [tone 2]; HAND REACHING OUT FOR CUP
(f) [positive]; clausal ellipsis
(g) conjunction : additive; ellipsis of Mood and Predictor; [tone 2]; HAND REACHING OUT FOR BISCUIT
(h) (i) [negative]; clausal ellipsis
(ii) ellipsis of Mood and Predictor

The first initiation, move (e), articulates the element Offer, the attitude-to-addressee 'tentative', and social shared knowledge (that, given the sequence element Offer and the attitude-to-addressee 'tentative', it is appropriate to choose from the intersecting thematic systems 'offers/coffee' a form of offer that involves [mental:affect] with addressee as Senser, [interrogative], and [modulation:inclination:oblique]. The second initiation, move (g), articulates Offer plus maximum knowledge of co-text, while the responses articulate Accept or Refuse together with the attitude-to-addressee 'friendly'.

4.4.5.2 The decoder's perspective

What have been analysed so far are the social discourse and practice choices, the components of situation, and the interactional processes that the encoder brings into play in producing his/her utterance, his/her meaning. But communication is a two-way process, and the question is: confronted with a configuration of grammatical and paralinguistic choices, how does the decoder 'interpret' the encoder's meaning? Indeed, does the decoder always interpret the encoder's meaning 'correctly'? Or, to put it another way, does the decoder bring into play the same interactional processes, components of situation and social discourses/practices as the encoder?

Micro-sequence 1 provides a good example of the flexibility the decoder has in NEGOTIATING MEANING with the encoder. As a reminder:

Neville: Jackie! It's coffee time!
Jackie: Coming!

Ignoring the [vocative] with [tone 5] and postural option STANDING AT THE DOOR LEANING IN, readily interpretable as a Summons, we may suppose that, if 'Jackie' has any problem here, it will be with the relational process in the declarative mood. As previously noted, these grammatical choices articulate the element Orient (pre-invitation) only in the context of specific shared social knowledge and attitude-to-addressee-and-social-situation. But suppose 'Jackie' does not share, or 'take up', the social knowledge that is evoked (perhaps as a new employee she does not know the procedure for coffee break in the organization); or suppose her attitude to 'Neville', or to the social situation (possibly unclear), or to the subject matter ('coffee break') articulates different choices in the social action semiotic systems 'gender roles' and 'relations between colleagues'. In that case she may take note of [key:high] and the postural option STANDING AT THE DOOR LEANING IN and interpret the utterance as a pre-invitation (Orient), but await a possible invitation instead of proceeding to Accept Invitation; or she may choose to ignore the high key and postural option, and interpret the utterance as, say, the Approach Indirect element in a casual conversation. Thus she will bring into play these interactional processes (the options in parentheses are those that 'Jackie' ascribes to 'Neville'):

Interaction sequence: (Orient Invite) or (Approach Indirect)
Attitude: (friendly;) tentative
Shared knowledge: ([social];) [not taken up]^[minimum]

and will equally bring into play this component of situation:

Purpose: ([regulatory]? [informative]?; [closeness]? [respect]?)

This combination of interaction sequence reading, 'tentative' attitude, inability or refusal to take up social shared knowledge leading to minimum evocation of co-text, and confusion as to purpose, is likely to result in an echo response with nominal substitution, along the lines of:

Jackie: Oh yes! So it is!

accompanied by the gestural option LOOKING AT WATCH and the tone of voice SURPRISED. 'Neville' then has two choices. Firstly, he can move on to the element Invite, change his attitude to 'tentative', and stop evoking social shared knowledge relating to the discursive formation 'industrial relations', in order to evoke social shared knowledge relating to the intersecting thematic systems 'invitations'/'coffee'. He could thus say (and remember that this is Unit 10 in a beginners' course):

Neville: Would you like to come to the cafeteria?

(As in Micro-sequence 3, 'Neville' evokes knowledge of a network of thematic system relations in which the grammatical configuration: addressee as Senser in a [mental:affect] process with [modulation:inclination:oblique] and interrogative mood, in conjunction with an appropriate interaction sequence element and attitude option, is recognized as the prelude to an invitation.)

The second choice that 'Neville' has is to fall in line with 'Jackie' and reinterpret the interaction sequence as an Approach Indirect, while maintaining the same attitude ('friendly'; 'casual'), but adopting a different shared knowledge strategy (by evoking straightforward knowledge of the environment). In this case he might say:

Neville: See you in the cafeteria!

(where Subject and 'the cafeteria' are recovered from the immediate or less immediate environment).

If 'Neville' responds with 'Would you like to come to the cafeteria?', 'Jackie' will most probably adopt the element Accept, the attitude 'interested' and the shared knowledge option [maximum]:

Jackie: Yes, sure!

If on the other hand 'Neville' replies with 'See you in the cafeteria!' she will in all probability maintain the interaction sequence element Approach Indirect, and the attitude 'friendly; casual' with the minimal response:

Jackie: Right!

(perhaps with the paralinguistic option SMILE).

'Neville' may now terminate the dialogue by his departure, or he may seek to prolong the dialogue by choosing the postural option HESITATE, in preparation for moving from Approach Indirect to another interaction sequence (that is, micro-sequence). He can make the move himself by adopting the element Offer, the attitude 'tentative', and social shared knowledge:

Neville: Shall I wait for you?

(The social shared knowledge evoked here is that of the thematic system 'offers' (offers of services rather than goods), which permits a form of offer in which the speaker is Actor in a material process clause that is in the interrogative mood and modulated by [obligation]).

A parallel move can also be made by 'Jackie':

Jackie: Shall I go with you?

By this time meaning should have been successfully negotiated, and the participants should be ready to terminate the interaction or to proceed to Micro-sequence 2.

4.5 CONCLUSION

4.5.1 Process in language

At the end of Chapter 3 I posed a number of questions, of which the most important were: how do we model the process of interpersonal negotiation? What is the best way to model a constantly changing context of situation? How do we represent what is conventional and iterable in language, and show the fluidity of meaning that flows from this? How can we model the non-particulate aspects of language? Should we bring the body into the act? These questions have all been addressed in the course of Chapter 4, and it is now time to sum up the findings, if not the answers, that have emerged.

The answer to the first question – how do we model the process of interpersonal negotiation? – lies in the twin encoder/decoder perspective that I have just illustrated. Interpersonal negotiation – or negotiation of meaning, as I shall now call it – occurs when a participant in an interaction (A, let us say) is uncertain as to the meanings of another participant (let us call the second one B); this uncertainty arises, I believe, because participant A does not know how to interpret one or more of the interactional processes, situational components or social discourses/practices that inform the language or paralinguistic options of participant B. The twin encoder/decoder perspective reveals any possible mismatch between what A is intending to mean, and the way B interprets A's meaning, and any meaning negotiation that does (or does not) ensue.

This also partly answers the second question: what is the best way to model a constantly changing context of situation? The encoder/decoder perspective makes it clear that the situation is always up for negotiation; and those ever-shifting interactional processes – interaction sequence, attitude and shared knowledge – betray just how fluid is the situation that they articulate.

The third question is: how do we represent what is conventional and iterable in language, and show the fluidity of meaning that flows from this? The first part of the question is easily answered: what is conventional and iterable in language is represented above all by the thematic systems. (This will become clearer when I present a thematic system in Chapter 6.) I am less confident, however, about answering the second part of the question. I suspect that any answer must start with the concept of PLAY: the experience of such a massive network of thematic systems is naturally a strong constraint, in the sense that we are constantly 'quoting' from the network, but the very fact that we can 'quote' from an almost endless variety of thematic systems also means that we can 'misquote' them, play with them. Let me give a simple and trivial example.

On the face of it, the utterance 'I'm tired' is drawn from a 'physical states' thematic system and affirms something about the bodily state of the speaker. But, as everyone knows, of course, 'I'm tired' can, according to context, intonation, tone of voice, posture, and other paralinguistic options, be a complaint, a sign of boredom, an exhortation (to a partner to leave a party, for example), an expression of a desire (to go to bed, for instance), or a refusal to do something requested. Admittedly, the intention of the speaker is usually fairly unambiguous, but the element of play is certainly there: if the 'intention', or perceived intention, of the speaker is challenged by the other participant(s), and seems likely to have negative consequences, the speaker can always fall back on the 'literal' meaning (a 'quote' from the physical states' thematic system) – a strategy that is often pursued in everyday life, though not always with marked success.

The last two questions concern how we model the non-particulate aspects of language, and whether we should bring the body into the act. The two questions are to some extent related, for the body, and the somatic sign systems that the body produces, are without doubt non-particulate and, in the spoken mode at least, crucial to an understanding of 'linguistic' interaction. So the answer is that we do bring the body into the act; and that what we have called paralinguistic options, together with analysis of the interpersonal and textual metafunctions, and of the interactional processes referred to as attitude and shared knowledge, are an attempt to model this non-particulate side of language.

4.5.2 Process and the communicative syllabus

Two further questions remain to be asked and answered: what are the implications of this process model of language for the learner of English, and how can the model be applied to the creation of a communicative syllabus? To the first question I can for the moment give only a provisional answer. For native speakers of English – and for the fictional participants – the dialogue I presented above is unproblematical. But a moment's reflection will make it clear that for a learner of English, still coming to grips with the thematic systems, social action semiotic, schemas, interaction sequences and paralinguistic codes of the English language and English (American, Canadian, Australian) people, this and a thousand other dialogues could be bristling with obstacles. A process model of language reveals in a systematic way what some of these obstacles are, thereby giving the learner the possibility of surmounting them.

But a learner can surmount such obstacles more easily if s/he has a teacher able to lend assistance. And a teacher is better able to lend assistance if equipped with a communicative syllabus based on a process model of language. The rest of this book will be concerned with outlining the principles and practices of a process-oriented communicative syllabus; but first of all I examine an early attempt at a communicative (more properly, functional-notional) course, *Building Strategies* (Abbs and Freebairn 1979). I do this not to praise or criticize the book, but to determine how 'communicative' it is, so that from its successes and its shortcomings I can draw some conclusion as to what is needed for a truly communicative course that helps learners of English develop the meaning negotiation skills through which all obstacles in everyday communication can be overcome.

5. The functional-notional syllabus: how communicative is it?

5.0 INTRODUCTION

Despite the criticisms made of it – and discussed at length in Chapter 1 – the functional-notional syllabus remained until recently perhaps the most developed expression of the movement towards a more communicative teaching of language. (I say 'until recently' because of the increasing claims made by the task-based syllabus, which I consider in Chapter 9.) The text chosen here to embody this movement, *Building Strategies* (Abbs and Freebairn 1979), is a pre-intermediate functional course book, the second in a series of four, that was written in the early days of the functional approach, and became widely known and used. It would be rash to claim that it is representative of all functional course books published, but probably fair to say that it exhibits features that at least some of its rivals share – features that illustrate quite clearly the potential strengths and weaknesses of the functional approach.

The criteria for judging these potential strengths and weaknesses are, of course, drawn from the meaning negotiation model of language outlined in Chapter 4. Thus I intend to examine the language taught in *Building Strategies* and see if I can assess the extent to which meaning is negotiated in the on-going communicative events, and specify the interactional processes, situation types, and social discourses and practices in operation. Or, to consider the question from the opposite perspective, I want to determine whether the language is predictable on the basis of the information supplied with regard to social discourses and practices and situation type, and whether it involves the negotiation of meaning that is so crucial in communication. To achieve my aim, I need to ask and answer four questions:

1. Are the social discourse and practice choices, situation types and interactional processes specifiable from the dialogues presented in the units?
2. Are the follow-up exercises linked to the dialogue that precedes them?
3. Are the follow-up exercises genuinely communicative?
4. Does negotiation of meaning occur in dialogues and/or follow-up exercises?

There are sixteen units in *Building Strategies*, of which four, an introductory unit and three consolidation units, will not be considered in the following survey. That leaves twelve units to be examined, but for fear of overburdening the reader I will present the analysis of only three of these, though I will use data from my analysis of the other nine units in subsequent discussion. Each of the three units analysed will address one of the questions 2–4 above – question 1 can be answered only by looking at all three units together. The analyses will be 'top-down' rather than 'bottom-up', even though we are in fact starting from the 'bottom' – the realization. The following abbreviations will be used:

SocDP	Social discourses and practices
DF	Discursive formation
TS	Thematic system
SAS	Social action semiotic
Sit	Situation type
SocSit	Social situation
SM	Subject matter
SocRel	Social relationship
Ch	Channel
SF	Symbolic function
Purp	Purpose
IntProc	Interactional processes
IS	Interaction sequence
At	Attitude
SK	Shared knowledge
LR	Linguistic realization
NVR	Non-verbal realization

In addition, the following symbols will be used:

- - - - -►	indicates a transition from one speaker's move to another speaker's move.
^	indicates a transition within the move of one speaker.
[x]	indicates that x is an option in a system.
M[A^B^C]	indicates that interaction sequence move M has embedded within it interaction sequence moves A^B^C.

A question mark (?) after a feature indicates that it cannot be determined from available data. Unless otherwise stated, channel will be 'spoken:face-to-face', and symbolic function will be 'ancillary'. Alphabetical letters signal moves, Roman numerals clauses within moves. In the detailed presentation of linguistic realizations, clauses are analysed for their experiential, interpersonal and textual features in that order, with each of these analyses separated by a semicolon (;).

One further note: only those sections of the dialogue relating to functions taught in the 'sets'-will be analysed. Thus the general procedure is that a key section of the dialogue will be analysed, followed by an analysis of the relevant 'set'.

5.1 THE COMMUNICATIVE VALUE OF A FUNCTIONAL-NOTIONAL COURSE

I now turn to my analysis of three units from *Building Strategies*, considering their communicative value in terms of the three questions posed above. The first unit to be analysed is Unit 2, and the question to be answered here is: are the follow-up exercises linked to the dialogue that precedes them?

5.1.1 The link between dialogue and follow-up exercises

Unit 2

Rod Nelson, a young electrical engineer from Canada, has just taken up a job at Weston Aeronautics in Bristol. One of his colleagues is Jack Cooper, who invites Rod to dinner. Before dinner Rod talks to Barbara, Jack's twenty-four-year-old daughter, who is manageress of a shoes shop. The photo accompanying the dialogue shows the two chatting: Barbara is attractive, smiling and nursing a dog; Rod has shoulder-length hair and is wearing a suit, but his head is turned away (to Barbara's mother?) so that his expression is not visible.

Micro-sequences 1 and 2

(a) *Barbara:* Do you like working at Weston, Rod?
(b) *Rod:* Yes, very much. The job's interesting and the people there are very friendly.
(c) *Barbara:* And do you mind living in a hostel?
(d) *Rod:* It's all right, but I want to find a flat of my own soon.

SocDP:

DF: ?
TS: 'work'; 'living conditions'; 'likes'; 'meeting someone for the first time'

Sit

SocSit: 'entertaining'
SM: 'work'; 'living conditions'
SocRel: 'host–guest'; 'male–female'
Purp: [heuristic]; [closeness]

IntProc

IS: Approach Direct
At: 'friendly' ---► 'enthusiastic'/'unenthusiastic'
SK: [personal] ---► [maximum] ^ [minimum] ---► [personal] -► [minimum]

LR

(a) [mental:affect] with addressee as Senser and material process clause as Phenomenon:Fact; [interrogative:polar] + [vocative]; interpersonal and topical Theme + personal shared knowledge as Given

(b) (i) [positive] + attitudinal submodifier + tone 5 + [quantifier:multal]; clausal ellipsis

(ii) [relational:attributive] with Carrier from 'work' lexical set, Attribute from 'enthusiastic' lexical set; [declarative]; Theme (synonym of *working*) as Given

(iii) as (b)(ii), but with [extension:addition], anaphoric reference, and Theme as collocate of *working*

(c) as (a), but without [vocative], and with [extension:addition]

(d) (i) [relational:attributive] with anaphoric pronoun as Carrier, and Attribute from 'unenthusiastic' lexical set; [declarative] + tone 4; Given as Theme, realized by anaphoric pronoun

(ii) [mental:affect] with speaker as Senser and material process clause as Phenomenon:Fact; [declarative]; [extension:adversative] + co-hyponym of *hostel* as minimum evocation of co-text

NVR

SMILE.

Details of social discourse and practice choices and situation type are well supplied in this micro-sequence, apart from the discourse formation (or is there a very discreet articulation of the discourse of sexuality?). The interaction sequence is the Approach Direct element of casual conversation (see Ventola 1979), which here articulates social situation, subject matter and purpose. The personal shared knowledge (that Rod works for Weston and lives in a hostel) articulates the ancillary nature of the symbolic exchange – ancillary, that is, to a network of social relationships in which Rod is a colleague of Jack Cooper and talks to him, and Barbara is daughter to Jack, who talks to her. The mental process in (a) articulates the interaction sequence element Approach Direct (which permits discussion of personal details of a more 'public' kind), the subject matter 'work' and, indirectly, the relevant systems of the social action semiotic, and the thematic system to which the lexical item *work* belongs – one of whose choices is to assign to *work* or one of its synonyms/hyponyms the role of Phenomenon in a mental process clause of the [affect] type (hence Barbara's question to Rod, and an anguished cry such as 'I hate marking exams!'). Responses (b) and (d) both have a similar form, in that both consist of a REPLY (defined as some equivalent of *yes, no* or *maybe* proffered in response to a demand for information) and a COMMENT (a type of explanation, qualification, etc.): this form articulates the thematic system 'likes', in which there is strong pressure to justify a (dis)like in a following clause or clause complex which, explicitly or implicitly, elaborates, extends or enhances the (dis)like. (See Halliday 1985: 196–7 for an explanation of these terms.) Finally a reminder that the shared knowledge choice [maximum] refers to a maximum evocation of co-text (in other words, ellipsis of some kind), while [minimum] refers to a minimum evocation of co-text such as lexical cohesion (the most minimal) or reference.

In Micro-sequence 1, then, it is possible to trace the relationship between social discourses and practices, situation type and realization. There is, however, no negotiation of meaning between fictional decoder and encoder, though the learner may need to negotiate on *hostel* if it belongs to a different, more positive thematic sub-system in his/her culture (otherwise *all right* may be seen as articulating the attitude 'enthusiastic').

I now turn to the two sets that follow Micro-sequences 1 and 2 – here and in the remaining analyses of Unit 2 dialogues and sets, I will not present linguistic realizations in detail but refer only to those realizations of particular interest, as the need arises.

Set 1 Express likes and dislikes

(a) Do you like cooking? (b1) Yes, very much.
(b2) It's all right.
(b3) Sometimes. It depends.
(b4) No, not much.
(b5) No, I hate it.

SocDP

DF: ?
TS: 'domestic activities'; 'likes'
SAS: ?

Sit

SM: 'cooking'; 'housework'
SocRel: ?
Purp: [heuristic]; ?

IntProc

IS: ?
At: ? – – – –► 'enthusiastic'/'unenthusiastic'/'hostile'
SK: ? – – – –► [maximum]/[minimum]/[maximum]^[social]/
[maximum]/[maximum]^[minimum]

NVR

?

In Set 1 a number of crucial components of the speech event cannot be specified, most notably systems in the social action semiotic, the on-going social situation, social relationship, interaction sequence, and non-verbal realizations. The result is that the grammatical realizations are unpredictable – or rather, since they have already been supplied by the textbook writers, unjustifiable. There is not even any indication of the circumstances in which it would be appropriate or inappropriate to use a response like (b5). And the response (b3) raises particular problems. The clause 'It depends', which can be analysed as a [relational:circumstantial], articulates shared knowledge of the thematic system 'likes' – and although a native or fluent non-native speaker of English knows that there is an implicit Attribute, and is aware of the range of lexical items (e.g. 'It depends on my mood') or embedded clauses (e.g. 'It depends on who's coming to dinner') which could realize that specific function, a pre-intermediate learner of English most probably does not know these things, and is not told in Unit 2. Nor is the learner warned that at this stage a decoder could well choose to negotiate meaning by asking, 'On what?' Thus explaining a thematic system choice is as important in some cases as specifying social situation or interaction sequence.

Set 2. Express personal opinions

1. (a) Do you like working at Weston, Rod?
   (b) Yes, very much. The job's interesting and the people there are friendly.

This exchange has already been analysed and needs no further comment.

2. (a) What do you think of the new theatre?
   (b) I think it's awful.
   (c) Do you? I think it's quite attractive. What do you think, Ann?
   (d) I don't like it. I think it's ugly.

(This dialogue is in the form of a photo of the National Theatre in London, with people standing outside it, out of whose mouths come speech balloons.)

SocDP

DF: 'architecture'
TS: 'buildings'; 'opinions'
SAS: ?

Sit

SocSit: ? or 'socializing'
SM: 'new (theatre) building'
SocRel: ?
Purp: [heuristic]; ?

IntProc

IS: ? or Approach Indirect
At: ? – – – – ► 'disapproving' – – – – ► 'approving'
'disapproving'

SK: [immediate] ---► [minimum] ---► [maximum]^
[minimum]^[maximum] ---► [minimum]

NVR
?

This exchange is at least provided with a definable environment, but otherwise the same crucial features are missing as in Set 1. It could be argued that the social situation 'socializing' and the interaction sequence Approach Indirect can be inferred from move (a), with the exophoric demonstrative reference of *the new theatre* implying a conversation between people who have just bumped into each other – but this is neither obvious nor certain, especially for a learner of English. Again it is possible to speculate on the relationship between the participants, but all that is really certain is that at least two of the speakers know each other, and one speaker is female. No negotiation of meaning occurs, although the opportunity exists: the first reply is not followed by a comment, thereby inviting the decoder to seek clarification (the simplest form of meaning negotiation).

Micro-sequence 3

(a) *Barbara*: Do you know many people yet?
(b) *Rod*: No, not many. Unfortunately.
(c) *Barbara*: Well, would you like to come and have a look round the shoe shop one day? In fact, what about coming next Saturday at lunch time? We close at one o'clock.
(d) *Rod*: Thanks. That's a great idea. Why don't we have lunch together?
(e) *Barbara*: Fine. I'm not so keen on big lunches, but we could have something light.
(f) Rod: Good. That's fixed, then.

SocDP

DF: ?
TS: 'getting to know people'; 'suggestions'
SAS: 'relations between host and guest'; 'gender roles'

Sit

SocSit: 'entertaining'
SM: 'friends'; 'visiting a workplace'; 'eating out'
SocRel: 'host–guest'; 'male–female'
Purp: [regulatory]; [closeness]

IntProc

IS: Centring [Orient^Suggest^Accept^Clarity]
At: 'friendly'; 'regretful'; 'enthusiastic'; 'unenthusiastic'
SK: [maximum]; [social]; [minimum]

NVR

SMILE or ?

(*Note.* In the interaction sequence the order of Accept and Clarify is not fixed)

As was the case with Micro-sequence 1, social discourse and practice choices and situational component choices are readily determinable. The interaction sequence is the Centring element of casual conversation, in which is embedded (hence the square brackets) a Suggest interaction sequence, whose beginning is marked by the continuative conjunction 'Well'. Barbara's first MOVE (to adapt the terminology used by discourse analysts like Sinclair, Coulthard and Burton) may seem like a continuation of the Approach Direct of Micro-sequences 1 and 2, with the mental process of 'Do you know many people' having the addressee as Senser and a poplar interrogative form – but in the event the fictional decoder does not 'read' it this way. Move (a), in fact, appears to be articulating the thematic system 'getting to know people' and the interaction sequence element Orient ('pre-suggestion'), as confirmed in the move (b) response by the Comment Adjunct 'Unfortunately', which anticipates (even invites) the subsequent Suggest – a fact which the language learner may not appreciate.

The first two clauses of move (c) articulate the Suggest and Clarify of the embedded interaction sequence. Both evoke (social) shared knowledge of the thematic system 'suggestions': the first ('would you like to come . . . '), of the configuration in which addressee is Senser in a poplar interrogative mental process clause modulated by [inclination:median] with the suggested activity a projected material process clause (see Halliday 1985: 337 and 196 for explanations of these terms); and the second ('what about coming . . . '), of the choice which assigns to the suggested activity the role of non-finite material process clause embedded in a prepositional phrase functioning as Circumstance: Matter in a minor clause whose only other element is 'what'. The second clause appears to be a suggestion (and is treated as such in Set 3) – but its status as Clarify is supported by the repetition ('come–coming'), and the fact that the two temporal elements 'next Saturday at lunchtime' have the status of New (information) in the clause.

At this point Rod continues the micro-sequence with his own Suggest ('Why don't we . . . '), evoking another choice in the thematic system – a choice permitting speaker and addressee both to function as Actor in a material process clause with negative polarity and [interrogative: wh-: Reason]. Barbara's Clarify ('I'm not so keen on . . . ') is articulated by a complex configuration of polarity ('not'), tone 4, attitudinal sub-modification ('so'), conjunction ('but') and antonymy ('big–light'). The second clause of her Clarify ('we could have . . . ') can also be treated as a suggestion – another choice in the thematic system giving both speaker and addressee the status of Actor in a material process clause with declarative mood and modalized by [modality:low].

Set 3. Making suggestions and plans

1. (a) What about coming next Sunday?
   (b) That's a good idea!
2. (a) How about meeting for lunch?
   (b) That's a great idea!
3. (a) Why don't we have lunch together?
   (b) Well, I'm not so keen on lunch. How about supper instead?

SocDP

DF: ?
TS: ?; 'suggestions'
SAS: ?

Sit

SocSit: ?
SM: 'eating out'
SocRel: ?
Purp: [regulatory]; ?

IntProc

IS: Suggest Accept Clarify
At: 'enthusiastic'; 'unenthusiastic'
SK: [social]; [minimum]

NVR

?

The crucial elements that were not specifiable in Sets 1 and 2 are equally impossible to determine here. It could be argued that the set refers back to Micro-sequence 3, but this is nowhere made clear, and the three exchanges are not even exactly the same as those in the dialogue.

To sum up Unit 2, the social discourse and practice choices and situational components articulated by the linguistic and non-verbal realizations are quite explicit in the micro-sequences of the dialogue, but are difficult, if not impossible, to determine in the three sets, whose link with the micro-sequences varies between tenuous and non-existent.

I now turn my attention to the third question I posed: are the exercises genuinely communicative? To answer this question I will consider Unit 7. Because of the simplicity of the language in this unit, no detailed analysis of the linguistic realizations will be made.

5.1.2 The communicative value of exercises

Unit 7

Rod Nelson (who by this time has escaped the hostel of Unit 2) and his new flatmate

Paul Blake have invited Barbara and Sue, Paul's girlfriend, to supper. They are in the kitchen getting supper ready.

Micro-sequence 1

(a) *Paul*: What have we got in the fridge, Rod?
(b) *Rod*: Nothing much. We've got some ham, eggs, cheese . . .
(c) *Paul*: Have we got any potatoes?
(d) *Rod*: I think so. Yes, we have.

SocDP

DF: ?
TS: 'cooking'
SAS: 'relations between flatmates'; 'relations between cook and helper'

Sit

SocSit: 'cooking'
SM: 'ingredients'
SocRel: 'friend–friend'
Purp: [regulatory]; [closeness]

IntProc

IS: Orient (^Prepare)
At: 'casual'
SK: [maximum]

NVR

?

The interaction sequence, as the continuation of Micro-sequence 1 reveals (Paul decides to make a potato salad), is one not previously mentioned, which might be termed Following a Recipe. Many of its realizations are non-verbal, but here the Orient consists in verbal checking to see whether the necessary ingredients are available – which is why the social purpose is analysed not as heuristic (the analysis to be expected when a series of questions is asked) but as regulatory.

Set 1. Ask and say what you have and haven't got

1. (a) Have we got any milk?
   (b) Yes, we've got lots of milk.
2. (a) Have we got any meat?
   (b) No, we haven't.

The two exchanges in Set 1, although appearing to be an extension of Micro-sequence 1, are actually supplied with a different context, namely a kitchen list, on which figure a number of items marked with a tick or a cross. So the analysis is:

SocDP

DF: ?
TS: ?
SAS: ?

Sit

SocSit: 'shopping'
SM: 'food'
SocRel: ?
Ch: 'written'
Purp: [informational]; [respect]

IntProc

IS: ?
At: 'informal'
SK: ?

NVR

DRAWINGS OF FOOD (pictorial code)

Set 1, which could have been simply an extension of the dialogue, has been rendered almost impossible to analyse by this contextualization. The problem is that it is partial – a list only, with no indication of possible use (e.g. Rod and Paul shopping in a supermarket). As a result, it has no obvious communicative purpose, and appears to be nothing more than a formal exercise in disguise.

Micro-sequence 2

(a) *Paul*: Where's the big red plastic bowl?
(b) *Rod*: On the bottom shelf in the cupboard under the sink.

SocDP

DF: ?
TS: 'cooking'
SAS: 'relations between flatmates'; 'relations between cook and helper'

Sit

SocSit: 'preparing a meal'
SM: 'utensils'
SocRel: 'friend–friend'
Purp: [heuristic]; [closeness]

IntProc
IS: (Orient^) Prepare
At: 'casual'
SK: [minimum] – – – ► [maximum]

NVR

CROUCHING AT SINK HOLDING BOWL

This exchange articulates the interaction sequence element Prepare, and the subject matter 'utensils', combined with the social purpose [heuristic]. The accompanying photo shows Paul crouching in front of the sink holding up a bowl; if, however, the kinesic choice were something like NO MOVEMENT TO SINK, then the social purpose could be read as [regulatory], and some sort of negotiation of meaning – verbal, non-verbal, or both – would ensue. But neither the dialogue nor the set exploits this possibility.

Set 2. Describe exactly where things are

(a) Where's the mayonnaise?
(b) In the cupboard.
(c) Which one?
(d) The small one.
(e) Where exactly?
(f) On the top shelf.

As this series of exchanges is apparently an extension of Micro-sequence 2, social discourses and practices, situation and interactional processes are identical, except that subject matter is 'ingredients'. However, the textbook writers have chosen here, for pedagogical reasons, no doubt, to split up the complex nominal group in the response in Micro-sequence 2 ('On the bottom shelf in the cupboard under the sink'): the first, embedded, prepositional phrase ('in the cupboard') of the complex prepositional phrase qualifying 'shelf' has become move (b); the equivalent of the second, embedded, prepositional phrase ('under the sink') in the prepositional phrase complex has become the Epithet ('small') in the nominal group of (d); and the main prepositional phrase ('On the bottom shelf') has become move (f). This may be pedagogically sound, but it articulates a very odd choice in the system of the social action semiotic regulating relations between cook and helper – one which implies a reluctant or incompetent helper, for example. From the point of view of social discourses and practices, then, Set 2 is of doubtful value.

Micro-sequence 3/Set 3. Ask people to do things

As the micro-sequence and the set are identical, they will require only one analysis.

(a) *Rod:* Could you get me the mayonnaise from the cupboard?
(b) *Paul:* Yes, sure.

SocDP

DF: ?
TS: 'cooking'; 'requests'
SAS: 'relations between flatmates'; 'relations between cook and helper'

SocSit: 'preparing a meal'
SM: 'ingredients'
SocRel: 'friend–friend'
Purp: [regulatory]; [closeness]

IntProc

IS: (Orient^) Prepare
At: 'casual'
SK: [social] ----► [maximum]

NVR

?

Set 3(a) articulates verbally the Prepare element of the interaction sequence, since it involves obtaining an ingredient of the recipe. It also evokes knowledge of the thematic system requests: this particular option ('Could you get . . . ') assigns the role of Actor to the addressee and assumes a low degree of inclination ('could') in the addressee. (Other options assign the Actor role but assume a higher degree of inclination ('would'), or assign the addressee the role of Senser with the requested action in an embedded clause ('would you like to . . . ').)

Set 4. Give instructions and advice

This set is based on a 'newspaper article' 'A holiday in the sun? Lovely! But be careful!'

> Don't lie in the sun for hours on your first day. Sunbathe for just half an hour.

SocDP

DF: ?
TS: 'holiday'; 'advice'
SAS: 'relations between media and public'

Sit

SocSit: 'giving advice'
SM: 'sunbathing'
SocRel: 'media–public'; 'adviser–advisee'
Ch: 'written'
SF: 'constitutive'
Purp: [regulatory]; [respect]

IntProc

IS: Advise
At: 'didactic'
SK: [minimum]

NVR

?

The cultural, situational and interactional process variables are all readily recoverable, and the main interest here is the linguistic realization. The first clause articulates the subject matter 'sunbathing' and through it the thematic system 'holidays' (as it is constituted in British society): when a holidaymaker is Actor and sun is Location, then Duration cannot be realized by a synonym of 'a long time'. In the same clause, meronymy refers to 'first day', considered as part of the previously mentioned 'holiday'. Also articulating minimum knowledge of co-text, in the second clause, is synonymy ('sunbathe–lie in the sun'), and antonymy ('hours–half an hour').

To sum up, the language of Set 4, like that of Set 3, is well motivated by social discourses and practices and by situation type, in contrast to Set 1, which is confused, and Set 2, whose extended question–answer form does not arise naturally from the relevant system of the social action semiotic, and completely undermines the communicative value of the exercise.

The final question to be considered is: does negotiation of meaning occur in dialogues and follow-up exercises? Our text this time will be Unit 8, and this time I will follow the precedent of Unit 2 and present a detailed linguistic analysis of the linguistic realizations of one micro-sequence.

5.1.3 Neogitation of meaning

Unit 8

Lynne, a secretary in Rod Nelson's office, is having family problems, and Rod has invited her round to his flat to talk about them. She is due to arrive at any moment when the phone rings.

Micro-sequence 1

(a) *Barbara:* Hello, Rod! Barbara here.
(b) *Rod:* Oh. Oh, hello, Barbara.
(c) *Barbara:* Er. . . are you busy?
(d) *Rod:* Well, yes, actually. I'm just having a shower.

SocDP

DF: ?
TS: ? or 'excuses'
SAS: 'telephone behaviour'

Sit

SocSit: 'telephoning'
SM: 'availability'
SocRel: 'male–female'; 'intimate–intimate'

Ch: 'spoken:telephone'
Purp: [heuristic]; [closeness]

IntProc

IS: Greet^Identify^Speaking Rights
At: 'friendly'/'tentative' -----► 'surprised'/'unwelcoming'
SK: [maximum]

NVR

(c) SURPRISED
(d) UNWELCOMING

It is difficult to see what, if any, thematic system is being articulated in this micro-sequence, unless it is 'excuses' (but is Rod *really* having a shower?). On the other hand, it is clear that the 'telephone behaviour' system of the social action semiotic is informing the dialogue. The interaction sequence Making a Telephone Call includes optional element Speaking Rights – that is, a check to see whether the person called is able to speak to the caller at that particular moment. The most interesting feature of the realization is the way that attitude is articulated not only by Mood Adjunct ('just') and tone of voice (e.g. UNWELCOMING), but also by continuatives ('oh', 'er', 'well') and by a Conjunctive Adjunct ('actually').

Set 1. Ask and talk about present actions

1. (a) Are you busy?
   (b) Well, yes, actually. I'm just having a shower.
2. (a) Am I ringing at a bad time?
   (b) No, I'm just watching TV, but that's all right.

Set 1(1) is taken from Micro-sequence 1, and needs no further comment. Set 1(2) belongs to the same context (the question, though not the reply, occurs in the continuation of Micro-sequence 1), so neither social discourses and practices nor situation type will be analysed again.

(Set 1(2))

IntProc

IS: Speaking Rights
At: 'friendly'
SK: [maximum] ^ [minimum]

Although Set 1(2) appears to be simply the 'welcoming version' of set 2(1), this is misleading: the reason for the denial of speaking rights may in this case (i.e. Rod's conversation with Barbara) be interpreted as a lie, whereas the reason dismissed as no obstacle to the granting of speaking rights may be presumed to be truthful. The apparent parallelism between 1(1) and 1(2) – and, presumably, the desire for pedagogical symmetry, encouraged by the discourse of language teaching – has led to an anomaly in the linguistic realization of 1(2). If 'just' is a Mood Adjunct of time, as it is in 1(1), then it seems more in keeping with the attitude 'unwelcoming' and a denial of speaking rights than with a 'permission to speak'. If, on the other hand, 'just' is a Mood Adjunct of intensity, indicating that the speaker places little value on the activity, then the adversative 'but' is inappropriate.

Set 1 (continued)

3. Could you answer the phone?
   I'm washing my hair.
4. Could you ring back later?
   We're having supper.
5. Could you phone back tomorrow morning?
   We're in the middle of painting the bathroom.

(These exchanges are not related to Micro-sequence 1, except perhaps distantly in the case of (4) and (5), and are contextualized by small drawings.

SocDP

DF: ?
TS: ?
SAS: 'telephone behaviour'

Sit

SocSit: 'telephoning'
SM: 'availability'
SocRel: ?
Ch: (3) spoken:face-to-face; (4) and (5) spoken : telephone
Purp: [regulatory]; ?

IntProc

IS: (3) (Summons) Answer:Other; (4) and (5) Speaking Rights
At: ?
SK: (3) [immediate] - - - - ► [social]; (4) and (5) [social]

A number of cultural, situational and interactional process variables are not clear in these three exchanges, although it might be possible to infer some of them. The 'telephone behaviour' system of the social action semiotic is articulated in (3) by the interaction sequence element Answer:Other – telephones must be answered, but in the middle of a hair-wash the task must be delegated; and in (4) and (5) it is articulated by the perceived necessity to offer a reason for denial of speaking rights. As in Set 1(1) and (2), the linking of these three moves is misleading: although (3) is formally similar to (4) and (5), it is in fact articulating a different channel and interaction sequence.

Micro-sequence 2

Lynne has just arrived,

(a) *Barbara*: Rod? It's me, Barbara. Am I ringing at a bad time again?
(b) *Rod*: No, no, that's all right. Is it something important?
(c) *Barbara*: No, not really. It's just . . . well, some American friends of mine are here for a few days and they wanted to go for a meal this evening. I thought maybe you'd like to come too.
(d) *Rod*: Well, that does sound fun, but . . . er . . . I'm afraid I've got a bad headache, to tell you the truth, and. . .

SocDP

DF: ?
TS: 'excuses'; 'invitations'
SAS: 'relations between boyfriend and girlfriend';
'telephone behaviour'

Sit

SocSit: 'telephoning'
SM: 'eating out'; 'friends'
SocRel: 'male–female'; 'intimate–intimate'
Ch: 'spoken:telephone'
Purp: [regulatory]; [closeness]

IntProc

IS: Identify^Speaking Rights^Orient^Invite^Excuse
At: 'friendly'/'tentative' – – – ► 'unwelcoming'/'nervous'
SK: [maximum]; [minimum]; [social]

LR

(a) (i) minor clause realized by [vocative] + tone 2
(ii) [relational:identifying] with speaker as Identifier; [declarative]; unmarked Theme, information focus
(iii) [material] with speaker as Actor (process and Time circumstantial from 'telephoning' schema) + [present in present]; [interrogative:polar]; unmarked Theme, information focus
(b) (i) [negative]; clausal ellipsis
(ii) [relational:attributive] with Attribute articulating Speaking Rights:Accept; [declarative]; anaphoric demonstrative as Theme
(iii) [relational:attributive] + Attribute from 'telephoning' schema; [interrogative:polar]; Attribute as New (configuration of grammatical choices articulates Speaking Rights:Accept + 'unwelcoming')
(c) (i) [negative] + Comment Adjunct (assertive); clausal ellipsis
(ii) [relational:identifying] with Identifier left unsaid; [declarative] + Mood Adjunct (intensity)
(iii) [relational:circumstantial] with carrier from 'friends' lexical set; [declarative]; Carrier as Theme + continuative ('Well')
(iv) [mental:affect] + projected material process clause from 'eating

out' schema; [declarative]; unmarked theme, information focus + [extension addition]
(v) [mental:cognition] with speaker as Senser; [declarative]
(vi) projected mental process clause with [probability:low] and [inclination:median], itself projecting a material process clause from 'eating out' schema
(d) (i) [relational:attributive] with Attribute from 'eating out' schema; [declarative] + tone 4 + stressed Finite ('does'); attribute as New + continuative ('Well')
(ii) [relational:possessive] with speaker as Carrier (process and Attribute articulate Excuse element of interaction sequence); [declarative] + Comment Adjunct of the admissive type ('to tell you the truth') + Comment Adjunct (desiderative) realized by [mental:affect] with speaker as Senser; [extension:adversative] + continuative ('er') – (Adjuncts and continuative articulate attitude 'nervous')

NVR

UNWELCOMING/TENTATIVE/NERVOUS.

Micro-sequence 2 is one of the most interesting fragments of dialogue in the course book (hence my decision to present a detailed analysis of the linguistic realizations). Of particular value to the learner is the articulation of the system in the social action semiotic 'relations between boyfriend and girlfriend'; of the interaction sequence elements Speaking Rights:Accept, Invite and Excuse; and of the attitude choices 'tentative', 'unwelcoming' and 'nervous'. The articulation of these variables can best be appreciated by examining part of Rod's first move (b)(iii), part of Barbara's second move (c)(v), and the whole of Rod's second move (d). In (b)(iii), Speaking Rights:Accept and 'unwelcoming' together produce an utterance ('Is it something important?') which the student may only partly understand unless made aware of interactional processes and tone of voice. In (c)(v) the interaction sequence element Invite (and so the thematic system 'invitations') combines with the attitude 'tentative' (itself an articulation of the 'boyfriend–girlfriend' system of the social action semiotic) to produce a clause of some complexity: the invitation, in the form of [mental:affect] with [modality:low] and [inclination:median], plus a projected material process clause, is itself projected by a [mental:cognition] clause. Finally, (d) articulates the interaction sequence element Excuse (actually a conflation of Refuse and Excuse), and through it the thematic system 'excuses', in combination with the attitude 'nervous' (and so the 'boyfriend–girlfriend' system of the social action semiotic, or at least the 'seeing other women' sub-system): the main realizations of this are tone of voice, the stressed Finite ('does'), intonation (tone 4 indicates reservation) and the continuative ('Well') in (d)(i), and the adversative ('but'), continuative ('er') and Comment Adjunct ('I'm afraid') in (d)(ii).

Set 2. Invite people to do things. Refuse invitations politely and make excuses

(a) Would you like to go out for a meal?
(b) Thanks very much. I'd love to but I'm afraid I've got a headache.

SocDP

DF: ?
TS: 'invitations'; 'excuses'
SAS: 'polite behaviour'

Sit

SocSit: ?
SM: 'eating out'; 'unavailability'
SocRel: ?
Purp: [regulatory]; ?

IntProc

IS: Invite ^ Refuse ^ Excuse
At: 'courteous'
SK: [social] ----► [maximum] [social]

NVR

?

There is no certainty that the exchange in Set 2 is related to the previous dialogue, so the components of the situation are difficult to specify. The initiation evokes knowledge of the thematic system 'invitations': it is assumed that the encoding of the addressee as Senser and action as projected clause in a polar interrogative, modulated, mental process clause ('Would you like to . . . ') will be recognized as an unmarked form of invitation. As for the response, the minor clause and the elliptical mental process clause articulate the 'polite behaviour' system of the social action semiotic and the 'invitations' thematic system. (Note that 'love' implies a slightly higher degree of commitment than 'like'.) The 'polite behaviour' system is articulated again, along with the 'excuses' thematic system, by the adversative 'but' and the Comment Adjunct 'I'm afraid' (which could also be analysed here as a mental process clause projecting a clause encoding 'unavailability', an analysis more consistent with certain of the thematic system patterns so far observed).

The final impression of Unit 8 is that the writers have created a dialogue which is culturally and situationally of great value to the learner, with considerable potential for negotiation of meaning, but have followed up the dialogue with exercises of relatively little interest. The path to real communication has been laid, but the students have been led along crude stepping stones.

5.2 CONCLUSION

The aim of this chapter has been to assess the communicative value of a functional-notional syllabus, represented by the pre-intermediate course book *Building Strategies*. During the analysis of three units of this course book a partial assessment was made, which I would now like to sum up. I say partial, because the full meaning of the word *communicative* will emerge only in the next chapter – until then *communicativeness* will be viewed more in terms of failed aspirations than positive achievements.

At the beginning of the chapter four questions were asked, which can now be answered – note that the answers will draw not only on the three units which were analysed here, but on four other units (3, 5, 14 and 15) whose analysis has not been presented in this chapter, but which have insights to offer us on the issues being discussed. The first question was: are social discourse and practice choices, situation type and interactional processes specifiable from the dialogues presented in the units? It is to the credit of the authors of *Building Strategies* that the answer to this question is an unequivocal yes. Cultural and situational variables, interaction sequence, attitude and shared knowledge are all readily specifiable, and are at times articulated by lively dialogues with great potential for negotiation of meaning: Unit 8, for example (the invitation–excuses dialogue between Barbara and Rod with Lynne the secretary hovering in the background); or this fragment of dialogue from Unit 14, in which Mike, a journalist, is interviewing Laura, a folk singer:

> *Mike*: And now you're a world-famous star, a composer and a mother. How do you manage to do it?
> *Laura*: Do what?
> *Mike*: Combine a career with a family?
> *Laura*: Are you married, with a family, Mr Sanders?
> *Mike*: Yes, but . . .
> *Laura*: Well, do you find it difficult to be a journalist and a father?
> *Mike*: But . . .
> *Laura*: Think about it, Mr Sanders. Goodbye!

The second question posed in the introduction was: are the follow-up exercises linked to the dialogue that precedes them? The answer to this, as indicated in section 5.1.1, is that although the models for each set are generally linked to the dialogue, all too often the follow-up exercises are neither linked to the dialogue in any but the most tenuous way, nor contextualized in any but the most perfunctory way. These exercises may be communicative, in that they usually permit students to communicate with each other, and even to ask and answer questions that may be of passing interest to them (as with Unit 2, Set 1, 'Express likes and dislikes'); but their value in a wider context – communicating in society – is debatable. This is underlined by two exchanges in Unit 5, Set 1:

3. May I use your phone?
   Well, actually, I'm expecting a phone call myself.
4. Can I use your phone?
   Sorry, but I'm expecting a call.

In these exchanges the 'refuse permission' is articulated without negative polarity: thanks to the absence of motivating context, the learner is given no indication as to situations in which a response of this form is appropriate.

The third question, addressed in section 5.1.2, was: are the follow-up exercises genuinely communicative, that is (since I have not yet fully characterized *communicative*), are they examples, no matter how artificial and stylized, of everyday communication between typical speakers of standard British English? To answer this question, we must be aware that *Building Strategies*, like any EFL textbook, articulates the pedagogical discourse of the time and place that gave birth to it, and thus articulates two *objects* (in the Foucaultian sense) of the discourse formation of second language education, *objects* that we might term AUTHENTICITY and LEARNABILITY, which are in constant tension, and therefore difficult to reconcile. The reason why authenticity and learnability are difficult to reconcile, and the effect this has on language learning exercises, can be illustrated by examining three unrelated sets in the course book. First consider Set 2 of Unit 3 – this is presented in the form of a health questionnaire, and contains the following language:

> 'Did you have more than three pieces of bread for breakfast?'
> 'Yes. I did. I had three. No, I didn't. I had only one.'

The students are invited in this exercise to complete this questionnaire for themselves and a partner. Now for the student to fill in a questionnaire for him/herself articulates the discourse of authenticity, while to fill in the questionnaire for a partner articulates the discourse of learnability, which advocates oral pair work as a highly valued practice essential for language learning. From the point of view of everyday communication, the resulting hybrid is not very satisfactory.

In Set 2 of Unit 7 ('Describe exactly where things are') – one of the units analysed in this chapter – authenticity is articulated by the 'preparing a meal' dialogue to which the set is linked, while learnability is articulated by the course book writers' decision to share the components of a complex nominal group occurring in the dialogue among the three responses in the mini-dialogue of the set. The language that results from this decision may well be easier for learners to cope with, but it is arguably language that is not worth learning, since at the very least it offends the system of the social action semiotic 'relations between cook and helper' and, more broadly perhaps, a number of social action semiotic systems relating to 'assistance in finding things'.

The last example concerns Set 1 of Unit 15, 'Ask and talk about travel arrangements', in which Barbara's father Jack and her mother Peggy are discussing their arrangements for travel to France, where Jack is taking up a job:

> *Peggy*: How will we get to the airport?
> *Jack*: A car will pick us up at 8.00 a.m.

The authenticity of this exercise is articulated by the 'travel arrangements' letter of the preceding Micro-sequence 1, to which the exercise is linked (though in this case, with social situation and interaction sequence unclear, the articulation of authenticity remains incomplete); while learnability is articulated by the question–answer form of the dialogue, which, despite the interspersed comments of Peggy, is actually a disguised variant of the pattern practice drill, a non-discursive practice motivated by the prevailing discourse on learnability of the 1950's and 1960's, apparently still alive and living a secret life in the 1970's. The result of this tension between authenticity and learnability is a dialogue which (as I interpret it) represents relations between men and women in a way which many people would find offensive, and few would regard as an example of everyday communication between typical speakers of standard British English. It is inevitable that learnability will always interfere to some extent with authenticity; but it is not inevitable that authenticity should be sacrificed to the extent that it has been in this and the other two sets examined above.

The fourth question to be asked in the introduction was: does negotiation of meaning occur in dialogues and follow-up exercises? As the analysis of Unit 8 seems to indicate, the authors probably did not see the teaching or learning of meaning negotiation skills as one of their goals, for even when meaning negotiation occurs in a dialogue (the second conversation between Barbara and Rod in Unit 8, for example), it is passed over in silence. It will be recalled that meaning must be negotiated when a decoder does not 'read' one or more cultural, situational or interactional process variables in the way they were 'intended' by an encoder, leading to a further move or moves to harmonize 'readings'. Thus in the Unit 8 dialogue, when Barbara is inviting Rod out for a meal, and Rod is making excuses while Lynne the secretary hovers in the background, it takes Barbara several moves to realize that Rod is not interpreting the 'boyfriend–girlfriend' system of the social action semiotic in the way she intended and expected him to. A similar problem occurs in the fragment of dialogue from Unit 14 quoted above. In this micro-sequence the folk singer Laura and the reporter Mike obviously do not interpret the system 'gender roles' in the same way, and Laura's attempts to negotiate these conflicting readings meet considerable resistance from the reporter. These two dialogues, from Units 8 and 14, provide an excellent opportunity to sensitize learners to negotiation of meaning, and even to develop exercises in meaning negotiation skills, but unfortunately are not exploited in this way.

Four points have been made in this final section: that cultural, situational and interactional process variables are readily specifiable in the dialogues; that the exercises in many sets are not linked to the dialogues or sufficiently contextualized; that a number of exercises are sufficiently contextualized but are undermined by the tension between authenticity and learnability; and that meaning negotiation skills are ignored, even when negotiation of meaning occurs in the dialogue. What we can learn from these four points, and the direction such knowledge can take us in, will be the subject of the next chapter.

6. Towards 'authentic' communication: a topical-interactional approach to language learning

6.0 INTRODUCTION

Chapter 6 begins by posing two questions. The course book *Building Strategies* is based in part on language functions (more formally, the illocutionary forces of speech act theory); the approach to communicative language learning that I am proposing here is based in part on social discourse and practice choices, and interaction sequences. The two questions are these. What precisely is a language function in the process model of language outlined in Chapter 4? What are social discourse and practice choices and interaction sequences in pedagogical terms? The answers to these questions should go some way towards showing how a theoretical model can give birth to a communicative language course.

6.1 SOCIAL DISCOURSES AND PRACTICES, INTERACTION SEQUENCES AND 'FUNCTION' IN *BUILDING STRATEGIES*

Table 6.1 shows social discourse and practice choices, and interaction sequences, in *Building Strategies*. Discourse formations are not listed separately, but are included with thematic systems; where the social discourse and practice choices, and interaction sequences of a micro-sequence or set, are identical to those of a preceding micro-sequence or set, they are not listed. Note that all units of *Building Strategies* except the introductory and consolidation units are included here.

Table 6.1 Social discourse and practice choices, and interaction sequences in *Building Strategies*

Thematic system	Social action semiotic	Interaction sequences
Unit 2		
MS 1, 2 'work'; 'living conditions'; 'likes'	MS 1, 2 'relations between host and guest'; 'gender roles'; 'first meeting behaviour'	MA 1, 2 Approach Direct

S 1 'likes'; 'domestic activities	S 1?	S 1 ?
S 2 'buildings'; 'opinions'	S 2?	S 2?
M S 3 'getting to know people'; 'suggestions'	MS 3 'relations between guest and host'; 'gender roles'	MS 3 Centring (Orient^Suggest ^Accept^Clarify]
S 3 'suggestions'	S 3?	S 3 Suggest^Accept^Clarify
Unit 3		
MS 1 'health' (+DF 'medicine')	MS 1 'hospital visiting'; 'mother–daughter relations'	MS 1 Greet^Approach Direct[Suggest^Accept]
S 2 'health'	S 2 'filling out questionnaires'	S 2 Question^Answer
Unit 4		
MS 1 'directions'	MS 1 'relations between strangers'	MS 1 Summons^ Orient^Enquire Directions^Direct
MS 3, 4 'community facilities' (+DF 'town planning'	MS 3, 4 'relations between media and public'	MS 3, 4 Introduce^ Orient^Analyse ^Conclude
Unit 5		
S 1 'renting accommodation'; 'permission'	S 1 'relations between buyer and seller'; 'relations between potential flatmates'	S 1 Greet^Orient ^Service^Display
S 1 (contd) 'permission', 'telephones'	S 1 (contd) ?	S 1 (contd) ?
S2(c) 'colour'	S2(c) 'relations between friends'	S2(c) Approach Direct
Unit 7		
MS 1 'cooking'	MS 1 'relations between flatmates'; 'relations between cook and helper'	MS 1 Orient^ Prepare

S 1 ? MS 3 'cooking'; 'requests'	S 1 ? MS 3 'relations between flatmates'; 'relations between cook and helper'	S 1 ? MS 3 Orient^ Prepare
S 4 'holidays'; 'advice'	S 4 'relations between media and public'	S 4 Advise
Unit 8		
MS 1 'excuses'	MS 1 'telephone behaviour'	MS 1 Greet^ Identify^Speaking Rights
S 1 (contd) ?	S 1 (contd) 'telephone behaviour	S 1 (contd) Summons^Answer: Other
MS 2 'excuses'	MS 2 'relations between boyfriend and girlfriend'; 'telephone behaviour'	MS 2 Identify^ Speaking^Rights ^Orient^Invite ^Excuse
S 2 'invitations'; 'excuses'	S 2 'polite behaviour'	S 2 Invite^ Excuse
Unit 9		
MS 1 'travelling' (+DF 'business')	MS 1 'relations between manager and assistant'	MS 1 Orient^ Arrange^ Sociability
S 1 'travelling'	S 1 ?	S 1 ?
Unit 10		
MS 1 'travelling'	MS 1 'relations between old school friends'; chance encounter behaviour'	MS 1 Greet^Approach Direct^Leave-taking^Goodbye
S 2 ?	S 2 'relations between reporter and interviewee'	S 2 Question Answer

Unit 12		
MS 1 'travelling'	MS 1 'relations between boyfriend and girlfriend'; 'airport meeting behaviour'	MS 1 Greet^Praise ^Regret^Evaluate
Unit 13		
MS 1 'missing person' (+DF 'the law')	MS 1 'relations between police and public'	MS 1 Identify^ Service Bid^ Service[Orient^ Recount^Describe] ^Goodbye
Unit 14		
MS 1, 2 'biography'	MS 1, 2 'relations between reporter and interviewee'; 'behaviour of public performer'	MS 1, 2 Greet^ Orient^Question ^(Clarify^) Answer
Unit 15		
MS 1 'travelling' (+DF 'business')	MS 1 'letter-writing conventions'; 'relations between organizer and organized'	MS 1 Orient Detail Wish
S 1 'travelling	S 1 'relations between husband and wife'	S 1 ?
MS 2 'living abroad'	MS 2 'relations between parents and children'; 'having drinks'	MS 2 Prepare^ Greet^Sociability ^Offer Drinks ^Toast

MS: micro-sequence. S: set.

6.1.1 Language functions

Turning first to the question of what a language function is in terms of our model, we notice that functions are listed under two categories, thematic systems and interaction sequences. Table 6.2 lists functions by thematic system and interaction sequence.

Table 6.2 Language functions by thematic system and interaction sequence

Unit 2	
MS 1, 2	'likes'; Approach Direct
MS3	'suggestions'; Orient^Suggest^Accept^Clarify
S 3	'suggestions'; Suggest^Accept^Clarify
Unit 4	
MS 1	'directions'; Summons^Orient^Enquire Directions^Direct
Unit 5	
S1	'permission'; Greet^Orient^Service^Display
Unit 7	
MS 3	'requests'; Orient^Prepare
S4	'advice'; Advise
Unit 8	
MS1	'excuses'; Greet^Identify^Speaking Rights
MS 2	'invitations/excuses'; Identify^Speaking Rights^Orient ^Invite^Excuse
S2	'invitations/excuses; Invite^Excuse

Note. The term 'language functions' here includes not only obvious illocutionary forces like *suggest* or *request* but also semantico-grammatical categories (notions) such as *likes* and hybrids such as *directions* (part function, part notion).

I will now look at each individual listing of the so-called functions. In Micro-sequences 1 and 2 of Unit 2, and in Set 1 (not listed here, owing to the absence of a specifiable interaction sequence) the function 'Express likes and dislikes' appears as the thematic system 'likes', but does not in fact figure overtly in the interaction sequence element, analysed as Approach Direct. Two proofs were given for the existence of a thematic system relating to 'likes': firstly, an expression of like or dislike tends to be followed by a clause, structurally related or unrelated to the 'like' clause, which explicitly or implicitly elaborates, extends or enhances the expression of like or dislike; and secondly, in the noncommittal response 'It depends' native speakers of English are aware of an unexpressed circumstantial Attribute, and of the set of lexicogrammatical items which could function as Attribute. As for the fact that the function does not figure overtly in the interaction sequence, this can be explained by saying that it is not necessary, since the thematic system 'likes' is regularly articulated by Approach Direct.

Moving on to Micro-sequence 3 and Set 3 of the same unit, the functions 'Make suggestions and plans', 'Agree and disagree with suggestions' appear as the thematic system 'suggestions' and the interaction sequence Orient^Suggest^Accept^Clarify. The question immediately arises: why the duplication, especially since it was judged unnecessary in the case of 'Express likes and dislikes'? The answer lies in the difference between the thematic system and the interaction sequence. A suggestion involves a performer and a performance, and a thematic system sets out the possible sociosemantic roles that may be played by each. Thus an addressee-performer may be Senser in an interrogative mental process clause with modulation:inclination ('Would you like to . . . ?'), in which case the performance is encoded as a projected clause; or an addressee-performer may be implicit ('ellipsed') in a *wh*-interrogative minor clause ('What/How about . . . ?'), in which the performance is encoded as Circumstance:Matter. A speaker-and-addressee performer may be Actor in in a *wh*-interrogative clause with negative polarity ('Why don't we . . . ?), in which the material process encodes the performance; or Actor in a declarative clause with modality:possibility ('We could . . . '), in which the performance is likewise encoded by the material process.

The thematic system 'suggestions' is, in short, the set of patterns used in making suggestions in present-day standard British English, together with certain conventions relating to appropriate usage – for example, when to choose and when to avoid the ellipsed addressee-performer pattern. What, then, is the interaction sequence element Suggest, or rather, more accurately, what is the interaction sequence Orient^Suggest^Accept^Clarify? An interaction sequence is motivated to some extent by social discourse and practice choices, and in Micro-sequence 3 the thematic system 'getting to know people' and the system of the social action semiotic 'relations between host and guest' deserve close attention. The system of the social action semiotic describes the range of duties that a host must perform, including befriending a guest newly arrived in the host's home town; the thematic system describes the set of activities permissible (at a given time in the given culture) in getting to know people, and assigns sociosemantic roles to the performer(s) and the performance. The interaction sequence is one of a number of possible meeting points between the system of the social action semiotic and the thematic system, and each element bears the imprint of the two systems: the Suggest element, for instance, is the reaction (not necessarily the only possible one) of a dutiful host to a guest who has activated the 'getting to know people' thematic system.

The most interesting element of the interaction sequence is Orient (the pre-suggestion or, as the case may be, pre-invitation, pre-request, etc., of the ethnomethodologists). This element is a component in so many interaction sequences that it may well articulate some very general system of the social action semiotic like 'getting things done' or 'getting other people to do things'. That its function is well understood can be illustrated in the following unremarkable exchange between a young man and his girlfriend:

YM. There's a great new film on at the Roxy.
G. Yeah, let's go to it.

This exchange could readily he analysed as Orient^Accept, eliminating the Suggest element altogether from the interaction sequence. Such exchanges underline the weakness of the 'function' label, especially in relation to what Searle called *indirect speech acts*, like the young man's initiation: to characterize such an utterance as a 'making a suggestion' would be misleading, for it does not articulate the thematic system' (pre-sequences are too 'wild' to be systematized); rather, it articulates an approach towards the interaction sequence element, or even a desire to avoid it. Hence the preference for thematic system and interaction sequence over language function.

Leaving the discussion on suggestions and pre-suggestions, we turn now to Micro-sequence 1 of Unit 4. The distinction just drawn between the the thematic system 'suggestions' and the interaction sequence element Suggest also holds good here. The thematic system 'directions' assigns sociosemantic roles – Actor to performer, material process with Location circumstantials to performance, and an appropriate lexical set. The element Direct in the sequence Summons Orient Enquire Directions Direct articulates not only the thematic system but a system of the social action semiotic, 'relations between strangers', which prescribes accepted behaviour towards strangers seeking directions.

In Set 1 of Unit 5 the functions 'Ask for, give and refuse permission' appear as the thematic system 'permission' and the element Display in the interaction sequence Greet Orient Service Display. Only two patterns in the thematic system are activated: both involve the speaker-performer as Actor in a modulated material process/polar interrogative clause, the only difference being in the modulation – [obligation: low] ('May I . . . ?') versus [potentiality] ('Can I . . . ?'). The Disply element, which should properly be analysed as two elements, Display Verbal (as on a telephone) and Display Visual (as in a shop), articulates the thematic system 'renting accommodation' and the system of the social action semiotic 'relations between buyer and seller'. In fact the 'permission' thematic system is brought into play to signal a transition between Display Verbal and Display Visual.

Micro-sequence 3 of the dialogue in Unit 7 illustrates the function 'Ask people to do things', which appears as the thematic system 'requests' and the element Prepare of the interaction sequence Orient Prepare. Only one pattern from the thematic system is presented: addressee-performer as Actor in a modulated – [inclination:low] – material process/polar interrogative clause ('Could you . . . ?'). The element Prepare articulates the thematic system 'cooking' and the system in the social action semiotic 'relations between cook and helper': the 'request' thematic system may be activated when, for example, an ingredient or utensil is required.

In Set 4 of the same unit the function 'Give instructions and advice' appears as the thematic system 'advice' and the interaction sequence element Advise. The thematic system patterns involve addressee-performer as Actor in material process/imperative clauses ('Sunbathe [for just half an hour]'); and performance as embedded material process/non-finite clauses functioning as Carrier in relational process clauses ('Swimming straight after meals [is dangerous]'). The interaction sequence element articulates the thematic system 'holidays' and the system of the social action semiotic 'relations between media and public', which empower newspapers to give readers holiday advice.

Turning to Micro-sequence 1 of Unit 8, we find the function 'make excuses' (the label is taken from Set 2, since Set 1 is actually entitled 'Ask and talk about present actions') appearing in the analysis as the thematic system 'excuses' and the interaction sequence element Speaking Rights. At this point only one pattern is presented: speaker-performer as Actor in a material process clause with tense present in present (i.e. present continuous) (I'm having a shower'). The interaction sequence element Speaking Rights:Reject articulates 'excuses' and the system in the social action semiotic 'telephone behaviour'.

In Micro-sequence 2 and Set 2 of the same unit the functions 'Invite people to do things', 'Refuse invitations politely and make excuses' appear as the thematic systems 'excuses' and 'invitations', and as the interaction sequence Orient Invite Excuse. Two patterns are activated from the 'invitations' thematic system: in the first pattern, addressee-performer is Senser in a modulated – [inclination:median] – mental process/polar interrogative clause which projects the performance ('Would you like to . . . ?'); the second pattern imitates the first, except that now the projecting clause of pattern 1 is declarative and modalized – [probability:low] – as well as modulated, and is itself projected by another mental process/declarative clause in which the inviter is Senser ('I thought maybe you'd like to . . . '). As for the 'excuses' thematic system, there are three new patterns: they all involve the speaker-performer as Senser in two mental process clauses in a paratactic adversative relation (I'd love to, but I'm afraid . . . '), the second of which projects three different types of clauses encoding the performances: (1) performer as Carrier, performance as relational:possessive with Attrubute from the 'bad health' lexical set (' . . . I've got a headache'); (2) performer as Actor, performance as material process modulated by [obligation:high] (' . . . I must write some letters'); (3) as type 2, but modulated by [obligation:median] (' . . . I ought to write some letters'). As for the interaction sequence elements Invite and Excuse, they both articulate the system of the social action semiotic 'relations between boyfriend and girlfriend' – in particular those sub-systems pertaining to 'shared activities' (in the case of Invite), and 'seeing other women' (as in the case of Excuse).

I am now in a position to say what a language function is in terms of the process model of language presented in Chapter 4. A language function is partly a thematic system – a cultural store of sociosemantic roles for a performer, processes for a performance, evaluations regarding the likelihood, necessity or desirability of the performance, together with affective judgements about it, and relevant lexical sets and logico-semantic relations. (Recall Derrida's argument, in 1982: 326, and Chapter 2.2 above, that the essential quality of speech acts is their iterability.) And it is also partly an interaction sequence element, articulating a system in the social action semiotic, and sometimes a thematic system as well. Note that a function need not appear as a distinct thematic system bearing the same name as a function – it may figure as an anonymous sub-system in an apparently unrelated thematic system. Thus in Unit 9, for example, 'Ask and talk about plans' and 'Remind people to do things' are treated as sub-systems of the thematic system 'travelling'.

6.1.2 Social discourses and practices, and interaction sequence

In order to better consider what thematic system and social action semiotic are in pedagogical terms, I will now group these two by 'affinity' (the meaning of this term will become clear presently). Table 6.3 shows this grouping. I would suggest that each group represents what is known in contemporary language teaching as a TOPIC (see van Ek 1975, Matthews and Read 1982, Bell 1985):

Group 1: Work
Group 2: Home life
Group 3: City life
Group 4: Health
Group 5: Media
Group 6: Travel
Group 7: The law
Group 8: The family

Note: the names of these topics – also known as THEMES – are not standardized.

Table 6.3 Thematic systems and social action semiotic by groups

Thematic system	Social action semiotic
Group 1	
'work' 'business' (DF) 'travelling:business'	'relations between manager and assistant' 'letter-writing conventions' 'relations between organizer and organized'
Group 2	
'living conditions' 'domestic activities' 'renting accommodation' 'telephones' 'cooking' 'colour'	'relations between host and guest' 'relations between buyer and seller' 'relations between (potential) flatmates' 'relations between cook and helper'
Group 3	
'buildings' 'directions' 'getting to know people' 'community facilities' 'town planning' (DF)	'relations between strangers'
Group 4	
'health' 'medicine' (DF)	'hospital visiting'
Group 5	
'biography'	'relations between media and public' 'relations between reporter and interviewee'

Group 6	
'holidays'	'chance encounter behaviour'
'travelling'	'airport meeting behaviour'
'living abroad'	
Group 7	
'missing persons'	'relations between police and public'
'the law' (DF)	
Group 8	
	'gender roles'
	'relations between parents and children'
	'relations between friends'
	'relations between boyfriend and girlfriend'
	'relations between husband and wife'

As Table 6.3 suggests, it is possible with the model I have proposed to break the the topic down into content units (thematic systems) and behaviour units (systems of the social action semiotic), which may prove valuable from a pedagogical point of view. I will return to the topic and its value as a teaching/learning tool after a brief consideration of the interaction sequence.

It was previously noted that an interaction sequence is an activity sequence (social situation/subject matter) shared between participants in a communicative event, and realized both verbally and non-verbally; and further affirmed that interaction sequence, in common with other interactional processes and certain situational variables, is not fixed, but may be interpreted in different ways by different participants, and is therefore open to negotiation. To the best of my knowledge, the interaction sequence does not correspond precisely to any current pedagogical unit. One unit that appears to come close to the interaction sequence is the guided role play, an example of which is the exercise from Unit 2 of *Building Strategies* shown in Table 6.4. This role play can be seen as an activity sequence shared between two or more participants in a communicative event, but all its elements are fixed – there is no potential for alternative interpretations and negotiation of meaning. So a guided role play is not an interaction sequence.

If the guided role play fails to satisfy the stated criteria for an interaction sequence, then we might well consider the claims made for drama techniques in language teaching. According to Wessels (1987: 11–12), the use of drama involves most aspects of 'genuine communication', including 'background, emotions, relationship, status, body language, and other paralinguistic features' (and presumably also 'misunderstandings', mentioned a few lines earlier as a feature of 'ordinary conversations'). Clearly there is a great potential in drama for alternative interpretations and negotiation of meaning, just as there must be in the simulations and role playing represented by a book such as *Imaginary Crimes* (Clark and McDonough 1982), which enables

Table 6.4 Guided role play, from *Starting Strategies*, Unit 2

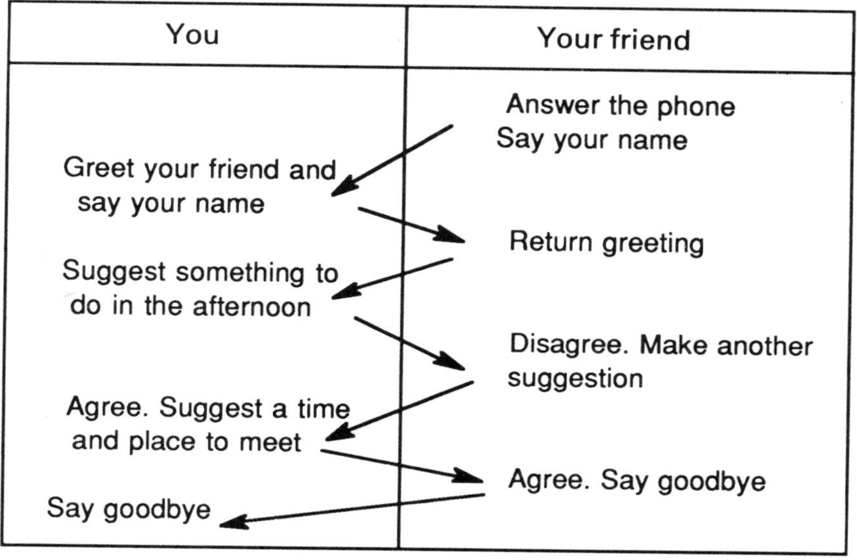

You	Your friend
	Answer the phone Say your name
Greet your friend and say your name	
	Return greeting
Suggest something to do in the afternoon	
	Disagree. Make another suggestion
Agree. Suggest a time and place to meet	
	Agree. Say goodbye
Say goodbye	

learners of English to act out the trials of people accused of a variety of crimes. However, while drama, simulations and role playing do force learners to negotiate meaning, they are not strictly activity sequences shared between two or more participants – they certainly activate a number of very valuable activity sequences, and undoubtedly have a role to play in the communicative language course that I am envisaging, but they are not interaction sequences.

In order be place the interaction sequence in a pedagogical context, we must return to the distinction between process and product discussed in Chapter 1, and to one of the advocates of the process-and-product approach, Christopher Brumfit. In his study of communicative methodology in language teaching (1984a: 88–92), Brumfit, reversing the usual state of affairs in which the content of a language course is a body of knowledge, a 'product', pleads for 'process' as the 'content' of a language course. Process, in Brumfit's view, has three aspects: (1) the process of using a language (1984a: 89); (2) the process of classroom methodology (1984a: 90); (3) the process of language acquisition (1984a: 92). Process in the first sense – the process of using a language – can be linked to our earlier use of process as the realization of a dynamic system such as Ventola's decision tree or flow chart to generate well formed schematic structures for service encounters; and to our interaction sequence, with elements open to alternative interpretation and subsequent negotiation. Thus an interaction sequence is not a unit – which is, of course, a product-based concept – but a process as defined by Brumfit and Martin.

For Brumfit, process and product have important implications for classroom methodology. Process can be identified with FLUENCY, which

Brumfit characterizes (1984a: 54) as 'speed and continuity, coherence, context-sensitivity, and creativity'; and product can be equated with ACCURACY, which Brumfit defines (1984a: 52) as 'a focus by the user, because of the pedagogical context created or allowed by the teacher, on formal factors or issues of appropriacy'. Both process/fluency and product/accuracy are essential to language teaching/learning – as Brumfit says (1984a: 117):

> We have . . . a product-based syllabus in order to ensure that there are some controls on the activity that takes place in the classroom. But it is clear that the syllabus must contain a process element, for otherwise it will not be a syllabus at all, but simply a statement of terminal behaviour of a restrictive kind.

In other words, product is a checklist of language items, and process is the use of those language items in an authentic context.

This brings us back to the *topic*. The topic is, of course, a product-based syllabus unit, but some doubt has been cast on its value as a checklist of language items. Brumfit quotes A. M. Shaw, in a 1977 article on 'recent' approaches to foreign language syllabus development, as denying that the topic approach is applicable to normal language teaching situations, 'because the language items will occur (except, no doubt, for some lexis) in a haphazard fashion' (Brumfit 1984a: 93). There are two possible responses to this view. The first response is to say — or, rather, query rhetorically — does it matter? That it may not matter is clear from the aims of the much-discussed Communicational Teaching Project (CTP) set up by Dr N. S. Prabhu in Bangalore (India), here outlined by Alan Davies (1983: 5):

> it was decided that a project should be set up which would aim to teach grammar through communicative activities. In other words, the orientation of the Project was from the start unique: it was to teach grammer through communication, *not* to teach communication (through anything) . . . The assumption behind the CTP was that form is best learnt when the learner's attention is on meaning (grammar *through* communication). As a consequence, there should be no planned progression in terms of language structure in any syllabus, no pre-selection of language in any lesson; no language-focussed activity in the classroom. Instead there should be the exploitation of: the learner's desire to solve problems; the preoccupation with meaning or thinking; the incidental struggle with language-use.

Not all communicative syllabus theorists agree that CTP lacks a planned progression in terms of language structures. Brumfit (1984a: 108) quotes Keith Johnson as claiming, in his 1982 work *Communicative Syllabus Design and Methodology*, that the 'conceptual development of Prabhu's "procedural syllabus" suggests that it may be a covert semantico-grammatical syllabus'. Brumfit does not agree with this claim:

> The concepts with which Prabhu is concerned are not stated specifically, and while they may be sometimes realised in linguistic items . . . , they will also appear as formal logical operations which may be realised as any of a large range of grammatical structures. Since the problems are embedded in knowledge of the world, as well as knowledge of the operations of the English language, the nature of the progression will not be defined by semantico-grammatical categories.

Semantico-grammatical categories may account for some of the linguistic items, but it is in the nature of concepts and problems not to remain bound by such a narrow categorization.

The second response to Shaw's criticism of the topic approach is to enquire whether the 'haphazard fashion' in which language items are said to occur is indeed haphazard, or whether it is possible to discern patterns which can be harnessed in the construction of a syllabus with 'planned progression in terms of language structure' and 'pre-selection of language' for each lesson. It was shown in the analysis of *Building Strategies* that there are recognizable patterns in thematic systems; and, although the matter was scarcely touched on, there are, equally, patterns in systems of the social action semiotic. But thematic system patterns are not individual language items; rather, they are regularly selected configurations of grammatical (standing for sociosemantic) choices, not necessarily amenable to the traditional structural grading which is still, to some extent at least, practised covertly in many communicative course books. This is, of course, not to deny the possibility of selecting patterns judged suitable for learners at a particular level. In this case, progression in terms of language patterns would be replaced by progression in terms of thematic system patterns. Such an approach needs to be illustrated, and this will be the aim of the next section.

6.2 SOCIAL DISCOURSES AND PRACTICES IN A TOPICAL-INTERACTIONAL APPROACH

Imagine that we are designing a course for learners of English who are at an elementary level (that is, they are not complete beginners), and that we have chosen Home Life as one of our topics. It is necessary to break this topic down into sub-topics: suppose that one of them is Renting Accommodation. How do we go about establishing patterns in the thematic system and the social action semiotic?

6.2.1 A fragment of a thematic system

The main problem that confronts anyone wishing to establish the patterns of a thematic system is that there is no accepted way of representing them. Lemke indicates a possible approach when he says (1985b: 24) that thematic items can be viewed as constituted by the relational networks they enter into, and the thematic relations as constituted by the typical item-relata they appear with.

The basic level of discourse for the discussion of meaning, he adds, is not an item, or the abstract thematic relations, but whole thematic systems, representable as relational networks. In short, patterns in the thematic system must be established through some form of relational network. There is also the lesser problem of terminology: as noted earlier, the terminology used is borrowed from grammatical systems such as transitivity, but the terms almost certainly stand for something more abstract (I have referred to thematic systems as a *sociosemantic* phenomenon), for which no satisfactory terminology exists (or exists only partially).

Figure 6.1 is a *very* partial fragment of a thematic system for Renting

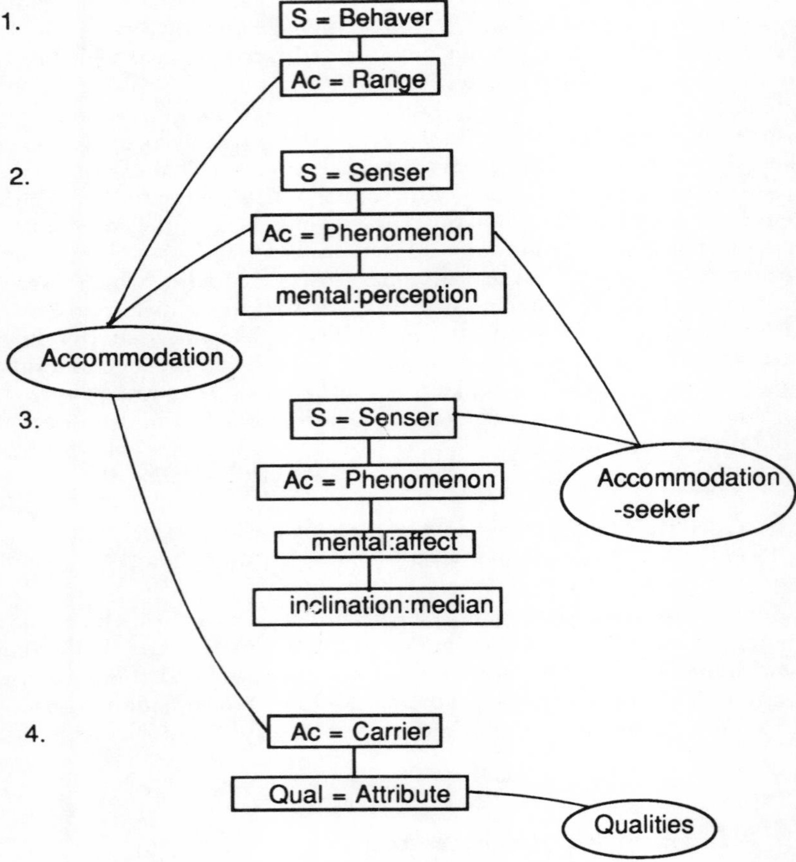

Figure 6.1 Very partial fragment of a thematic system for the sub-topic Renting Accommodation. *Ac* types of accommodation, *Am* amenities, *Pro* accommodation-provider, *Qual* qualities (of accommodation, etc.), *Ro* rooms/furniture/facilities, *S* accommodation-seeker, *Ser* services

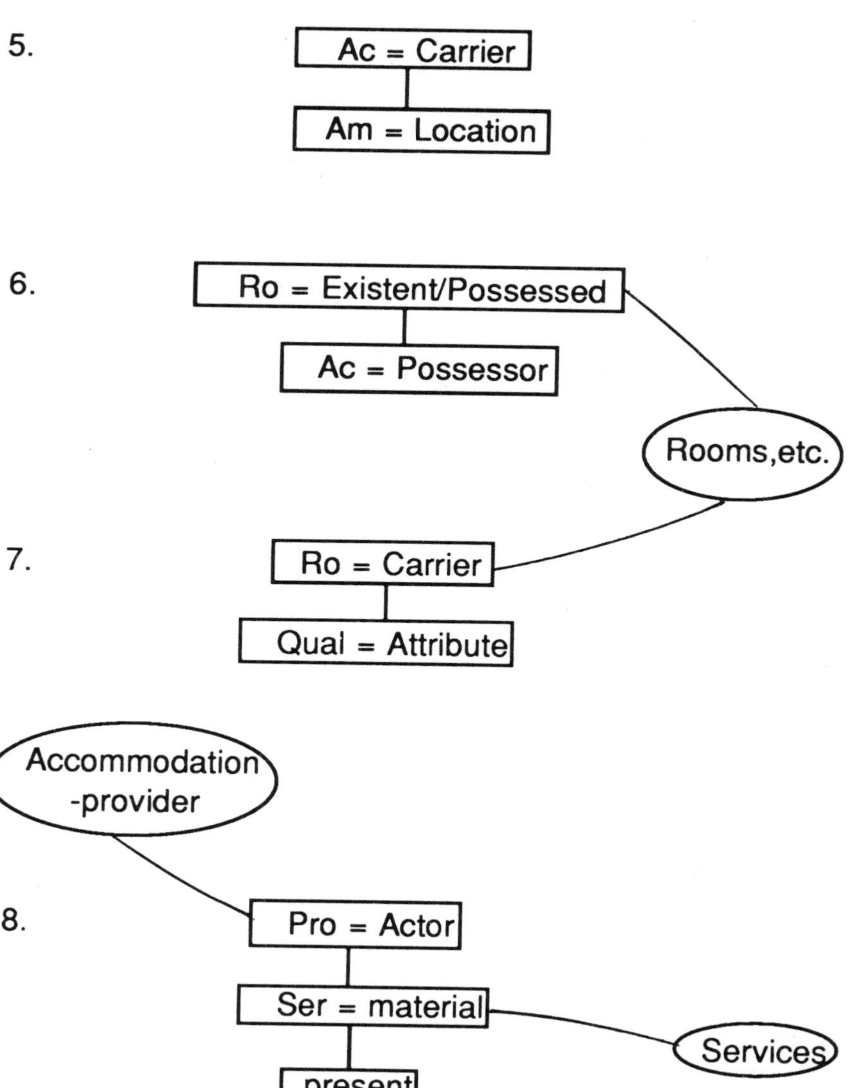

Figure 6.1 (continued)

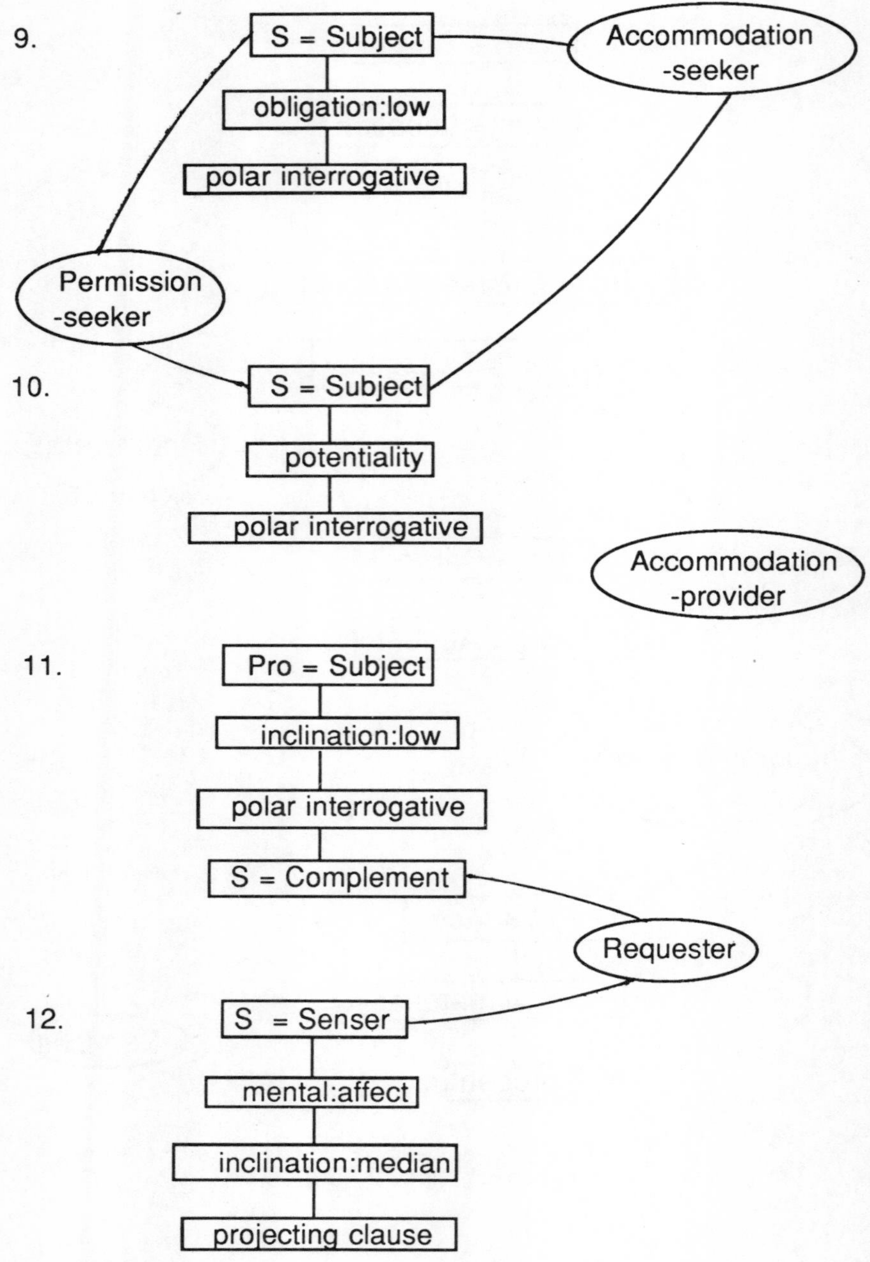

Figure 6.1 (continued)

Accommodation. Figure 6.1 is a form of relational network showing the different relations that individual thematic items can enter into (Accommodation, for example, is Range, Phenomenon and Carrier), and the other thematic items with which a given thematic item enters into a relation (for instance, Accommodation enters into different relations with Accommodation-seeker, Qualities (of the accommodation), and Amenities. Nos. 1–8 are patterns involving thematic items directly related to the semantic field of renting accommodation – for the sake of convenience, I will henceforth refer to these as *topical* thematic systems; Nos 9–12 are patterns belonging to the thematic systems 'permission' (9 and 10) and 'requests' (11 and 12), which I propose, rather unsatisfactorily, to call *interactional* thematic systems (*interactional* because these thematic systems provide the socially sanctioned patterns for 'doing things with words' *to* another participant). It would obviously be useful to give examples of utterances motivated by these patterns, but first I need to consider briefly the social action semiotic.

6.2.2 A fragment of the social action semiotic relevant to renting accommodation

Figure 6.2 represents a fragment of the social action semiotic relevant to renting accommodation. The relational network shows four of the relations into which an accommodation-seeker may enter. Each of these relations is a system in the social action semiotic, one of which (the 'accommodation-seeker/landlord or landlady' system) is illustrated, with some of the least delicate options shown. Note that 'telephone' is enclosed by a rectangle rather than an oval: the rectangle indicates that the entity entering into a relationship with 'accommodation-seeker' is inanimate, with obvious implications for the nature of the relation.

6.2.3 Linguistic articulation of social discourses and practices

In the present model, social discourses and practises are articulated by components of the situation, which are in their turn articulated by interactional processes, which are realized by language and non-verbal codes. However, in what follows I am going to bypass the intermediate planes and go straight from social discourses and practises to language, my excuse being that these are citation forms, not real communication. What I am in fact going to do is illustrate the thematic system patterns with utterances motivated by patterns in topical, or topical plus interactional, thematic systems, conjoined with one of the systems of the social action semiotic presented in Figure 6.2

1. (Patterns 1 and 12 + 'accommodation-seeker/agent')
   I'd like to look at the flat in Smith Street.
2. (Patterns 2 and 10 + 'accommodation-seeker/agent')
   Can I see the flat in Smith Street?
3. (Patterns 2 and 11 + 'accommodation-seeker/agent')
   Could you show me the flat in Smith Street?

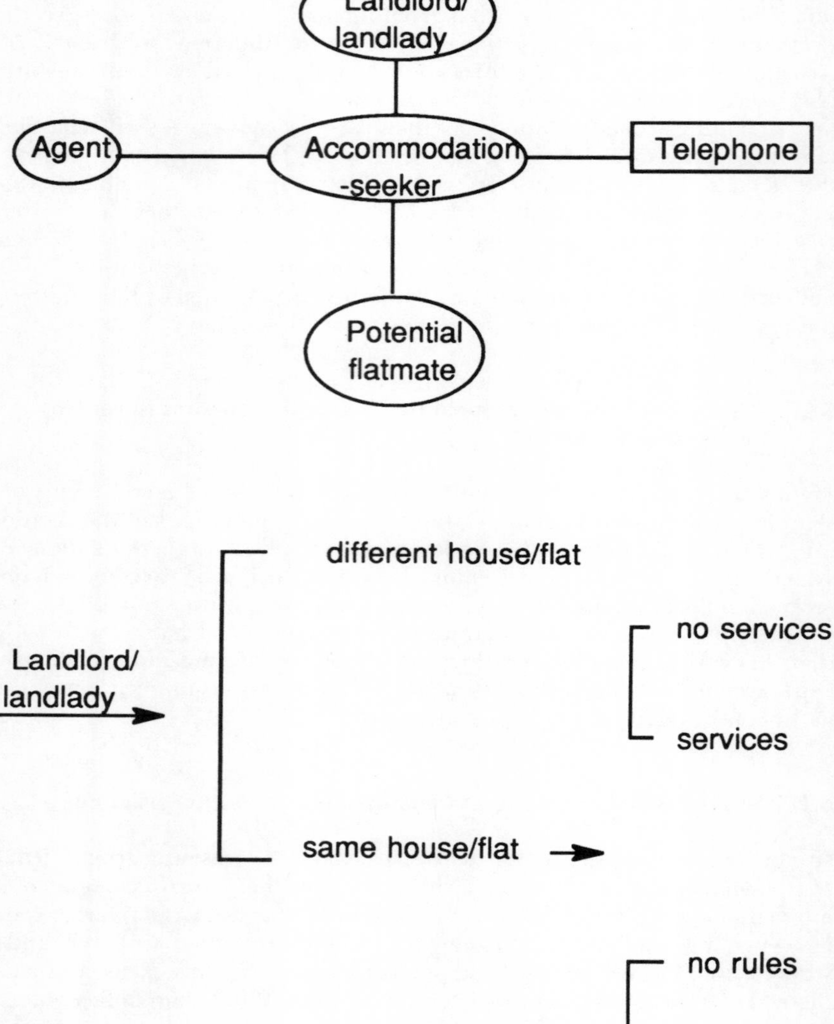

Figure 6.2 Fragment of the social action semiotic relevant to renting accommodation

4. (Patterns 2 and 9 + 'telephone' + 'accommodation-seeker/landlord or landlady')
   May I see the flat this evening?
5. (Pattern 3 + 'accommodation-seeker/agent')
   I'd like a large room.
6. (Pattern 4 + 'accommodation-seeker/landlord or landlady')
   The flat is too small.
7. (Pattern 5 + 'accommodation-seeker/agent')
   The flat is on a bus route.
8. (Pattern 6 + 'accommodation-seeker/landlord or landlady')
   Is there a washing-machine?
   Has it got a separate entrance?
9. (Pattern 7 + 'accommodation-seeker/landlord or landlady')
   The sitting room is lovely.
10. (Pattern 8 + 'accommodation-seeker/landlord or landlady')
    Do you provide meals?

Abstracting from these utterances a list of language items like those found in most EFL course books, we arrive at the following:

(a) I'd like to . . .
(b) Can I . . . ?
(c) May I . . . ?
(d) Could you . . . ?
(f) X is Y (copula + adjective).
(g) X is on . . . (copula + prepositional phrase).
(h) Is there . . . ?
(i) Has it got . . . ?
(j) Simple present.

As regards the suitability of these items for an elementary course: items (f), (g), (h), (i) and (j) are uncontroversial, while items (a), (b), (c), (d) and (e) are at least defensible. Thus we have here the basis for a progression in terms of thematic system patterns.

6.3 CONCLUSION

In the next chapter I propose to demonstrate a progression in terms of thematic system patterns, and the mechanics of a topical-interactional course, through two units at differing levels, both revolving around the topic Home Life.

7. Fragments of a topical-interactional course

7.0 INTRODUCTION

In this chapter, two units of a topical-interactional course will be presented – one for learners at elementary–intermediate level, and one for students at elementary–advanced level. The topic motivating the first unit will be Home Life, while the second unit will articulate a combination of Home Life and Family Life. For each unit there will be three interwoven sections: (1) the social discourse and practice variables (SocDP), components of situation (Sit), and interactional processes (IntProc) motivating a dialogue or exercise; (2) the dialogues and exercises – topical and interactional – as they will be presented to the learner; and (3) analytical commentary on 1 and 2. Following the procedure adopted in the analysis of *Building Strategies* (and to make the chapter more 'reader-friendly'), linguistic and non-verbal realizations will be presented in full for the first dialogue, and thereafter will be referred to only if they throw some particular light on the process that occurs in passing from SocDP/Sit/Int Proc to actual discourse.

7.1 UNIT AT ELEMENTARY–INTERMEDIATE LEVEL

7.1.1 The specifications for Dialogue 1

SocDP

DF: 'business'
TS: 'renting accommodation'
SAS: 'relation between accommodation-seeker and landlady'

Sit

SocSit: 'inspecting accommodation'
SM: 'rooms'/'services'
SocRel: 'buyer–seller'; 'older–younger'
P: [regulatory]; [respect]

IntProc

IS: Summon ^ Reply ^ Greet ^ Identify ^ Service ^ Display ^ [Orient to Request^Accept] ^Resolution
At: 'pleased'/surprised'/'sad'/sympathetic'/'uncertain'/'happy'
SK: [immediate]/[minimum]/social]/[maximum]

LR

(a) (i) NVR articulating Summons
(ii) NVR articulating Reply
(b) (i) minor clause realizing Greet
(ii) [relational:identifying] with Identified/Identifier articulating Identify element of IS; [declarative];
(iii) clause complex α' β:
projecting clause – [mental: affect] with speaker as Senser; [declarative] + [inclination:median]; projected clause – [behavioural] with Range from 'accommodation' schema; non-Finite
(c) (i) [material] with speaker as Range, Actor from 'accommodation' schema; [declarative]; continuatives
(ii) [material] with addressee as Actor; [imperative]
(iii) [relational:identifying] with Identified recoverable from environment; Identifier from 'accommodation' schema; [declarative]; exophoric demonstrative
(d) (i) [relational:attributive] with Carrier recoverable from environment, Attribute from 'pleased' lexical set; [declarative] + tone 5
(ii) [relational:attributive] with Carrier from environment, Attribute from 'pleased' lexical set; [declarative] + tone 5 + attitudinal submodifier; reference
(iii) [relational:attributive] with Carrier from 'room' schema, attribute from 'pleased' lexical set; [declarative] + tone 5; [extension:addition]
(iv) minor clause realized by nominal group consisting of interrogative deictic, epithet and head + tone 5 + conjunctive adjunct (additive)
(e) (i) clausal ellipsis + [positive]; [relational = attributive] with Carrier from environment or discourse, Attribute from 'accommodation' schema + [past]; [declarative]; anaphoric/exophoric pronoun + repetition
(f) [mental:perception] with speaker as Senser, Phenomenon from 'room' schema; [interrogative:polar] + [obligation:low]
(g) clausal ellipsis + [positive]
(h) (i) [relational:attributive] with Carrier recoverable from environment, Attribute from 'pleased' lexical set; [declarative] + tone 5; exophoric demonstrative + conjunctive adjunct (additive)
(ii) [material] with addressee as Actor, Goal and process from 'services' schema; [interrogative:polar]; continuative

(j) [material] with speaker as Actor, Goal and process from 'services' schema; [declarative]; continuative

(k) (i) [relational:attributive] with Carrier from 'services' schema; [declarative] + tone 5; anaphoric demonstrative

(ii) [relational:attributive] with Carrier and Attribute from 'accommodation' schema; [declarative] + attitudinal submodifier; [enhancement:causal–conditional]

(l) (i) clausal ellipsis + [positive] + continuative

(ii) [material] with addressee as Actor, Range from 'accommodation' schema; [imperative]

(m) minor clause realized by greeting + [vocative]

(n) (i) [relational:attributive] with Attribute from 'sad' lexical set; [declarative] + attitudinal submodifier; anaphoric pronoun

(ii) [relational:attributive] with speaker as Carrier, Attribute from 'sad' lexical set; [declarative]

(iii) [material] with speaker and other as Actor + Circumstance:Purpose; [declarative] + [negative] + (usuality:high]; [extension:addition]

(o) minor clause realized by continuative + nominal group (Epithet from 'worried' lexical set + Thing) + tone 5

(p) (i) [material] with addressee as Actor; [imperative]

(ii) [mental:perception] with addressee as Senser, Phenomenon from 'accommodation' schema; [imperative]; [extension:addition]

(q) [relational:attributive] with Attribute from 'pleased' lexical set; [declarative] + attitudinal submodifier + tone 4; anaphoric pronoun

(r) (i) clausal ellipsis + [positive]

(ii) [relational:attributive] with Carrier from 'accommodation' schema and Attribute from 'sad' lexical set; [declarative]; [extension:adversative] + meronym of *garden*

(iii) [relational:attributive] with Carrier from 'accommodation' schema, Attribute from 'sad' lexical set; [declarative] + attitudinal submodifier; anaphoric pronoun

(s) clause complex $\alpha'\beta$:
projecting – [mental:affect] with speaker as Senser; [declarative] + [inclination:median]
projected – [material] with Goal from 'accommodation' schema; non-Finite

(t) clausal ellipsis + [positive] + [probability:high] + [vocative]

(u) (i) [material] with speaker as Actor, Range from 'accommodation' schema + Circumstance:Purpose; [interrogative:polar] + [potentiality]; [extension:addition] + repetition (*Mitzi, take . . . for walks*)

(ii) [material] with Goal from 'accommodation' schema; ellipsis of Mood + [extension:addition] + repetition (*garden*)

(v) minor clause realized by continuative + gratitude + [vocative] + tone 5

NVR

(a1) KNOCK ON DOOR
(a2) OPEN DOOR
(b) SMILE
(c) PLEASED
(k) SURPRISED
(m) PATTING DOG
(n) SAD
(o) SYMPATHETIC
(q) UNCERTAIN
(r) SAD
(v) HAPPY

7.1.2 For the student: Dialogue 1

Susan Brown is a university student. She is going to look at a room that Mrs Lake is letting in her house.

(a1) *Susan*: (KNOCKS AT DOOR).
(a2) *Mrs Lake*: (OPENS DOOR).
(b) *Susan*: (SMILES). Hello. My name's Susan Brown. I'd like to look at your room.
(c) *Mrs Lake*: (SMILES). Oh yes, the agent rang me. Come in. (THEY GO UPSTAIRS.) This is the room.
(d) *Susan*: (SHE LOOKS AROUND. SHE IS VERY PLEASED). That's lovely! It's so clean. And the table's nice and big. What pretty curtains, too!
(e) *Mrs Lake*: Yes, it was my daughter's room.
(f) *Susan*: May I see the bathroom?
(g) *Mrs Lake*: Yes. (THEY GO TO THE BATHROOM.)
(h) *Susan*: Mmm, that's pretty, too! Er . . . do you provide meals?
(j) *Mrs Lake*: Yes, I do breakfast and dinner.
(k) *Susan*: (SURPRISED). Oh, that's amazing! The room is very cheap, then.
(l) *Mrs Lake*: Oh yes. (THEY GO DOWNSTAIRS TO THE KITCHEN.) Meet my little dog, Mitzi.
(m) *Susan*: Hellow, Mitzi. (PATS DOG)
(n) *Mrs Lake*: (SAD). She's very fat. I'm old and we don't often go for walks.
(o) *Susan*: (SYMPATHETIC). Oh, poor Mitzi.
(p) *Mrs Lake*: Come and see the garden. (THEY GO OUTSIDE.)
(q) *Susan*: (UNCERTAIN). It's very nice.
(r) *Mrs Lake*: (SAD). Yes, but the grass is long and it's so untidy.
(s) *Susan*: I'd like to rent the room.
(t) *Mrs Lake*: Yes, of course, dear.
(u) *Susan*: And can I take Mitzi for walks and look after the garden?
(v) *Mrs Lake*: (HAPPY). Oh, thank you, my dear.

A. Comprehension exercise

Complete these sentences:

1. Susan is a ______________________________
2. Susan is going to ____________________ in Mrs Lake's house.
3. The room is ______________________________
4. The table is ______________________________
5. The bathroom is ______________________________
6. Mrs Lake provides ______________________________
7. Mitzi is fat because ______________________________
8. The garden is ______________________________

B. Group work

1. Does Mrs Lake know that Susan is coming?
2. Why does Susan want to rent the room?
3. Why is Mrs Lake happy at the end of the dialogue?
4. Why is the room cheap?

7.1.3 Commentary on Dialogue 1

I would like first to examine the specifications for Dialogue 1. Social discourses and practices is straightforward: thematic system and social action semiotic have already been discussed; and obviously a topic such as Renting Accommodation will articulate the discourse formation 'business'. Social situation and subject matter articulate the thematic system 'renting accommodation'; and social relationship and purpose articulate 'relation between accommodation-seeker and landlady' (though obviously the option 'older–younger' will not occur in all circumstances). The interaction sequence is largely a service encounter, articulating social situation and social relationship ('buyer–seller' only). Embedded in the service encounter is an Orient to Request^Accept, which articulates in a very interesting way the subject matter 'services', the purpose [regulatory], and the social relationship 'older–younger' – and indirectly certain objects and subject positions of the discourse of business. Attitude manifests partly 'inspecting accommodation' and 'buyer–seller', partly 'services', [regulatory] and 'older–younger'. Shared knowledge articulates thematic system – [social] —, 'inspecting accommodation' – [immediate] —, spoken mode – [maximum, —, and the explicitness generally associated with the everyday situation of an accommodation-seeker discussing accommodation with a landlady (minimum evocation of co-text is 'safer' than evoking context of culture – social or personal – in such asymmetrical encounters, unless, of course, one participant in the encounter is being deliberately implicit, as the discussion below will reveal).

Let us now turn to the linguistic realizations. The first two moves are non-verbal, but are included here as being the sole articulators of the interaction sequence elements Summons and Reply. Moves (b) (i)] and (b) (ii), 'Hello. My name's Susan Brown,' articulate the interaction sequence elements Greet and Identify, while (b) (iii), 'I'd like to look at your room,' articulates both the interaction sequence element Service and social shared knowledge (of the thematic system 'requests'). Move (c) (i), 'Oh yes, the agent rang me,' also articulates social shared knowledge, this time of the thematic system 'renting accommodation' and the social situation schema that derives from it. Move (c) (ii), 'Come in,' articulates the seller's contribution to Service, while (c) (iii), 'This is the room,' articulates the seller's initiating of the element Display, Move (d), 'That's lovely!', articulates the buyer's contribution to Display, together with the attitude 'pleased' and shared knowledge of the immediate environment. Move (e), 'Yes, it was my daughter's room,' articulates the larger thematic system 'home life' (or possibly 'family life'), which regularly collocates the adjective *pretty* (as Epithet in a nominal group or Attribute in a relational process) with *daughter . . . room* or *daughter's room* (*daughter* as Possessor in a relational process or Classifier in a nominal group). Moves (f) and (g), 'May I see the bathroom?' and 'Yes,' re-articulate the element Service, while (h) (i), 'Mmm, that's pretty, too!', is a return to the Display element (buyer's contribution). Moves (h) (ii), (j), (k) and (l) (i), from 'do you provide meals?' to 'Oh yes,' re-articulate the Service element; move (k), 'Oh, that's amazing!', also articulates the attitude 'surprised'. Moves (l) (ii) to (r), from 'Meet my little dog, Mitzi,' to 'Yes, but the grass is long,' may be analysed as articulating the interaction sequence element Orient to Request (or pre-request) – they obviously entail negotiation of meaning on the part of the buyer, and will be discussed at greater length below. Move (s), 'I'd like to rent the room,' articulates the interaction sequence element Resolution and social shared knowledge of the thematic system 'requests'; while move (t), 'Yes, of course, dear,' articulates the seller's contribution to Resolution. Moves (u) and (v), 'And can I take Mitzi for walks?' and 'Oh, thank you, my dear,' articulate the element Accept (Request), and will also be discussed below.

The non-verbal realizations (tone of voice and kinesic options) are clear, and need no comment. Note that these non-verbal realizations are included in the dialogue (capital letters, in parentheses). At the end of the dialogue there are two exercises of different types: the first exercise, a written one for individual work, concentrates on the topic Renting Accommodation; while the second exercise, an oral one for group work, which involves problem-solving, stresses the interactional side and prepares the learners for the subsequent negotiation of meaning exercise(s).

7.1.4 Exercise 1(topical)

Exercise 1 is what I shall call a topical exercise, relating to the lexicogrammer that articulates the relevant thematic system, or, rather, to an aspect of the lexicogrammer – in this case, the tense [present] — and material process with accommodation-provider as Actor and both process and Goal from the 'services' schema.

7.1.4.1 Specifications

SocDP

DF: 'business'
TS: 'renting accommodation'
SAS: 'relation between accommodation-seeker and landlady'

Sit

SocSit: 'inspecting accommodation'
SM: 'services'
SocRel: 'buyer–seller'
P: [regulatory]; [respect]

IntProc

IS: Service
At: 'pleased'; 'surprised'
SK: [maximum]

7.1.4.2 For the student: Exercise 1

You are looking for a room in Mrs Lake's house, and you ask her questions about services. When she answers, you are pleased or surprised.

Example

Meals?

You: Er . . . do you provide meals?
Mrs Lake: Yes, I do.
You: Oh, that's amazing.

Use one of these words to show you are pleased or surprised: good, wonderful, fantastic, terrific, extraordinary.

1. Washing?
2. Ironing?
3. Packed lunches?
4. Change the sheets?
5. Clean the room?
6. Do meals at weekends?
7. Cook for guests?
8. Cater for parties?

7.1.5 Exercises 2–4 (interactional)

It was noted above that moves (l) (ii) to (r) articulate the interaction sequence element Orient to Request, but obviously entail negotiation of meaning on the part of the buyer. It is quite possible for the buyer to interpret Mrs Lake's utterances in a different way, as will now be demonstrated.

7.1.5.1 Dialogue 1: a decoder perspective

Moves (l) (ii) to (r) may be specified as follows (only specifications differing from those of the encoder perspective will be listed):

Sit

SM: 'facilities'
SocRel: 'older–younger'
P: [informational]

IntProc

IS: Display

To read moves (l) (ii) to (r) as Orient to Request, the buyer must be aware of certain conditions:

1. The discourse formation 'business' is still being articulated.
2. The subject matter 'services' is still being articulated.
3. The 'buyer–seller' relation is still very much in play.
4. The pragmatic purpose is still [regulatory].
5. The interaction sequence element Display is no longer in force (or rather, to be more exact, it has been turned into a pre-request).

Any exercise must somehow make the leaner aware of the problems the buyer may have in decoding Mrs Lake's moves, and why such problems might arise.

7.1.5.2 For the student: Exercise 2

Here is the last part of the dialogue between Susan and Mrs Lake. The ending is different. Explain the difference between the two endings.

Susan: Er . . . do you provide meals?
Mrs Lake: Yes, I do breakfast and dinner.
Susan: (SURPRISED). Oh, that's amazing! The room is very cheap, then.
Mrs Lake: Oh yes. (THEY GO DOWNSTAIRS TO THE KITCHEN.) Meet my little dog, Mitzi.
Susan: Hello, Mitzi. (PATS DOG.)
Mrs Lake: She's very fat. I'm old and we don't often go for walks.
Susan: (SYMPATHETIC). Oh, poor Mitzi.
Mrs Lake: Come and see the garden. (THEY GO OUTSIDE.)
Susan: (UNCERTAIN.) It's very nice.
Mrs Lake: (SAD). Yes, but the grass is long and it's so untidy.
Susan: I'd like to rent the room.
Mrs Lake Yes, of course, dear.

Susan: Can I move in tomorrow?
Mrs Lake: Er . . . yes. Um . . . Could you sometimes take Mitzi for walks and mow the lawn, though?

Multiple-choice questions

1. Mrs Lake wants Susan to meet Mitzi because:
   (a) She is sad.
   (b) Susan likes dogs.
   (c) Mitzi is fat.
2. Mrs Lake and Susan go into the garden because:
   (a) The garden is nice.
   (b) The grass is long.
   (c) Susan likes gardens.
3. In your opinion, Mrs Lake is:
   (a) Old and clever.
   (b) Old and sad.
   (c) Old and talks too much.
4. In your opinion, Susan:
   (a) Is lazy.
   (b) Has a busy life.
   (c) Didn't understand Mrs Lake.

7.1.5.3 For the student: Exercise 3

The new dialogue between Susan and Mrs Lake ends like this:

Susan: Can I move in tomorrow?
Mrs Lake: Er . . . yes. Um . . . Could you sometimes take Mitzi for walks and mow the lawn, though?

The dialogue is not finished. Working in groups, finish it in three different ways:

Ending 1. Susan didn't understand Mrs Lake.
Ending 2. Susan is lazy.
Ending 3. Susan has a busy life.

7.1.5.4 For the student: Exercise 4

Susan doesn't like dogs and hates gardens. What will Susan say to Mrs Lake? Rewrite the dialogue, starting like this:
Susan: Er . . . do you provide meals?
Mrs Lake: Yes, I do breakfast and dinner.
Susan: (SURPRISED). Oh, that's amazing! The room is very cheap, then.

Mrs Lake: Oh yes, (THEY GO DOWNSTAIRS TO THE KITCHEN.) Meet my little dog, Mitzi.

7.1.5.5 Commentary on interactional Exercises 2–4

The dialogue of Exercise 2 makes Mrs Lake's requests explicit: questions 1 and 2 attempt to show that Mrs Lake's moves (n) and (r) are not Display but Orient to Request, while question 3 indicates that Mrs Lake is speaking in full knowledge of her purposes, and question 4 asks learners to speculate why learners may not have interpreted Mrs Lake's move as Orient to Request. Exercise 3 takes up the last question of Exericse 2 and asks learners to complete the dialogue in three possible ways. Exercise 4 varies Susan's attitude in a crucial way and invites learners to rewrite the dialogue – a fairly sophisticated task. Thus all three exercises attempt to lay bare the mechanics of meaning negotiation and make learners participants in the negotiating process.

7.1.6 The specifications for Dialogue 2

SocDP

DF: 'business'
TS: 'renting accommodation'
SAS: 'relation between accommodation-seeker and landlord'; 'relations between potential flatmates'

Sit

SocSit: 'inspecting accommodation'
SM: 'rooms'; 'inconveniences'
SocRel: 'buyer–seller'
P: [regulatory]; [respect]

IntProc

IS: Summons^Reply^Greet^Identify^Service^Orient to Resolution^ Resolution
At: 'unhappy'/'pleased'/'satisfied'/'unfriendly'
SK: [social]/[immediate]/[maximum]/[minimum]

7.1.7 For the student: Dialogue 2

Jack Smith wants to share his flat with someone. He puts an advertisement in the newsagent's window. Bill Green comes to see the flat. He is carrying a guitar, and has long hair.

(a1) *Bill*: (KNOCKS ON DOOR).
(a2) *Jack*: (OPENS DOOR).
(b) *Bill*: (A BIG SMILE). Hello. My name's Bill Green. I saw your ad in the newsagent's window.

(c) *Jack*: (A SMALL SMILE, UNFRIENDLY) Oh yes, come in. (THEY GO INTO THE FLAT.) Do you play the guitar?
(d) *Bill*: Yes, I'm in a band.
(e) *Jack*: (UNHAPPY.) Oh. (POINTING.) This is the bedroom.
(f) *Bill*: (PLEASED). It's nice and big! Good for guitar practice.
(g) *Jack*: But it's very noisy – it's on a main road. (POINTING.) And this is the sitting room.
(h) *Bill*: (PLEASED). Mmm. Very nice! Great for parties.
(j) *Jack*: Oh no, it's too small. (POINTING.) And this is the kitchen.
(k) *Bill*: It's very modern.
(l) *Jack*: Well, the cooker doesn't work very well.
(m) *Bill*: (SATISFIED.) Right! Can I move in immediately?
(n) *Jack*: (UNHAPPY). Er . . . I don't know. I don't think this flat is suitable for you, really.

A. Comprehension exercise

Complete these sentences:

1. Jack wants to ______________________________
2. Bill ______________ hair.
3. Bill plays ______________________________
4. The bedroom is good ______________________
5. The sitting room is great ___________________
6. The kitchen ______________________________

B. Group work

1. Does Jack want to share his flat with Bill Green? Why?
2. What does Jack say about:

   (a) The bedroom?
   (b) The sitting room?
   (c) The kitchen?

   Why does he say these things?

7.1.8 Commentary on Dialogue 2

The semiotic specifications for Dialogue 2 do not differ greatly from those listed for Dialogue 1. The main difference is the bringing into play of the system in the social action semiotic 'relations between potential flatmates', here articulated by the decision to activate the subject matter schema 'inconveniences', the interaction sequence element Orient to Resolution (which we might also term *pre-refusal*), the attitudes 'unhappy' and 'unfriendly', and their corresponding non-verbal realizations.

Now a brief consideration of the linguistic realizations. Moves (a1) and (a2), which are non-verbal, realize the interaction sequence elements Summons and Reply. Move (b) (i), 'Hello,' realizes Greet, (b) (ii), 'My name's Bill Green,' realizes Identify, and (b) (iii), 'I saw your ad in the newsagent's window', partly articulates Identify and partly articulates Service, which is also realized by moves (c) (i), 'Oh, yes,' and (c) (ii), 'Come in.' From the seller's point of view, (c) (iii), 'Do you play the guitar?', is the first move in the interaction sequence element Orient to Resolution (in this dialogue, a pre-refusal), articulating two subject positions in the social action semiotic, landlord and potential flatmate; (d), 'Yes, I'm in a band,' and (e) (i), 'Oh,' are the response and follow-up to Jack's initiation. Moves (e) (ii), 'This is the bedroom,' and (f), 'It's nice and big! Good for guitar practice,' are the seller's and the buyer's contributions to the articulation of the interaction sequence element Display; in moves (g) (i) and (g) (ii), 'But it's very noisy – it's on a main road,' the seller rearticulates the element Orient to Resolution (pre-refusal) by introducing a subject matter normally avoided by a seller, the 'inconveniences' schema, which itself articulates social shared knowledge (of the two systems of the social action semiotic currently in play, which permit a landlord/potential flatmate to decide that s/he is incompatible with the potential tenant/flatmate). This alternation between Display and Orient to Resolution continues until move (m), 'Right! Can I move in immediately?', when the buyer articulates his version of the Resolution element (a decision-to-purchase), thereby inviting the seller to proceed with the sale or articulate a clear refusal-to-sell. Move (n), 'I don't think this flat is suitable for you, really,' again articulating social shared knowledge of the two social action semiotic subject positions landlord and potential flatmate, is obviously the first step in a refusal-to-sell, althouth the outcome is still open to negotiation.

7.1.9 Exercise 5 (topical)

This exercise is based on the Display/Orient to Resolution alternation of Dialogue 2, and requires no further specification. The exercise draws on three patterns of the thematic system, of which the first is Pattern 7, where the thematic item Room/Furniture/Facilities is Carrier in a relational process with Qualities as Attribute. The second and third are patterns not yet referred to, in which a Facility (Fac) has a malfunction (Mal), represented either as a process (13) or as an attribute (14) (Figure 7.1). Thus the exercise is concentrating on *is* followed by an adjective, and on the simple present with positive or negative polarity, and adverbs of frequency.

7.1.9.1 For the student: Exercise 5

Jack Smith is showing you his flat. He shows you something, and you are pleased, but then he says something bad about it.

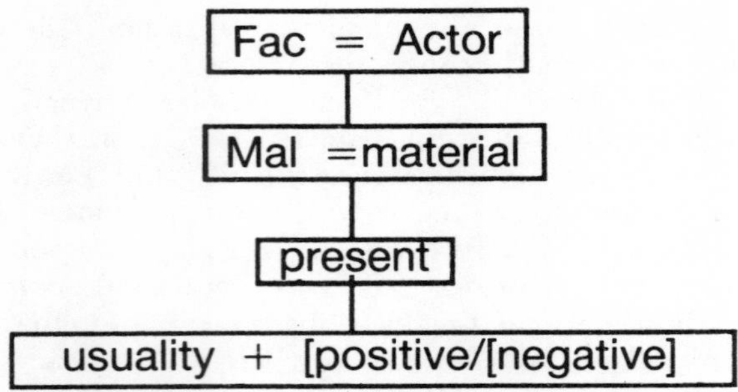

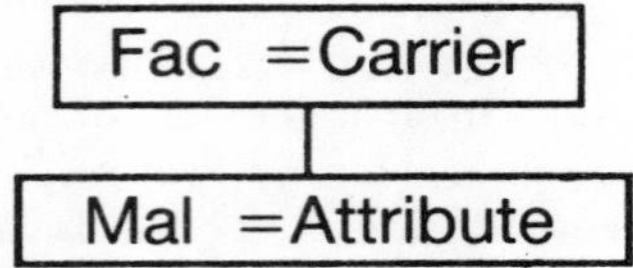

Figure 7.1 Continuation of the thematic system presented in Figure 6.1. *Fac* facilities, *Mal* malfunction

Example

kitchen/very modern/cooker doesn't work

Jack: And this is the kitchen
You: It's very modern.
Jack: Yes, but the cooker doesn't work very well.

1. fridge/nice and big/often breaks down
2. bathroom/very nice/water often runs cold
3. TV/good make/old and picture is bad
4. sofa/looks comfortable/springs are broken
5. washing machine/convenient/sometimes overflows
6. attic/charming/roof is too low

7.1.10 Exercise 6–8 (interactional)

The buyer appears quite unwilling or unable to interpret moves (c) (iii), (g) (ii), (j) (ii) and (1) as articulating the interaction sequence element Orient to Resolution (pre-refusal), so the buyer is clearly 'reading' certain semiotic variables in a different way than that 'intended' by the seller.

7.1.10.1 Dialogue 2: decoder perspective

The Orient to Resolution moves of Dialogue 2 may be specified as follows (only those differing from the encoder perspective will be listed):

SocDP

SAS: 'relations between accommodation-seeker and landlord'

Sit

SM: 'rooms'
P: [heuristic]/[informational]

IntProc

IS: Sociability Display
At: 'friendly'

In order for the buyer not to 'read' the six moves mentioned above as articulating Orient to Resolution, he must:

1. Ignore or not fully understand the system in the social action semiotic 'relations between potential flatmates' (assuming buyer and seller belong to the same culture).
2. Be unaware of, or consider unimportant, the subject matter 'inconveniences'.
3. See the moves as [heuristic] (c iii) or [informational], articulating the system in the social action semiotic 'relations between accommodation-seeker and landlord' (the 'honest landlord' sub-system).
4. See the moves as articulating Sociability (c iii) or Display
5. Fail to notice the attitude 'unhappy' articulated by move (e) (i).

The learner needs to be made aware of this, and of possible strategies the seller can deploy to make the buyer conscious of the pre-refusal moves.

7.1.10.2 For the student: Exercise 6

Look at these four short dialogues. Two of them are from Dialogue 2, the other two are about the same subject but are different. How are they different?

A. (i) *Jack*: (POINTING). This is the bedroom.
Bill: (PLEASED). It's nice and big! Good for guitar practice.
Jack: But it's very noisy – it's on a main road.
(ii) *Jack*: (POINTING). This is the bedroom
Bill: (PLEASED). It's nice and big! Can I practise my guitar here during the day?
Jack: Yes, sure.
B. (i) *Jack*: (POINTING). And this is the sitting room.

Bill: (PLEASED). Mmm. Very nice! Great for parties.
Jack: Oh no, it's too small.

(ii) *Jack*(POINTING). And this is the sitting room.
Bill: (PLEASED). Mmm. Very nice! Can I have small parties here sometimes?
Jack: Yes, sure.

Group work

1. In two of the dialogues Bill doesn't think of Jack's feelings. Find the dialogues, and say what Bill does.
2. In the other two dialogues Bill is polite. What does he do?
3. Do you think that Jack likes Bill in all four dialogues? Why?

7.1.10.3 For the student: Exercise 7

Jack doesn't like the guitar and big parties. What will he say to Bill, and what will Bill answer?

Jack: (POINTING). This is the bedroom.
Bill: (PLEASED). It's nice and big. Good for guitar practice.
Jack: ______________________________
Bill: ______________________________
Jack: (POINTING). And this is the sitting-room.
Bill: (PLEASED). Mmm. Very nice! Good for parties.
Jack: ______________________________
Bill: ______________________________

7.1.10.4 For the student: Exercise 8

The dialogue between Jack and Bill is not finished. Write an ending for it. Start like this:

Bill: (SATISFIED). Right! Can I move in immediately?
Jack: (UNHAPPY. Er . . . I don't know. I don't think this flat is suitable for you, really.

7.1.10.5 Commentary on interactional Exercises 6–8

The mini-dialogues of Exercise 6 contrast a Bill unaware and a Bill aware of the responsibilities of a potential flatmate as prescribed by the social action semiotic of the particular sub-culture of which be is a member. The questions for group work encourage learners to examine the approaches of Bill-unaware and Bill-aware, and their possible effect on Jack. Exercise 7 asks the learners to rewrite parts of Dialogue 2, permitting Jack to voice his disapproval of Bill more directly; and Exercise 8 requires learners to supply an ending for Dialogue 2, in the light of their knowledge of the types of strategies that Bill and Jack have at their disposal.

7.1.11 Conclusion: general comments on the unit

Two dialogues and eight exercises of an elementary–intermediate unit have been presented and analysed here. The emphasis has been on the interactional – there are only two topical exercises, revolving around patterns 7 and 8 of the thematic system, plus the two additional outlined in 7.1.9 above: in other words, the structure *copula* + *adjective*, Simple Present, and adverbs of frequency – because topical exercises represent little more than a culturally and situationally explicit extension of a type of exercise that already exists, whereas interactional exercises constitute a relatively new departure for language teaching and need to be explored as thoroughly as possible.

One area that was not touched on in discussion of the interactional exercises, but certainly needs to be taken into account, is what might be called coding orientation. The concept of code, which came to prominence with the work of Bernstein, is defined by Halliday (1978: 111) as 'the principle of semiotic organisation governing the choice of meanings by a speaker and their interpretation by a hearer' and as 'the grid' or subcultural angle on the social systems'. Thus the coding orientation may position speaking subjects in differential ways in relation to the on-going communicative event. Now the dialogues and exercises of this fragment of a topical-interactional course all suppose that the fictional participants in the communicative events have the same (middle-class, British) coding orientation, which will obviously, to a greater or lesser degree, not be shared by the real-life participants (the learners) in the parallel communicative event (the learning of English). In the case of Dialogue 1, for learners from societies which accord considerable respect and obedience to older people, the question of witholding an offer of assistance to Mrs Lake would not arise; and with regard to Dialogue 2, learners who like guitar music and parties and are not averse to noise may not consider Bill thoughtless, but rather find Jack rude and churlish. Given the range of possibilities – in theory as diverse as the cultures using the course – the question of coding orientation cannot be dealt with in the student's book; the only feasible approach is to sensitize the teacher to the problem, so that s/he is aware of how the cultural baggage of his/her students may affect the way in which they 'read' the dialogues and, in effect, negotiate with the (fictional and real-life) emitters of the dialogue.

7.2 UNIT AT INTERMEDIATE–ADVANCED LEVEL

Before proceeding to the unit at intermediate–advanced level, it will be necessary to make some additions to the partial thematic system and fragment of the social action semiotic presented in Chapter 6.

7.2.1 A further fragment of a thematic system

Figure 7.2 is a continuation of the relational network for the thematic system Renting Accommodation.

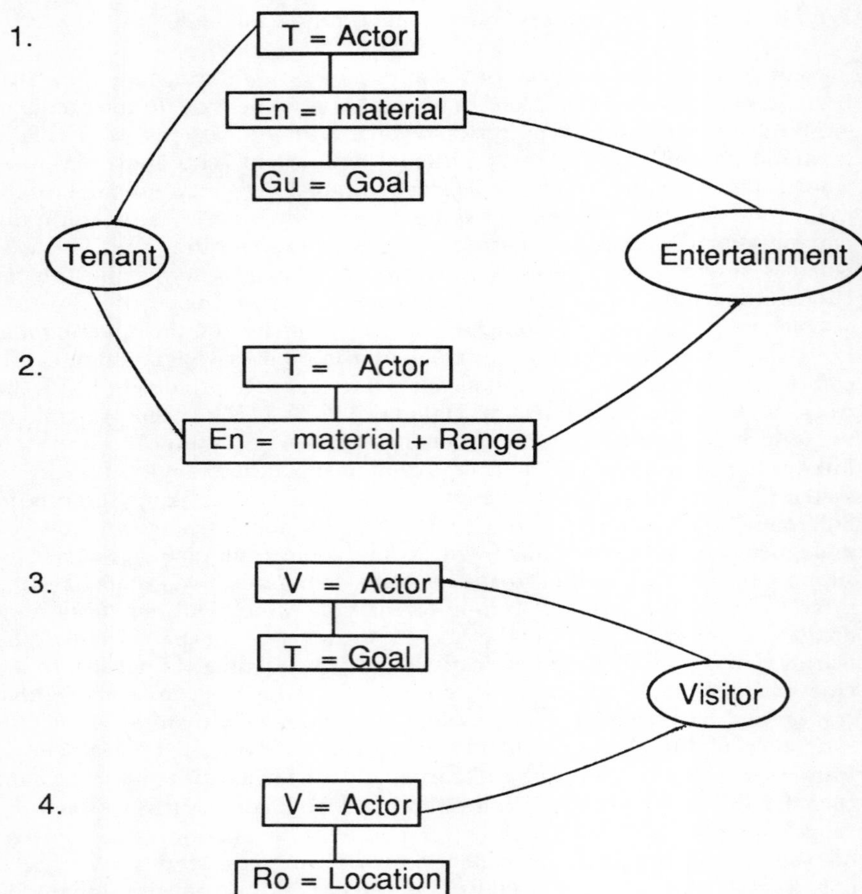

Figure 7.2 Continuation of a very partial fragment of a thematic system for the sub-topic Renting Accommodation. *Dom* domestic chores, *En* entertainment, *Fl* flatmate, *Gu* guest, *Pro* accommodation-provider, *Rul* rules, *T* tenant, *V* visitor

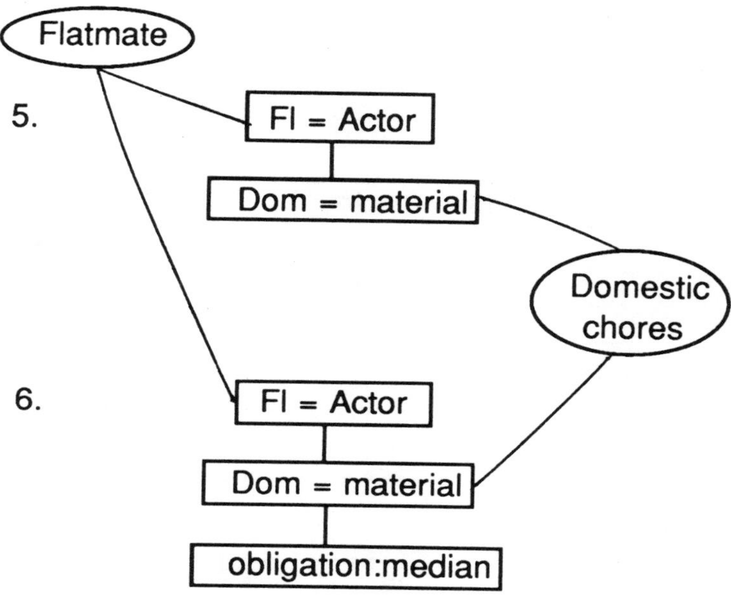

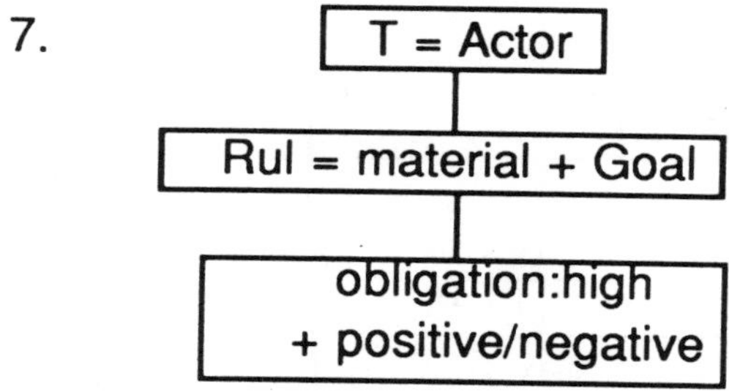

Figure 7.2 *continued*

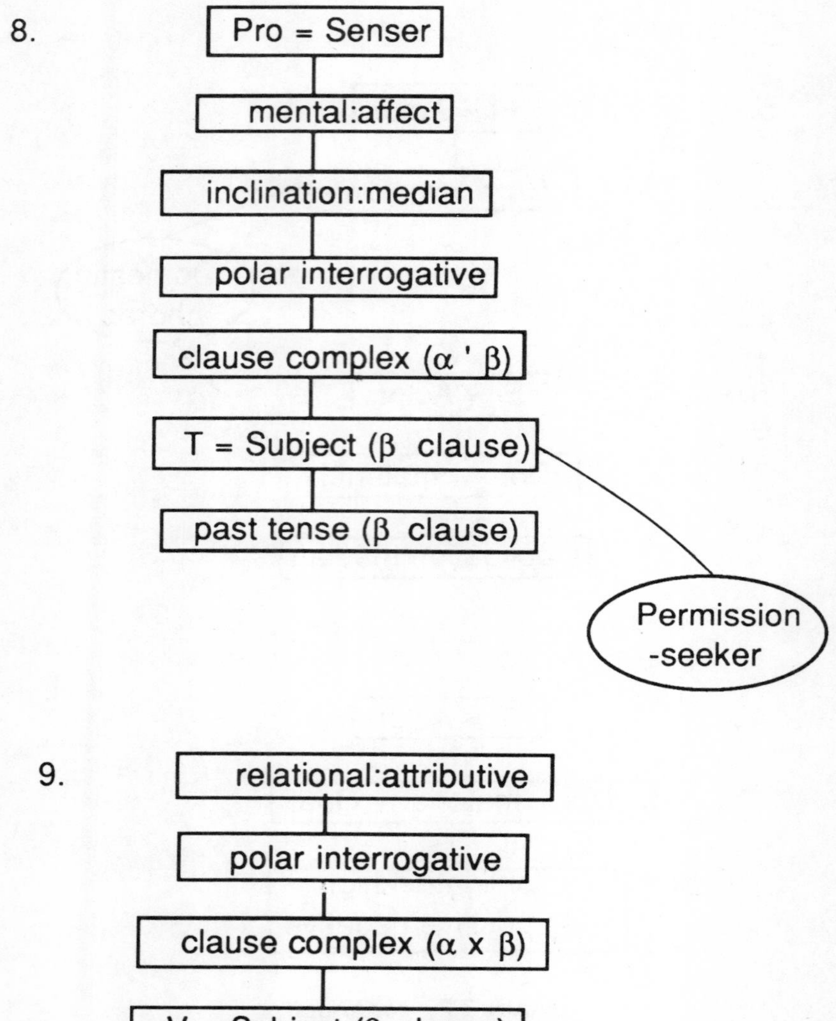

Figure 7.2 *continued*

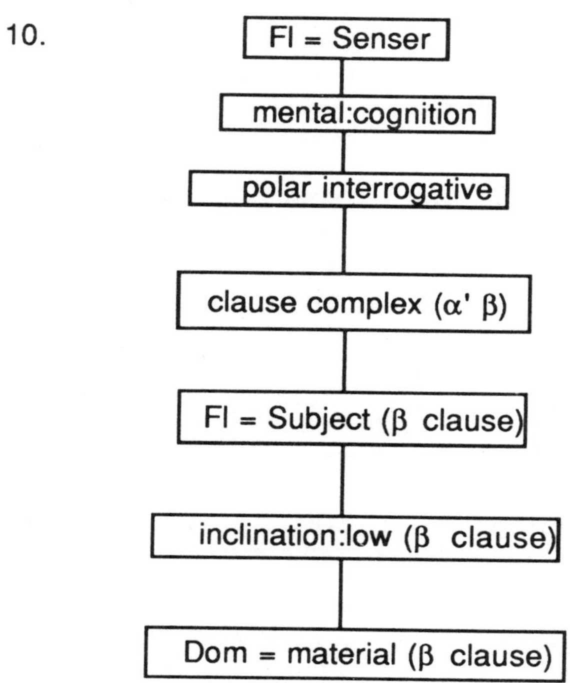

Figure 7.2 *continued*

7.2.2 A further fragment of the social action semiotic relevant to renting accommodation

Figure 7.3 represents a further fragment of the social action semiotic relevant to renting accommodation, to supplement the fragment already sketched in Chapter 6. The figure shows in the simplest possible way the relationships into which a tenant may enter in the course of functioning as a tenant.

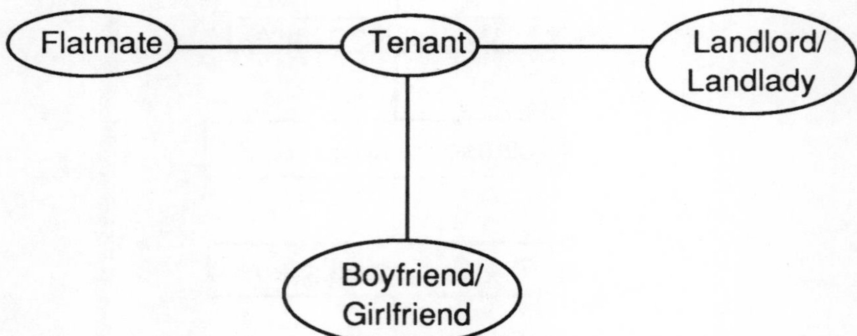

Figure 7.3 A further fragment of the social action semiotic relevant to renting accommodation

7.2.3 Articulation of the thematic system patterns

The following utterances articulate the topical (1–7) and/or interactional (8–10) thematic system patterns of Figure 7.1, together with a relationship of the social action semiotic (Figure 7.2). As was the case with the sentences in Chapter 6 illustrating the first fragment of the thematic system, the utterances are citation forms, and do not arise from any real communicative event.

1. (Pattern 1 + 'tenant/landlord or landlady')
   I'm entertaining a few friends this evening.
2. (Patterns 2, 8 + 'tenant/landlord or landlady')
   Would you mind if I had a small party on Saturday?
3. (Patterns 4, 9 + 'tenant/landlord or landlady')
   Is it allright if a friend stays in my room?
4. (Pattern 3 + 'tenant/landlord or landlady')
   Some people from the office are visiting me this evening.
5. (Patterns 5, 10 + 'tenant/flatmate')
   Do you think you could do the cooking?
6. (Pattern 6 + 'tenant/flatmate')
   You should do the washing up.
7. (Pattern 7 + 'landlord or landlady/tenant')
   You mustn't keep pets.

These yield the following language items:

(a) Would you mind if . . . ?
(b) Is it all right if . . . ?
(c) First Conditional.
(d) Second Conditional.
(e) Do you think you could . . . ?
(f) You should . . .
(g) You must/mustn't . . .

Let us now turn to the unit itself, beginning with the specifications for Dialogue 1.

7.2.4 Specifications for Dialogue 1

SocDP

DF: 'business'
TS: 'renting accommodation:the rules'; 'family'
SAS: 'relation between tenant and landlady'

Sit

SocSit: 'discussion'
SM: 'rules of the house'; 'family'
SocRel: 'insider–outsider'; 'buyer-seller'
P: [regulatory]; [dominance]

IntProc

IS: Conditions of Contract^Accept^Orient^Seek Permission^Grant Permission^Suspend/Cancel Contract
At: 'unenthusiastic'/'unfriendly'/'nervous'/'reluctant'/'indifferent'/ 'cheerful'
SK: [maximum]/[minimum]/[social]/[personal]

7.2.5 For the student: Dialogue 1

Alan Jones is renting a room in Mrs King's house. Mrs King is explaining the rules of the house.

(a) *Mrs King*: Did I tell you the rules, Alan?
(b) *Alan*: No, Mrs King, you didn't.
(c) *Mrs King*: Well, there are three. You mustn't have parties, you mustn't share your room with anyone, and you mustn't keep pets.
(d) *Alan*: (UNENTHUSIASTIC). Right.
(e) *Mrs King*: You don't sound very happy, dear.
(f) *Alan*: Um . . . the problem is, it's my birthday next week and I've invited a few friends over.

(g) *Mrs King*: (UNFRIENDLY). Oh yes.
(h) *Alan*: (NERVOUS). Would you mind if I had a small birthday party next Friday?
(j) *Mrs King*: (RELUCTANT). Well, just this once, Alan.

(*A few weeks pass*)

(k) *Alan*: (AT BREAKFAST). My brother's visiting me next week. I haven't seen him for two years.
(l) *Mrs King*: (INDIFFERENT). That's nice, dear.
(m) *Alan*: (NERVOUS). Is it all right if he stays in my room for two nights?
(n) *Mrs King*: (VERY RELUCTANT). Well, I don't normally allow it . . . All right, just this once.

(*A few weeks pass*)

(o) *Mrs King*: (CHEERFUL). My sister's visiting me next week. I haven't seen her for ten years. I've promised her your room, so I'm afraid you'll have to leave, Alan.

A. Comprehension exercise

Complete these sentences:

1. In Mrs King's house:
   (a) Parties ______________________
   (b) The room ______________________
   (c) No pets ______________________
2. Alan was unhappy because ______________________
3. Mrs King ______________________ to have a small birthday party.
4. It was ten years ______________________
5. Mrs King allowed ______________________
6. As a result of the vist of Mrs King's sister, ______________________

B. Group work

1. Did Alan behave in a reasonable way towards Mrs King?
2. Did Mrs King behave in an unreasonable way towards Alan?
3. Mrs King was unfriendly towards Alan. What should he have done to change her attitude?
4. Will Mrs King let Alan return to his room after her sister has gone?

7.2.6 Commentary on Dialogue 1

Examining first the specifications for Dialogue 1, I will say nothing further about social discourses and practices, except to note that Renting Accommodation continues to articulate the discourse formation 'business' even after the initial commercial arrangement has been concluded, and beyond the regular paying of rent. Social situation and subject matter articulate the two thematic systems 'renting accommodation:rules' (represented by Pattern 7 in the second fragment of the thematic system), and 'family'; and social relationship and purpose articulate the system in the social action semiotic 'relations between tenant and landlady'. The interaction sequence, which we might call Signing a Contract, directly articulates the subject matter 'rules of the house' and the social relationship – and indirectly the discourse formation 'business', the thematic system 'renting accommodation:rules', and the system in the social action semiotic 'relations between tenant and landlady'. Note that here the elements Seek Permission ^Grant Permission are not part of an embedded interaction sequence but are integral to Signing a Contract – they might better be termed Seek Permission to Waive Conditions and Grant Permission to Waive Conditions. Attitude articulates various combinations of 'rules of the house', 'insider–outsider' and [dominance] or its opposite [subordination].

Now to consider the linguistic realizations. Moves (a) to (c), from 'Did I tell you the rules?' to '. . . you mustn't keep pets', articulate the interaction sequence element Conditions of Contract, and social shared knowledge (of the 'rules' sub-system of 'renting accommodation'). Move (d), 'Right,' articulates the interaction sequence element Accept and the attitude 'unenthusiastic' – and also, perhaps, a transition to the interaction sequence element Orient (to Seek Permission). Moves (e), (f) and (g), from 'You don't sound very happy' to 'Oh yes,' articulate the Orient element, while (h), 'Would you mind if I had a small birthday party?', articulates Seek Permission, and (j), 'Well, just this once,' articulates Grant Permission plus the attitude 'reluctant'. Moves (k) and (l), 'My brother's visiting me next week' and 'That's nice' rearticulate Orient; move (m), 'Is it all right if he stays in my room?', rearticulates Seek Permission; and (n), 'Well, I don't normally allow it,' rearticulates Grant Permission plus the attitude 'very reluctant'. Finally, move (o), 'I'm afraid you'll have to leave, Alan,' articulates Suspend/Cancel Contract, social shared knowledge of the thematic system 'renting accommodations:the rules', in which even bending the rules may mean that a tenant is asked to leave), minimum shared knowledge of co-text ('sister . . . room' echoes the earlier 'brother . . . room'), and personal shared knowledge (Alan should have known how reluctant Mrs King was to waive the rules, particularly the second time).

7.2.7 Exercise 1 (topical)

7.2.7.1 For the student: Exercise 1

You are living in Mrs King's house. She has a number of rules for her tenants, but you are hoping she will make an exception for you.

Example

Rule: No parties.

You: It's my birthday next week, and I've invited a few friends over.
Mrs King: (UNFRIENDLY). Oh yes.
You: (NERVOUS). Would you mind if I had a small birthday party next Friday?

1. Rule: No pets.
(Your brother has a dog – can you look after if for a week?)
2. Rule: Don't hang anything on the walls.
(You went to an exhibition and bought a poster.)
3. Rule: Tenants may not use the back garden.
(Some friends are visiting and the weather is glorious.)
4. Rule: No overnight guests.
(Your friend has missed the last bus – it's after midnight.)
5. Rule: No repairs or alterations without permission.
(Your room is green – you think it's a cold colour.)
6. Rule: No noise after 10.00 p.m.
(You want to watch the election results on television.)
7. Rule: Don't dry washing on the radiator.
(The laundrette is closed and you need clean clothes urgently.)
8. Rule: No visitors after 10.00 p.m.
(Your friend has just had a fight with his/her spouse and wants to talk to you – and it's 1030 p.m.)

7.2.7.2 Commentary on Exercise 1

The aim of this exercise is to practise the permission-seeking form *Would you mind?* and the Second Conditional, although there is also scope for practising the Present Perfect. Unlike Exercise 1 in the elementary–intermediate unit (7.1.4.2), this exercise is not entirely mechanical, in that it requires learners to manipulate and/or expand the language provided in the cues.

7.2.8 Exercises 2–4 (interactional)

All the possibilities of negotiation of meaning here lie in the attitude options chosen by the landlady and apparently not interpreted correctly by the tenant.

7.2.8.1 Dialogue 1. A decoder perspective

SocDP

DF: ?
SAS: 'relation between two people sharing a house'

Sit

SocRel: 'insider–insider'
P: [respect]

IntProc

At: ?/?/'nervous'/?/?/'cheerful'

It is assumed that the tenant does not interpret the dialogue as articulating the dicourse formation 'business' (the question mark indicates uncertainty as to what his alternative interpretation might be); it is furthermore assumed that he sees the system in the social action semiotic motivating the dialogue not as 'tenant–landlady', but as 'two people sharing a house'. Consequently, he will interpret the social relationship as 'insider–insider' (ignoring 'buyer–seller'), and the purpose not as [dominance] but as [respect]. Finally, we may suppose that he either ignores, or minimizes the significance of, the attitude options 'unenthusiastic', 'unfriendly', 'reluctant' and 'indifferent'. Any interactional exercise must attempt to make learners aware of the tenant's differing or deficient 'reading' of these variables.

7.2.8.2 For the student: Exercise 2

Look at this segment of Dialogue 1. How does it differ from the original Dialogue 1? (Mrs King has just told Alan the rules.)

Alan: (UNENTHUSIASTIC). Right.
Mrs King: You don't sound very happy, dear.
Alan: Um . . . the problem is, it's my birthday next week, and I've invited a few friends over.
Mrs King: (UNFRIENDLY). Oh, yes.
Alan: (THINKING.) But we could go to a pub, or get together at my girlfriend's flat.
Mrs King: (ALMOST FRIENDLY). Oh, since you've already arranged it, Alan, they can come here.
Alan: (WARMLY). That's very kind of you, Mrs King.

Group work

1. Why does Mrs King seem unfriendly at first when Alan mentions inviting a few friends over?
2. Why does Alan suggest going to a pub or his girlfriend's flat?
3. How does Mrs King react to Alan's suggestion?
4. Alan uses two approaches in this and the original fragment of Dialogue 1.

   (a) Asking permission for a party at Mrs King's house.
   (b) Suggesting that he and his friends go to a pub or his girlfriend's flat.

   Which approach is more effective, and why?

7.2.8.3 For the student: Exercise 3

Complete this segment of conversation from Dialogue 1. Alan will use the same approach as in Exercise 2.

Alan: (AT BREAKFAST). My brother is visiting me next week. I haven't seen him for two years.
Mrs King: (INDIFFERENT). That's nice, dear.

7.2.8.4 For the student: Exercise 4

Dialogue 1 is incomplete. There are two possible endings: (a) Alan loses his room, (b) Alan returns to his room after a few days. Working in groups, write these endings. Begin like this:

Mrs King: (CHEERFUL). My sister's visiting me next week. I haven't seen her for ten years. I've promised her your room, so I'm afraid you'll have to leave, Alan.

7.2.8.5 Commentary on interactional Exercises 2–4

Exercise 2 shows a fragment of the dialogue as it would be if Alan interpreted all the social discourse and practice, situation, and interactional process variables as they are 'intended' by Mrs King. Exercise 3 asks students to rewrite another fragment of Dialogue 1 with the same interpretation holding. Exercise 4 invites students to imagine two endings to Dialogue 1 – one unfaviourable to the Alan of Dialogue 1, and one favourable to the Alan of Exercises 2 and 3.

7.2.9 Specifications for Dialogue 2

SocDP

DF: 'business'
TS: 'renting accommodation:sharing'
SAS: 'relation between flatmates'; 'relation between boyfriend and girlfriend.

Sit

SocSit: 'discussion'/'performing domestic chores'
SM: 'domestic chores'; 'sharing'; 'going out'; 'work'
SocRel: 'insider–outsider'; 'buyer–seller'; 'male–female'; 'intimate–intimate'
P: [regulatory]; [dominance]

IntProc

IS: Conditions of Contract^Accept^Orient to Request^Accept^Defer^Orient

to Request^Refuse Acknowledgement^Greet^Orient to Request^Refuse Request
At: 'irritated'/'cool'
SK: [minimum]/[social]/maximum]/[personal]

7.2.10 For the student: Dialogue 2

Alan Jones and his girlfriend, Anna, have decided to live together in her flat. They are discussing the sharing of domestic chores.

(a) *Alan*: Well, since I can't cook, do you think you could cook for both of us?
(a) *Anna*: Yes, but in that case I think *you* should do all the housework.
(c) *Alan*: Okay, that's fair.
(d) *Anna*: And we should each do our own washing and ironing.
(e) *Alan*: Oh yes, of course.

(*A few days pass.*)

(f) *Anna*: (IRRITATED). The kitchen's looking pretty filthy, Alan.
(g) *Alan*: ((READING A BOOK). Er . . . yes . . . I'll do it tomorrow. (*Later.*) (CALLING OUT) I don't understand how your iron works, Anna.
(h) *Anna*: (SAYS NOTHING).
(j) *Alan*: (CALLING OUT). Anna? . . . Damn!

(*Next morning.*)

(k) *Alan*: Oh hell! We're going out to the theatre this evening and I haven't got a clean shirt, Anna. And I've got to go now or I'll be late.
(l) *Anna*: (SAYS NOTHING).

(*In the evening.*)

(m) *Alan*: Hello, Anna. How are you?
(n) *Anna*: Fine. I had a good day at work.
(o) *Alan*: Great! What's for dinner? I'm starving!
(p) *Anna*: (COOL). Nothing.

A. Comprehension questions

Complete these sentences:

1. Alan suggested that Anna ________________________________
2. Anna agreed, but only if________________________________
3. It was decided that they ________________________________
4. The kitchen was ____________________ because Alan ________
5. Alan had trouble with Anna's iron and wanted her____________

6. Alan didn't have time ______________________________
7. When Alan got home, he found ______________________________

B. Group work

1. Why was Anna irritated by the dirty kitchen?
2. In your opinion, how did Anna feel when Alan said, 'I'll do it tomorrow'?
3. Why did Anna twice 'say nothing' in reply to Alan?
4. Why didn't Anna cook dinner?

7.2.11 Commentary on Dialogue 2

As regards the specifications for Dialogue 2, the dialogue articulates the discourse formation 'business', in that the sharing of domestic chores is in part at least an arrangement between a landlady (Anna) and a tenant (Alan). Other social discourse and practice variables have already been discussed above (7.2.1–2). Social situation and subject matter articulate the thematic system 'renting accommodation:sharing'; the social relationships 'insider–outsider' and 'buyer–seller' articulate the system in the social action semiotic 'relation between flatmates', while 'male–female' and 'intimate–intimate' articulate the social action semiotic system 'relation between boyfriend and girlfriend'. As for purpose, [regulatory] and [dominance] articulate 'relation between flatmates' and 'relation between boyfriend and girlfriend' respectively. (In the case of the option [dominance], I am assuming that Alan is consciously or unconsciously adhering to a traditional version of the social action semiotic in which males hold the dominant position in a relationship.) The interaction sequence Signing a Contract articulates the social situation 'discussion', the subject matter 'domestic chores' and 'sharing', and the social relationship 'insider–outsider' and 'buyer–seller', as far as the elements Conditions of Contract and Accept are concerned; with regard to the elements Orient to Request (for the Waiving of Contract Conditions) and the various responses, they articulate the social situations 'performing domestic chores', the subject matter 'domestic chores', 'going-out' and 'work', and the social relationships 'male–female' and 'intimate–intimate'. Attitude articulates a combination of the subject matter 'sharing', the social relationships 'male–female' and 'intimate–intimate', and the purpose [regulatory] and [dominance].

Now to the linguistic realizations. Moves (a) to (e), 'Well, since I can't cook . . . ' to 'Oh yes, of course,' articulate the interaction sequence elements Conditions of Contract and Accept (moves (a), (b) (ii)–(iii) and (d) are Conditions of Contract articulators, moves (b) (i), (c) and (e) are Accept articulators). Move (f), 'The kitchen's looking pretty filthy,' articulates the interaction sequence element Orient to Request, the attitude 'irritated', and the shared knowledge options [personal] – Alan knows as well as Anna that he undertook to do the housework – and [social] – the obligations of a flat-sharer as represented by Pattern 6 in the 'renting accommodation' thematic system ('You should do the washing up'). Moves (g) (i) and (g) (ii), 'Er . . . yes . . . I'll do it tomorrow,' articulate the elements Accept and Defer, while (g) (iii–iv), 'I don't understand how your iron works,' and (j), 'Anna? . . . Damn!', instantiate a second articulation of Orient to Request, together with the shared knowledge choices [personal] – Alan knows he has to do his own ironing – and [social] – the 'malfunctioning facility' pattern of the 'renting accommodation' thematic system, outlined in 7.1.9 above, but this time with the more normal case of the 'tenant' reporting the malfunction to the 'landlady'; and Anna's intervening move (h) – silence, of course – is an articulator of the element Refuse Acknowledgement. Moves (k), 'We're going out to the theatre . . . ', and (l) 'SAYS NOTHING, rearticulate the elements Orient to Request plus [personal] and [social] and Refuse Acknowledgement respectively. Move (m), 'Hello, Anna. How are you?', articulates the interaction sequence element Greet, while (n), 'Fine. I had a good day at work,' articulates Greet plus the attitude 'cool', and (o) (i), 'Great!', completes the Greet series of moves. Moves (o) (ii) and (o) (iii), 'What's for dinner? I'm starving!', articulate once more Orient to Request and the shared knowledge options [personal] – Anna is supposed to do the cooking – and [social] – the obligations of a flat-sharer as represented by Pattern 5 of the 'renting accommodation' thematic system ('Do you think you could do the cooking?'); while move (p), 'Nothing,' articulates Refuse Request and the attitude 'cool'.

7.2.12 Exercise 5 (topical)

This is a two-part exercise which practices two forms found in the dialogue (*Do you think you could . . . ?* and *I think you should . . .*) in the first part, and a form not found in the dialogue (*you should have . . .*) in the second part – still in the 'domestic chores' framework.

7.2.12.1 For the student: Exercise 5

Part A

You are sharing a flat with your friend, and you are trying to decide who will do various domestic chores.

Example

cook/do all the housework

You: Well, since I can't cook, do you think you could do all the cooking?
Your friend: Yes, but in that case, I think you should do all the housework.

1. iron/do all the washing
2. clean windows/clean the toilet
3. clean carpets/do the gardening
4. sew on buttons/clean the bath and sinks
5. do odd jobs/do the washing-up
6. mend clothes/take the garbage out
7. polish floors/do all the sweeping
8. do dusting/make the beds

Part B

Your friend doesn't do his/her domestic chores, and you are annoyed.

Example

kitchen/filthy

You: The kitchen's looking filthy. You should have cleaned it this morning.
Your friend: Oh sorry, I'll do it now.

1. clothes/dirty
2. toilet/filthy
3. garden/full of weeds
4. bath/grey
5. breakfast dishes/still in sink
6. garbage bin/overflowing
7. kichen floor/covered with muck
8. table/thick with dust

7.2.13 Exercise 6–8 (interactional)

The specifications for Dialogue 2 represent an idealized consensus view of the social discourse and practice, situational and interactional process variables motivating the dialogue. In order to consider how meaning is (or is not) negotiated in this dialogue, we need to separate the perspectives of each participant.

7.2.13.1 Dialogue 2. A dual perspective

	Alan	*Anna*
DF:	Ø	'business'
SAS:	'relation between boyfriend and girlfriend	'relation between flatmates'
SocRel:	'male–female'; 'intimate–intimate'	'insider–outsider'; 'buyer–seller'

P:	Alan	Anna
	[regulatory]];	[regulatory];
	[dominance)	[respect]

There are four points to be noted:

1. Anna is contextualizing the dialogue within the framework of the discourse formation 'business', while Alan is not.
2. Anna sees the interaction as motivated by the system in the social action semiotic 'relation between flatmates'; for Alan, 'relation between boyfriend and girlfriend' is the dominant system.
3. Alan is performing the social relationships 'intimate–intimate' and 'male–female' (in its most traditional and asymmetrical form), whereas Anna is performing 'insider–outsider' and 'buyer–seller' – though it could be argued that 'intimate–intimate' and 'male–female' (in a more symmetrical contemporary form) are being articulated by Anna's two refusals to acknowledge and her final response, 'Nothing.'
4. Alan's purpose is one of [dominance], while Anna's is one of [respect].

These four points should be taken into account in the interactional exercises.

7.2.13.2 For the student: Exercise 6

Compare the two scenes in this dialogue with the same scenes in Dialogue 2.

Anna: (IRRITATED). The kitchen's looking pretty filthy, Alan.
Alan: (READING A BOOK – GUILTY LOOK). Oh, I'm sorry, Anna. I've been so busy lately. I'll do it right now. (GETS UP) (*Later.*) (CALLING OUT) Is there something wrong with your iron? The light's not on and it's not heating up.
Anna: (CALLING OUT). The light's not working, but the iron's OK – just slow.

Group work

1. How does Alan's behaviour in the kitchen scene differ in the two dialogues?
2. In the iron scene, why does Anna say nothing in one dialogue and give Alan information in the other?

7.2.13.3 For the student: Exercise 7

Rewrite the clean shirt scence, changing the behaviour of Alan and Anna as in Exercise 6.

7.2.13.4 For the student: Exercise 8

Dialogue 2 is unfinished. Write an ending for it. Begin like this:

Alan: Hello, Anna. How are you?
Anna: (COOL). Fine. I had a good day at work.
Alan: Great! What's for dinner? I'm starving!
Alan: Nothing.

7.2.13.5 Commentary on interactional exercises 6–8

Exercise 6 represents two scenes from Dialogue 2 as they would be if Alan interpreted the social discourse and practice parameters, and situational variables, in the same way as Anna. Exercise 7 asks learners to rewrite a third scene from Dialogue 2 from the same perspective. In the light of insights gained from these exercises, learners are then invited in Exercise 8 to supply an appropriate ending to (the original) Dialogue 2.

7.2.14 General comments on the unit

As was the case in the elementary–intermediate unit, the emphasis is on interactional rather than topical exercises. There are two topical exercise, 1 and 5: Exercise 1 is based on Pattern 8 of the fragment of thematic system outlined earlier in this chapter, separated from, but still dependent on, Pattern 7 (the 'rules' pattern); Exercise 5, part A, is based on Patterns 5, 6 and 10, while part B is based on Pattern 5, a variant of Pattern 5 formed by [past], [negative] and, in some cases, collocation (e.g. 'didn't clean' – – – ► 'filthy'), and on Pattern 10 extended by [past in present] and a Time circumstantial.

As regards the six interactional exercises, no account has been taken of coding orientation, of cultural or sub-cultural angles on social discourse and practices. Dialogue 1 and poses few problems in this respect: only Mrs King's reaction to the visit of Alan's brother may cause puzzlement, especially in cultures which place a high value on family and family solidarity. Dialogue 2 is another matter. Apart from the fact that Alan and Anna's cohabiting is inconceivable or even offensive in many cultures, Anna's assumption that Alan should do domestic chores is likely to arouse mirth or incomprehension, and Alan's apparent reluctance to perform his chores may well be seen as 'natural', especially by male learners. Of course, at an intermediate–advanced stage, after considerable exposure to the culture of the target language, such reactions are less probable, but need to be foreseen by the teacher.

7.3 CONCLUSION

I have presented two units of what I call a topical-interactional course, concentrating on the part that a modified systemic-functional model can play in understanding the sociocultural motivation of everday interactions, the process of meaning negotiation that is often required to bring such interactions to a successful conclusion, and the role that should be assigned to structures and functions in the pedagogic enterprise. Now four wider issues need to be addressed: the contibution that a topical-interactional approach can make to the new process linguistics foreshadowed in Chapter 2; the implications of the new approach for the teaching of English; how the present attempt to model discourse in the context of language teaching compares with other contemporary approaches to discourse within a pedagogical framework; and finally, to what extent a topical-interactional syllabus might resemble or differ from the most influential approach to communicative syllabus design to emerge recently, the task-based syllabus. The first two issues will be addressed in Chapter 8, and the other two issues will be the subject of Chapter 9.

8. The topical interactional syllabus: a process approach to language and language teaching?

8.0 INTRODUCTION

I have presented two units of a topical-interactional course without commenting on the implications that the material, and the model out of which the material has grown, might have for the process linguistics I spoke of in Chapters 2 and 3, as an amalgam of Derrida's views on speech act theory and Halliday's speculations on indeterminacy in language; and for communicative language teaching, still struggling to reconcile the claims made by advocates of a process-oriented syllabus like Breen and Candlin (see Chapter 1) or Prabhu (see Chapter 6) with the certainties of a product-based (structural and/or functions) syllabus. In this chapter I will examine these implications, starting with the insights that the two units of a topical-interactional course can offer to the nascent process linguistics.

8.1 MEANING NEGOTIATION AND PROCESS LINGUISTICS

The twin aims of process linguistics, as already stated, are to account for not only the particulate in language, but also what Halliday calls the wavelike and the fieldlike, that is, the indeterminate; and to find a way of representing what is conventional and iterable in language (at the semantic level, that is – the formal level has already been codified), and of showing the fluidity of meaning that follows from this (differance or dehiscence, in Derrida's terms). In what follows I will attempt to demonstrate that the model developed in Chapter 4 and applied in Chapters 5 and 7 fulfils these twin aims, and I shall do this by examining the four dialogues in Chapter 7 that form the basis for the topical-interactional syllabus, looking for waves and/or fields of meaning, and seeking to understand how the iterable can become ambiguous and liable to misunderstanding.

The first dialogue presented in Chapter 7 is the dialogue between Susan Brown and Mrs Lake, which I reproduce here for the sake of convenience:

Susan: (KNOCKS AT DOOR).
Mrs Lake: (OPENS DOOR).

Susan: (SMILES). Hello. My name's Susan Brown. I'd like to look at your room.
Mrs Lake: (SMILES). Oh yes, the agent rang me. Come in. (THEY GO UPSTAIRS.) This is the room.
Susan: (SHE LOOKS AROUND. SHE IS VERY PLEASED). That's lovely! It's so clean. And the table's nice and big. What pretty curtains, too!
Mrs Lake: Yes, it was my daughter's room.
Susan: May I see the bathroom?
Mrs Lake: Yes, (THEY GO TO THE BATHROOM.)
Susan: Mmm, that's pretty, too! Er . . . do you provide meals?
Mrs Lake: Yes, I do breakfast and dinner.
Susan: (SURPRISED). Oh, that's amazing! The room is very cheap, then.
Mrs Lake: Oh yes. (THEY GO DOWNSTAIRS TO THE KITCHEN.) Meet my little dog, Mitzi.
Susan: Hello, Mitzi. (PATS DOG.)
Mrs Lake: (SAD). She's very fat. I'm old and we don't often go for walks.
Susan: (SYMPATHETIC). Oh, poor Mitzi.
Mrs Lake: Come and see the garden. (THEY GO OUTSIDE.)
Susan: (UNCERTAIN). It's very nice.
Mrs Lake: (SAD). Yes, but the grass is long and it's so untidy.
Susan: I'd like to rent the room.
Mrs Lake: Yes, of course, dear.
Susan: And can I take Mitzi for walks and look after the garden?
Mrs Lake: (HAPPY). Oh, thank you, my dear.

It was hypothesized that a particular segment of the dialogue, roughly beginning with 'Meet my little dog, Mitzi,' and ending with 'Yes, but the grass is long and it's so untidy,' could well provoke uncertainty in the minds of accommodation-seekers, and that its meaning might therefore need to be negotiated. It was suggested that the reason for this was that an accommodation-seeker need not see the situation in the same way as Mrs Lake: for while Mrs Lake, we suppose, sees that particular segment of the dialogue as still reflecting the discursive formation 'business' (in particular that discursive object we might call PAYMENT BY SERVICES RENDERED), as well as the social relationship 'buyer – seller', and as representing a move away from the interaction sequence element Display to the element Orient (pre-request), it would be perfectly possible for the accommodation-seeker to assume that 'business' was no longer in play, that the social relationship 'older – younger' was at least as important as 'buyer – seller', and that the segment was a continuation of the Display element that started with 'This is the room.'

According to the theory proposed earlier (in Chapter 3), this potential 'misunderstanding' should be reflected if not in the particulate meanings of the communicative event, then at least in its waves and fields, and that this should somehow be detectable in the linguistic and/or somatic (paralinguistic) features of the on-going transaction, particularly in those relating to the textual and interpersonal metafunctions. And this is indeed the case. One aspect of the textual function, and therefore of wavelike meanings, is lexical cohesion, since words that are related to each other, through synonymy or antonymy, for example, form the 'peaks' of a wave running through the text. So consider the following four lexical chains:

Chain 1	*Chain 2*	*Chain 3*	*Chain 4*
room	lovely	dog	very fat
agent	clean	walks	old
room	nice and big	garden	very nice (+ UNCERTAIN)
table	pretty	grass	long
curtains	pretty		so untidy
room	amazing		poor
bathroom	very cheap		
meals			
breakfast			
dinner			
room			
rent			

Chain 1 is obviously a renting-a-room chain: 'agent', 'room' and 'rent' are collocates (that is, words which frequently appear together in the same 'text' and 'curtains' are meronyms of 'room' (that is, they are in a part–whole relationship to 'room'); 'bathroom' is a co-meronym of 'room' (they are both part of a house); 'meal' collocates with 'room' and 'rent'; and 'breakfast' and 'dinner' are hyponyms of 'meal' (that is, they are both members of the category 'meal'). Chain 2 is a positive-virtues chain, in praise of the room and the benefits that attach to renting it, and as such is part of the fieldlike meaning, which I discuss below. Chain 3 might be presumed to belong to Chain 1 — after all, rooms are in houses, and houses often have dogs and gardens – but for the fact that it is firmly linked with negative-features Chain 4. Now what is interesting here is that while 'dog' and 'garden' do not clash overmuch with Chain 1 (they are relevant to the matter at hand, though only peripherally), 'fat', 'old' and 'untidy' *appear* to be irrelevant to the service encounter in progress, and certainly clash with the positive field built up in the early part of the transaction. Not surprisingly, Chains 3 and 4 coincide with Mrs Lake's Orient, or pre-request, and, coming as an interruption to Chain 1 and, as I shall demonstrate, to Chain 3, represent a disjunction in the on-going communicative event. This is reinforced by what might be called the somatic chains:

SMILES	SAD
SMILES	SYMPATHETIC
PLEASED	UNCERTAIN
SURPRISED	SAD
HAPPY	

As with the lexical cohesion, a negative-feelings chain interrupts a positive-feelings chain.

This brings me back to the fieldlike meanings. As Chains 2 and 4, and the two somatic chains, show quite clearly, there are two, or possibly three, meaning fields in the encounter, signalled both grammatically and somatically: the field that builds up between Mrs Lake and Susan during the inspection of the room and bathroom; the field that Mrs Lake builds up when talking about Mitzi and her garden; and, possibly, the sympathy field that Mrs Lake awakes in Susan.

The conclusion to be drawn from all this is that the point at which meaning may become unclear and need to be negotiated is marked by a disjunction in the waves and fields of meaning. The wave formed by a lexical chain whose peaks are meronyms, co-meronyms or collocates of 'room' is interrupted by a small dog-and-garden chain of doubtful relevance, and the positive charge of the field built up between Mrs Lake and Susan is interrupted by a negative charge, reinforced by a switch in the somatic signals from warmth to melancholy.

What does this tell us about our attempt to represent the conventional or iterable and the slipperiness of meaning that follows from this? To answer the question, I need to consider the implications of the iterability of speech acts. Another term that Derrida uses for iterability is citationality, meaning of course that linguistic items (in this case, speech acts) can be *quoted*.Now in the transaction between Mrs Lake and Susan, the speech acts that are of greatest interest are the two statements/pre-requests that Mrs Lake makes about her dog and her garden, namely:

1. She's very fat. I'm old and we don't often go for walks.
2. Yes, but the grass is long and it's so untidy.

Suppose that, after her encounter with Mrs Lake, Susan is giving a report of the event to a friend of hers. It is quite possible that two fragments of the conversation might go like this:

3. *Susan.* And she has a dog. She seems worried about it.
   Friend. What do you mean?
   Susan. Well, she said that the dog was fat because she was too old to take it for walks much.

4. *Susan.* Then she showed me the garden. She didn't seem too happy about that, either.
   Friend. What's the problem there?
   Susan. Oh, she said that the grass was too long and it was untidy.

While there is a certain amount of interpretation here, as evidenced by 'seems worried', 'didn't seem too happy' and 'too long', it would be fair to say that this represents a more or less straight report of Mrs Lake's statements/pre-requests which does not take any position on whether Mrs Lake's utterances are only informational statements or also function as pre-requests. Of course, it would also be possible to take a stand on this issue:

5. *Friend*: The room's really cheap! It sounds like you've been very lucky.
   Susan: Yes, but there is a catch. After she told me the rent, she asked me in a roundabout way to walk her dog and do some work in the garden.

In this case Susan is firmly opting to interpret Mrs Lake's statements as pre-requests.

So far meaning has been preserved, if it is assumed that Mrs Lake was 'intending' that her statements should function as pre-requests, an assumption I shall return to presently. But it is very easy to imagine *quotations* that do not preserve the meaning that has been assigned to the statements. Imagine that the somewhat insensitive Bill Green of Dialogue 2 had gone to Mrs Lake's house seeking accommodation, and that the transaction had been the same, at least until Mrs Lake's comments on her garden. Bill's report to his friend could well have been rather different:

6. *Friend*: Why didn't you take the room? It's so cheap!
   Bill: Yes it is, but the landlady's a pain in the neck. She kept whingeing about her fat dog and her overgrown garden. So I decided the room was not for me.

7. *Friend*: Why didn't you take the room? It's so cheap!
   Bill: Yes, but I think the old woman's senile. She kept going on about her dog and her garden. I think she'd drive me crazy.

8. *Friend*: Why didn't you take the room? It's so cheap!
   Bill: Yes, and you know why? The wily old girl wants to turn me into an odd-job man — walking the dog, cleaning up the garden, and doing any other thing that takes her fancy. It's just exploitation.

This, of course, is only a sample and not exhaustive.

By what processes did Mrs Lake's statements produce the three assessments of her meaning contained in the responses of exchanges 6, 7 and 8? In exchange 6 Bill characterizes Mrs Lake as a 'pain in the neck' and accuses her of 'whingeing': here it seems that Bill has failed to jump from one wave to another, tc leave one field and enter the next, and has interpreted the disjunction as the unmotivated self-pity of an old woman. In exchange 7 Bill accuses Mrs L. of being 'senile' and of 'going on': again Bill has failed to make the leap from one wave or field to another, and sees the disjunction as the ramblings of senility. In exchange 8 he describes Mrs L. as 'wily' and accuses her of 'exploitation': in this case Bill has recognized (correctly, in the present interpretation) that the landlady's statements are still part of the service encounter and the discourse of 'business', and has therefore judged the disjunction as a clever strategy, without taking into account that the sadness may be genuine or, if it is indeed a strategy, 'unconscious'. (I ignore here the possibility that there may be other somatic signals reinforcing Bill's interpretation.)

Which brings me to another point. I have assumed that Mrs Lake's statements about her dog and garden were pre-requests and 'intended' as pre-requests, and concluded the transaction on that basis. But Mrs Lake may not *believe* them to be pre-requests, and so Dialogue 1 could well end like this:

9. *Susan*: I'd like to rent the room.
   Mrs Lake: Yes, of course, dear.
   Susan. And can I take Mitzi for walks and look after the garden?
   Mrs Lake: Oh no, my dear. I'm going to pay my neighbour's son to do those little jobs for me.
   Susan: Oh, are you sure I can't help?

If, however, Mrs Lake suddenly became aware that she might have been thinking of asking Susan to lend a hand, then she could well reply to Susan's question like this:

10. *Mrs Lake*: Well, if you ever have a spare moment, I'd appreciate any little help you could give.

I'll conclude this section by saying what must already be quite clear: that the key to understanding Derrida's assertions lies in the wavelike and fieldlike aspects of meaning. Bill's interpretation of Mrs Lake's statements in exchanges 6 and 7 is linked crucially with the fact that he is aware of the disjunction in the meaning waves and fields, and has interpreted it as unmotivated self-pity or senile rambling. The interpretation that motivates exchange 8 is quite the opposite: Bill imagines the disjunction to be not only motivated by business principles but wholly intentional, despite the uncertainty introduced by the SAD tone of voice and facial expression. To understand this and exchanges 9 and 10 fully, it is necessary to consider a passage from 'Limited Inc abc . . .' (Derrida 1977: 216):

> at the 'origin' of every speech act, there can only be Societies which are (more or less) anonymous with limited responsibility and liability – Sarl – a multitude of instances, if not of 'subjects', of meanings highly vulnerable to parasitism – all phenomena that the 'conscious ego' of the speaker and hearer . . . is incapable of incorporating as such and which . . . it does everything to exclude. Without ever fully succeeding, since incorporation, in 'psychoanalytical' terms, requires that the defending body of the subject make place 'inside' for that which it excludes. And yet how can the theory of speech acts in its current state account for this kind of incorporation, which nevertheless registers essential effects on all languages?

The two concepts here that can advance our understanding of exchanges 8, 9 and 10 are the assertions that at the origin of every speech act there can only be 'anonymous Societies', and that incorporation 'registers essential effects on all languages'. The implications of these assertions are wide-ranging, and a proper discussion of them is beyond the scope of this present work, but they do also have an immediate application to the three exchanges. If speech acts are 'Societies', each of whose 'shareholders' leaves an imprint on language and the body (I have taken Derrida's argument one step further, justifiably, I think), then it could be argued that in a video of a real-life, rather than imagined, encounter between a 'Mrs Lake' and a 'Bill' there might well be linguistic and somatic signs of the different 'shareholders' in the statements of a real 'Mrs Lake' that give grounds for Bill's interpretation in exchange 8 and for Susan's apparently more benign view, or that would equally permit Mrs Lake to deny in exchange 9 any desire to oblige Susan to do chores or odd jobs for her, then relent in exchange 10 and accept the 'offer'. And what would the nature of these linguistic or somatic signals be? They would, of course, be waves or fields of meaning.

I now pass to the second dialogue of the elementary–intermediate unit, which I reproduce below:

Bill: (KNOCKS ON DOOR).
Jack: (OPENS DOOR).
Bill: (A BIG SMILE). Hello. My name's Bill Green. I saw your ad in the newsagent's window.
Jack: (A SMALL SMILE, UNFRIENDLY). Oh yes, come in. (THEY GO INTO THE FLAT.) Do you play the guitar?
Bill: Yes, I'm in a band.
Jack: (UNHAPPY). Oh. (POINTING.) This is the bedroom.
Bill: (PLEASED). It's nice and big! Good for guitar practice.
Jack: But it's very noisy – it's on a main road. (POINTING.) And this is the sittingroom.
Bill: (PLEASED). Mmm. Very nice! Great for parties.
Jack: Oh no, it's too small. (POINTING.) And this is the kitchen.
Bill: (PLEASED). It's very modern.
Jack: Well, the cooker doesn't work very well.
Bill: (SATISFIED). Right! Can I move in immediately?
Jack: (UNHAPPY). Er . . . I don't know. I don't think this flat is suitable for you, really.

If the analysis carried out for the first dialogue has any validity, then a similar analysis should throw light on those areas of the second dialogue where negotiation of meaning is required. Consider, then, the following lexical chains:

Chain 1	*Chain 2*	*Chain 3*	*Chain 4*
ad	nice and big	very noisy	guitar
newsagent	very nice	too small	band
bedroom	Great (for parties	(doesn't work well)	
sittingroom			

kitchen	very modern	[not] suitable
cooker		
flat		

Note: 'doesn't work well' is in parentheses because it is only partly a lexical item.

And consider these somatic chains:

Chain 1	*Chain 2*
BIG SMILE	SMALL SMILE
PLEASED	UNFRIENDLY
PLEASED	UNHAPPY
SATISFIED	UNHAPPY

The obvious point to make about the lexical chains is that accompanying the wave of lexis relating to 'renting a room in a flat' there are two other waves, one, ridden by Bill, that creates a positive field, and another, ridden by Jack, that creates a negative field, with these two fields being reinforced by a positive and a negative somatic chain. The less obvious point is that the small chain 'guitar–band' may be interpreted as part of the Approach Direct element of a casual conversation, and therefore as a disjunction in the service encounter, rather than, as I have made it, the first step in an Orient (pre-refusal).

The problem in this transaction, then, is not so much that there is a disjunction (Chain 4 constitutes only a minor disturbance) but the Chain 3 is more a ripple than a wave, and a very weak field, even allowing for somatic chain 2. Are these sufficient grounds, however for Bill Green to *misquote* Jack? The following are possible reports that Bill might give to a friend of his transaction with Jack:

1. He was very honest – he told me how noisy the bedroom is, and said the cooker doesn't work very well.
2. He seemed impressed that I play in a band.
3. He seems very negative – didn't have a good word to say for anything.
4. He kept running everything down – maybe he doesn't really want to share with anyone.

All these are plausible *misquotations* of Jack's statements or single question, plausible because of the strung-out nature of Jack's 'inconveniences' wave and the weakness of the negative field.

I turn now to the first dialogue of the intermediate–advanced unit:

Mrs King: Did I tell you the rules, Alan?
Alan: No, Mrs King, you didn't.
Mrs King: Well, there are three. You mustn't have parties, you mustn't share your room with anyone, and you mustn't keep pets.
Alan: (UNENTHUSIASTIC). Right.
Mrs King: You don't sound very happy, dear.

Alan: Um . . . the problem is, it's my birthday next week and I've invited a few friends over.
Mrs King: (UNFRIENDLY). Oh yes.
Alan: (NERVOUS). Would you mind if I had a small birthday party next Friday?
Mrs King: (RELUCTANT). Well, just this once, Alan.

(*A few weeks pass.*)

Alan: (AT BREAKFAST). My brother's visiting me next week. I haven't seen him for two years.
Mrs King: (INDIFFERENT). That's nice, dear.
Alan: (NERVOUS). Is it all right if he stays in my room for two nights?
Mrs King: (VERY RELUCTANT). Well, I don't normally allow it . . . All right, just this once.

(*A few weeks pass.*)

Mrs King: (CHEERFUL). My sister's visiting me next week. I haven't seen her for ten years. I've promised her your room, so I'm afraid you'll have to leave, Alan.

The analysis of this transaction is somewhat more problematic than that of the preceding two, largely because there are no clear-cut lexical chains to carry the waves of meaning. All the fluidity of meaning lies in the fields of meaning, and even here problems arise. The transaction begins with a brief but very strong field made up of the model 'mustn't' repeated three times in one sentence – this field is so strong that it creates a kind of science fiction 'force field' which is very difficult to penetrate. There are three ways for Alan to react to this 'force field': he can either give up all hope of trying to penetrate it, blast his way in, or look for cracks in it. In linguistic terms two of these options are a way of bridging the gap between 'you mustn't' and 'you can', either through a 'can I?' strategy (the storming option), or through a 'possible alternatives' tactic (the looking-for-cracks option). The looking-for-cracks option was explored in the exercise in which Alan disarmed Mrs King by considering alternative venues for his birthday party; the storming tactic is the one Alan employs in the dialogue, and it is clear from the fields of meaning that accompany this tactic that it is (as the conversational analysts say) socially 'dispreferred':

Field 1	*Field 2*
UNENTHUSIASTIC/Right	UNFRIENDLY/Oh yes
Um . . . the problem is	RELUCTANT/Well, just this once
NERVOUS/Would you mind if?	INDIFFERENT/That's nice
NERVOUS/Is it all right if?	VERY RELUCTANT/ Well, I don't normally allow it . . . All right, just this once

Alan apparently realizes that his strategy is a dispreferred one, if we are to judge by his nervousness; and Mrs King is apparently not only aware that Alan is using a dispreferred strategy but also resents it, as is evidenced both by her tone of voice – variously unfriendly, reluctant or indifferent – and by linguistic signals such as the minimal acknowledgement represented by 'Oh yes,' the repetition of the continuative 'Well,' and of the modalized adverbial phrase 'just this once', and the use of the clause 'I don't normally allow it,' which is a personalized equivalent of the impersonal 'normally you couldn't' (personalized in the sense that the agent behind the prohibition, in this case 'I,' is clearly revealed).

Thus linguistic and somatic signals reveal the presence of a field of resentment in Mrs King – resentment against the dispreferred option chosen by Alan. But since the force of the field only builds up over a number of weeks – indeed, if Alan had not asked Mrs King whether his brother could stay in his room the field might well have dissipated – it could well escape Alan's notice, so that the following *misquotations* of Mrs King's statements by Alan, in conversation with a friend, might not surprise us:

1. *Friend*: Where's the party going to be?
   Alan: Oh, at my place.
   Friend: Really? I thought you said your landlady doesn't allow parties.
   Alan: Well, that's what she says, but I asked her if I could have it there, and she didn't seem bothered.

2. *Friend*: So your brother's going to stay with you?
   Alan: Yes . . . It'll be really nice.
   Friend: Doesn't your ladylady object?
   Alan: No, she thinks it's nice for me.

3. *Friend*: I hear you're looking for accommodation again. What happened?
   Alan: Well, it's odd really. I thought the landlady was nice and easy-going, but she suddenly turned round and chucked me out because her sister's coming to visit her.

Which proves that, in statements where particulate meaning does not mesh well with one or more field of meaning, there is a risk that the particulate meaning will be the meaning that is most readily perceived.

Now for a consideration of the second dialogue in the unit at intermediate–advanced level:

Alan: Well, since I can't cook, do you think you could cook for both of us?
Anna: Yes, but in that case I think *you* should do all the housework.
Alan: Okay, that's fair.
Anna: And we should each do our own washing and ironing.
Alan: Oh yes, of course.

(*A few days pass.*)

Anna: (IRRITATED). The kitchen's looking pretty filthy, Alan.
Alan: (READING A BOOK). Er . . . yes . . . I'll do it tomorrow. *(Later.)* (CALLING OUT) I don't understand how your iron works, Anna.
Anna: (SAYS NOTHING).
Alan: (CALLING OUT). Anna? . . . Damn!

(*Next morning.*)

Alan: Oh hell! We're going out to the theatre this evening and I haven't got a clean shirt, Anna. And I've got to go now or I'll be late.
Anna: (SAYS NOTHING).

(*In the evening.*)

Alan: Hello, Anna. How are you?
Anna: (COOL). Fine. I had a good day at work.
Alan: Great! What's for dinner? I'm starving!
Anna: (COOL). Nothing.

The analysis of this dialogue also raises some problems, as the following will make clear:

Field 1		*Chain 1*		*Field 2*
should	----►	housework		
		'kitchen . . . filthy'	---►	IRRITATED/'pretty filthy'
should	----►	ironing		
		"(don't understand how) iron works"	---►	SAYS NOTHING
	----►	washing		
		"[no] clean shirt"	----►	SAYS NOTHING
		cooking		
		"dinner"		
		"starving"		
		'[no dinner]'	◄-------	COOL/'Nothing'

Note: single quotation marks ('x') indicate Anna's words, while double quotation marks ("x") indicate Alan's words.

As in the previous dialogue, a king of linguistic force field is established at the beginning with the repeated 'should', indicating a moral obligation on Anna and, more particularly, Alan to carry out their allotted duties. These duties form a lexical chain: the first item in the chain is 'housework' (the arrow from 'should' signals that it is a duty), which is Alan's task; this collocates with 'kitchen . . . filthy', for keeping the kitchen clean is an obvious aspect of housework, and failure to do so is a dereliction of Alan's duty which leads to the largely somatic Field 2, passing through Anna, that starts with IRRITATED. The third item in the lexical chain is 'ironing' (Alan is responsible for his own ironing), which collocates with the not strictly lexical '(don't understand how) iron works', since knowing how to operate an iron is an essential part of knowing the ironing schema; this lack of knowledge on Alan's part, combined with the previous IRRITATED , leads to the second item in Field 2, SAYS NOTHING. The next item in the lexical chain is 'washing', a duty with the same status as 'ironing'– '[no] clean shirt' collocates with 'washing' in much the same way as 'kitchen . . . filthy' collocated with 'housework', and not surprisingly provokes the third item in Field 2, a repetition of SAY NOTHING. The last three items in the lexical chain relate to 'cooking', the major task allotted to Anna: 'starving' and 'dinner' both collocate unproblematically with 'cooking', while '[no dinner]' (an explication of Anna's laconic 'Nothing') is a logical consequence of the final item in Field 2, namely COOL, which is itself a logical consequence of the previous somatic items.

The analysis of this dialogue differs from previous analyses in that there is a strong causal link between the two fields and the chain, and the main field is largely somatic, with 'pretty filthy' being the closest that Anna comes to a grammatical realization of her feelings. Are Anna's statements, however, still open to *misquotation*? Consider the following possible statements that Alan might make later in conversation with a friend:

> She complained about the kitchen and I told her I'd clean it, but she still seemed annoyed with me. Then I asked her how her iron worked and she ignored me. Next morning I asked her nicely to wash a shirt for me, because I was running late, and she ignored me again. But the worst thing is , when I got home in the evening there was no dinner – and it's her job to do the cooking.

Such a report of Alan's dispute with Anna suggests that somatic signals can be interpreted correctly but still cause puzzlement, and that causal links between chains and fields can be overlooked.

8.2 THE COMMUNICATIVE SYLLABUS: PRODUCT AND/OR PROCESS?

8.2.0 Introduction

The four dialogues of a topical-interactional course, then, can be properly analysed only by a linguistic model that deals in waves and fields, and in the *dehiscence* which means that all utterances can be 'quoted' in a myraid of ways. They can, in short, be analysed only by a process model of language. From this it may seem to follow that a topical-interactional course embodies a mainly process approach to language teaching, but, as the discussion in Chapter 8 shows, this is not necessarily the case. In the remainder of Chapter 8, I consider to what extent a topical-interactional course *is* and *should be* process-based; and, with these two questions resolved and a balance struck, the implications that such a balance could have for exploiting the course in the classroom.

8.2.1 Is a topical-interactional course process-based (and should it be)?

It was noted earlier, in Chapter 6, that Brumfit (1984a) pleads for process as content, citing three processes: the process of using a language, the processes of classroom methodology, and the process of language acquisition. At the same time it was remarked that the process of using a language could be linked to Martin's use of process, and that the interaction sequence was thus best seen not as a unit but as a process. Since these remarks were made, it has become clear that the interaction sequence is only part of a larger process that I have called negotiation of meaning, but this merely reinforces the obvious point: that the *interactional* side of the dialogues I have presented is an attempt to transform the process of using a language into (at least part of) the content of a course.

How is this done? In the first dialogue at elementary-intermediate level – the dialogue between Mrs Lake and Susan – the content of the interactional exercises is the interpretation, at the point where Mrs Lake shows Susan her dog and garden, of the discourse formation, subject matter, social relationship, pragmatic purpose and interaction sequence element that are in play at the time, and how this interpretation affects the on-going communicative event. In the dialogue between Jack and the insensitive Bill Green, the content is understanding Bill Green's reaction to Jack's negative comments about the flat, in terms of differing views of the social action semiotic, subject matter, interaction sequence moves and attitude choices motivating Jack's comments. In the first dialogue at intermediate–advanced level, between Mrs King and Alan, the content is Alan's inability to see that the dialogue is articulating the discourse formation 'business', the social action semiotic 'tenant–landlady', the social relationship 'buyer–seller', the purpose [dominance], and a number of negative attitude options. Finally, in the dialogue between Alan and Anna, the content is the differing perspectives that Anna and Alan have of the dialogue: Anna sees the dialogue in the context of the discourse formation 'business', while Alan does not: they interpret differently the system of the social action semiotic in play; they are not performing the same social relationship; and their purposes are at odds.

In other words, the content of the course, or at least of the meaning negotiation component of the course, is the possibility of participants in on-going transactions 'reading' key parameters in different ways, and possible strategies for reconciling different 'readings'. But that, of course, is not the only content, for each dialogue has its topical exercises, which, in focusing on particular grammatical structures deemed of particular importance in the dialogue, appear to introduce the familiar 'product-content' into the course. In this respect, then, does it differ from any conventional structural or functional course with a topical overlay?

To answer this question requires a consideration of the thematic systems which allegedly underpin topical-interactional dialogues. Thematic systems, it will be recalled, are networks of sociosemantic relations into which events, abstract entities, people, places and things enter, as processes, participants or circumstances, as social roles or discourse roles, and, finally, as players in the logical structure of the discourse. They thus represent a storehouse of sociosemantic knowledge that learners of English need to plug into. There are probably a number of ways of helping learners to plug in, and among these is careful attention to certain aspects of grammatical structures and communicative functions.

To demonstrate this, I return to the dialogues. In Dialogue 1 the grammatical structure that is the focus of the first part of the unit at elementary–intermediate level is the Simple Present, but in the context of the thematic system pattern in which the landlord/landlady is the provider of services. In the second dialogue, the two structures – *be* + Adjective and Simple Present – are practised within the context of two thematic system patterns, one in which a room or its facilities are attributed with some particular quality, and the other a pattern in which a facility is Actor and a malfunction is material process. In the first dialogue at intermediate–advanced level the focus is on the function Asking Permission, in the framework of the thematic system pattern in which the landlord/landlady is Senser in a modalized mental: affect process in the interrogative mood, and the activity for which permission is sought (another pattern from the Renting Accommodation thematic system) is projected by (that is, dependent on) the mental process clause. In the second dialogue the spotlight is on the function Requesting, this time in the context of two thematic system patterns: both start with one flatmate as Senser in a mental:cognition process, though in the first the mood is interrogative and in the second it is declarative; both continue with the activity requested encoded in a projected (dependent) clause, in both cases a modalized material process clause with the other flatmate as Actor, though in the first pattern the modality is [inclination:low], and in the second [obligation:median].

The conclusion that can be drawn from this is that grammatical structures and communicative functions, if contextualized, can become part of the process of using language, since contextualized grammer can build up social meaning (e.g. landlords or landladies are people who regularly do or do not provide a range of services), and contextualized functions can make transparent some of the conventional strategies that speakers of middle-class British English use to get things done (e.g. the desired activity is put in a dependent clause projected by a mental process often in the interrogative mood, the whole heavily modalized).

But these contextualized grammatical structures and communicative functions are not only part of the process of using language, they are also part of the process of meaning negotiation. In Dialogue 2 of the elementary–intermediate unit Jack uses the manifestations of a thematic system pattern (e.g. 'it's very noisy', 'the cooker doesn't work well') as a pre-refusal strategy. In Dialogue 1 of the intermediate–advanced unit Mrs King's two instances of Grant Permission (arguably part of the thematic system, though not recorded as such) can be seen as preludes to her breaking of the contract. To return to the language of Derrida, these are perfect examples of dehiscence exploding the meaning of iterable signs.

The two linked questions asked in the title of this section can now be answered. A topical-interactional course does focus on product, in the sense that it takes as one of its goals the ability to manipulate spectific grammatical structures and communicative functions. But it sees this product as part of the process of using language, in that the product is always contextualized as part of a cultural storehouse, and potentially part of the process of meaning negotiation. As to whether a topical-interactional course, or indeed any course, should focus on product, I think the answer to that questions has already been given: grammatical structures and communicative functions are a legitimate — indeed, necessary — part of any language course, provided they are inserted in a clear context and perform a clear sociosemantic function, for in this way they help the learner to build up his/her storehouse of cultural knowledge.

8.2.2 Exploiting a topical-Interactional course

How could a topical-interactional course be used? Of course, no such course exists, except in the fragments I have presented, but it is not difficult to imagine how such a course would look, with a number of units covering a wide variety of everyday situations, out of which different grammatical structures, communicative functions and meaning negotiation sequences would naturally arise. (The fact that everyday situations play such a large part in this course suggests that it might better suit learners of ESL, or learners of English studying in an English-speaking country). But the four dialogues and accompanying exercises that do exist give a sufficiently clear indication of how the course could be used.

No guidelines for the use of the topical (i.e. grammatical or functional) exercises are required, since such exercises, in one form or another, are the meat and drink of EFL teachers. In fact, the topical exercises could well be omitted, though, for the reasons mentioned above, such an omission could well be counterproductive. If the topical exercises do indeed plug into a storehouse of cultural knowledge, they have a valuable function over and above their normal function; though whether and how the teacher could exploit this 'cultural storehouse' function is unclear to me.

On the other hand, guidelines for the use of the interactional exercises seem called for. Of course, they are a type of role play or problem-solving exercise such as every teacher is familiar with, but they do have certain specificities. One of these is that a meaning negotiation situation is one in which two participants (or possibly more) are trying to work out what the other participant is 'getting at', implying that in any meaning negotiation role play there should be some uncertainty in the minds of the learners taking part in the role play. Now all four dialogues presented were unfinished, and each could be completed in one of two ways, a 'positive' way or a 'negative' way. Thus the only way to keep some element of uncertainty is to divide a class into two sets of groups and send one set of groups out of the classroom, Some groups would be cued to perform the 'positive' ending, and some the 'negative' ending, and the culmination of the exercise would be when an in-class student role-played with an out-of-class student, neither knowing which ending to expect.

It might be objected that this seems too much like 'rehearsing' language, since most of the dialogue is given, and the learners are guided carefully to one of two endings. The second objection is easily answered: the guidance can be easily withdrawn, or at least reduced. But the first objection is more difficult to counter, and does in fact require a different kind of exercise, what I have called, rather unhappily, a psycho-schema or idio-schema. Consider this narrative and the group work that follows it:

Unresolved idio-schema: Renting a room

Shinichi had seen the advertisement for the room in the Accommodation Office – or was it in the newspaper? Or on a notice board? Or even in an estate agent's window? He'd seen so many advertisement lately – and had phoned the person mentioned in the ad (Mr Jones? Mr James?), who sounded rather odd on the phone. 'Perhaps he couldn't understand you,' said Buddhi, who'd been in the country for years. 'Or maybe he just doesn't like foreigners.' Shinichi didn't find this very encouraging. 'Well, I don't like *them* very much,' he said aggressively. The phone coversation had been short: Shinichi had just mentioned the ad (where *had* he seen it?) and asked if he could see the room; the man had hesitated and said, 'Yeah, OK,' and arranged a time, but he didn't seem very enthusiastic. Now here was Shinichi walking up to the front door of a suburban house. He knocked nervously – he wasn't sure if the man had said ten o'clock or two o'clock. He wished he knew if it was Jones or James. The door was opened by an elderly man who seemed rather annoyed. He greeted Shinichi, and seemed even more annoyed when Shinichi returned the greeting, but invited him to enter and look at the room. By now Shinichi was even more nervous and a little angry, but he followed the man. The man spoke slowly and clearly to Shinichi as if he was a child; he told him what the rent was, and said he could use the kitchen as long as he cleaned up after his 'Chinese cooking'.

Group work

In groups, discuss possible answers to the following questions (there are no 'right' answers):

1. Why did Mr Jones/James sound 'odd' on the telephone?
2. Why didn't the man sound 'enthusiastic' on the telephone?
3. Why did the man seen 'annoyed' when he opened the door?
4. Why did he seem 'even more annoyed' when Shinichi greeted him?
5. Why was Shinichi 'angry'?
6. Why did the man speak 'slowly and clearly' to Shinichi?

How do you think the meeting between Shinichi and Mr Jones/James might have ended?

This 'idio-schema' was conceived when I was teaching English in Australia to students mainly from Japan, Indonesia and Thailand. Australians, traditionally insulated from the Asian region by the White Australia policy, happily abandoned some twenty years ago, do still exhibit a degree of antipathy towards immigrants or students from Japan or South East Asia, a fact which was borne home to me one day by an Indonesian student's reporting to me an incident of what he saw as racist behaviour towards him. Mindful of the importance of incorporating the learner's feelings into the learning process, I determined to combine my interest in schemas (those iterable offspring of thematic systems and the social action semiotic) with the student's perceptions of real or imagined prejudice (a fertilizer guaranteed to promote dehiscence) – and the result was the idio-schema. The schema is the familiar renting-a-room schema, and the need to negotiate meaning arises because Shinichi and Mr Jones/James, either through Shinichi's carelessness or unclear English, or through Mr Jones's deafness or attitude towards 'foreigners', seem to be getting on very badly. All these possible obstacles to clear meaning are discussed in the group work, and then, in groups as segregated from each other as conditions permit, a resolution of the situation is sought: when representatives from the groups come together, they have to role-play the situation on the basis of the unresolved narrative, without knowing how the other participant sees the resolution of the situation. This is not authentic communication, but, as far as simulating the world outside the classroom goes, it may be the closest we can get to authentic communication.

8.3 CONCLUSION

I have discussed in this chapter the implications that the meaning negotiation component of the topical-interactional dialogues has for a process model of linguistics; how a topical-interactional course fits into the product/process dichotomy outlined in Chapter 1; and procedures for exploiting the interactional exercises that follow the dialogues, together with a suggestion for going beyond the dialogue/interactional exercise format. What I have not done so far is compare my model of discourse with other pedagogical models of discourse, examine my approach to process in language teaching in the light of other approaches to process in language teaching. I propose to remedy this omission in the next and final chapter by exploring the model(s) of discourse advocated by the applied linguist Guy Cook (1989) and the task-based syllabus presented by another applied linguist, David Nunan (1989), thereby placing the present work in the context of other on-going investigations into language and language teaching.

9. Discourse and syllabus: contemporary approaches to process in language teaching

9.0 INTRODUCTION

At the end of Chapter 8, I noted that I had not yet compared my model of discourse with other pedagogical models of discourse, or examined my approach to process in language teaching in the light of other approaches to process in language teaching. As proposed, I will now remedy this omission by exploring the model(s) of discourse advocated by the applied linguist Guy Cook (1989) and the task-based syllabus presented by another applied linguist, David Nunan (1989), and so situate the present work in the context of other on-going investigations into language and language teaching which see language as a process, and focus on process in language pedagogy.

9.1 AN ALTERNATIVE APPROACH TO THE TEACHING OF DISCOURSE

9.1.1 The model

In his book entitled *Discourse* the applied linguist Guy Cook presents (1989: 80) a model of discourse which bears striking similarities to mine, as Figure 9.1 shows.

Social relationship, says Cook (1989: 89), can be seen in terms of three factors: office, status and role. Office is a 'relatively permanent position within the social structure to which someone is appointed or qualified'; status is a general

Social relationships Shared knowledge Discourse type Discourse structure Discourse function Conversational mechanisms Cohesion (Grammer and lexis) (sounds and letters)

Figure 9.1 Guy Cook's model of discourse
Source: After Cook 1989: 80.

term for 'social importance influenced by facts like age, wealth, education'; and role is a 'temporary interactional stance, involving the performance of certain types of perlocutionary and illocutionary acts'. Shared knowledge, according to Cook (1989: 90), involves 'hypotheses about the degree of knowledge we share with [people we are communicating with] and the degree to which the schemata they are operating correspond to our own'; this assessment, he adds, 'affects every level of discourse, from the quantity and ordering of information, to cohesion, the use of the article, and grammatical structure'. Discourse type, in Cook's words (1989: 95), is not an 'academic abstraction' but 'something we all use every day in order to orient ourselves towards the communication in which we are involved'; discourse types range from recipes and jokes to reports and essays. Discourse structure, as Cook makes clear (1989: 103–5), is the equivalent of generic structure or interaction sequence, while discourse function, as he shows (1989: 109), is the string of rhetorical functions that make up a 'move' in discourse structure. Conversational mechanisms, says Cook (1989: 117), include the 'gaining, holding, and yielding of turns, the negotiation of meaning and direction, the shifting of topic, the signalling and identification of turn type, the use of voice quality, face, and body'. Cohesion (see Cook 1989: 127) includes reference, substitution, ellipsis, conjunction and lexical cohesion, as discussed in Chapter 3 of the present work.

9.1.2 The model applied

Some of the components of Cook's model are very close to certain of the components of the model used in the present work, so would be natural to assmue that he would apply his model in much the same way that I have applied mine, that is, to processes in spoken discourse like negotiation of meaning. But such is not the case. To begin with, the procedure in Cook's explication of his model differs from mine in that he presents specific tasks for each component of the model before he goes on to tasks that involve the model as a whole. But, more important perhaps, the kinds of tasks that he presents focus not only on spoken but also on written language. The implications of these two points will become clearer if I give an overview of the range of tasks that follow from Cook's model.

The first component of the model is social relationship, with its constituents office, status and role; only one task is presented here – for teachers rather than learners – and that involves examing a dialogue from a language teaching textbook to determine whether it has 'successfully captured some of the effects of the social relationship' (1989: 90). For the second component, shared knowledge, two tasks are worth mentioning: the first (1989: 92) takes a short biographical sketch of Ernest Hemingway and expands it with information that learners are likely to share with the teacher, then asks leaners to cut out the unnecessary shared knowledge; the second task (1989: 93–4) takes the same short biographical sketch and changes many of the articles (from *a* to *the* or vice versa), then asks learners to make any necessary corrections.

The third component is discourse type, of which Cook says (1989: 97):

> perception of discourse type is a factor in discourse processing and production which brings together our perceptions of sender/receiver, topic, function . . . What is important from a pedagogic point of view is that we should, as early as possible, alert students to different discourse types, so that they may classify the interaction they are involved in, and make as productive a use of that classification as we do ourselves.

Thus Cook recognizes the crucial importance of discourse type, just as the present model attaches great importance to interaction sequence; unfortunately, although he does present several tasks designed to make teachers aware of discourse types and their relation to functions and topics, he is not very explicit about how we should 'alert students to different discourse types'. The fourth component is discourse structure (which is the 'skeleton' of discourse type), and here Cook refers (1989: 104) to tasks such as recognizing and understanding the various parts of a textbook (e.g. *list of contents*, *preface*, *appendices*), or associating discourse parts like *headline*, *salutation* or *list of ingredients* with their discourse types. The fifth component (the 'skeleton' of discourse structure) is discourse function: this is more familiar ground, and Cook presents a number of tasks, representative of which is a recombination exercise (1989: 110–11), which takes a short paragraph on the biology of birds and splits it up into eighteen sentences, then asks learners to combine the sentences into a paragraph, following the principle that such recombining work will help learners to understand better the function of the sentences in the paragraph.

The sixth component of Cook's model is conversational mechanisms, and for this particular area Cook makes a number of suggestions (1989: 117–22): teaching phrases, words or noises associated with particular turn types; asking learners to compare invented conversations from language teaching books with authentic conversations; and using flow diagrams of conversations that give the topic or function of each utterance but not the realization. The last component of his model is cohesion: the main task Cook proposes here (1989: 129–31) is to take a passage and replace reference or ellipsis with the full form.

Thus far all the tasks discussed refer to only one component of the model, so before I make further comment I will present a task which, says Cook (1989: 134), 'can develop discourse skills without concentration on any one aspect in isolation'. In this activity, borrowed from Melville *et al.*'s *Towards the Creative Teaching of English* (see Cook 1989: 135), each student is given a piece of paper on which is written one sentence of the following story:

> There were four people sitting in a train in Vietnam in the late sixties.
> The four people were as follows: a young Vietnamese who loved his country, an old Vietnamese grandmother, a beautiful young girl of about eighteen, and an ugly American soldier.
> Suddenly the train went into a tunnel.
> There was the sound of a kiss.
> All four people heard a slap.
> When the train came out of the tunnel, the Vietnamese could see that the G.I.'s face was red.

The beautiful young girl glanced at the granny and the soldier in astonishment.
The granny was asleep in the corner of the compartment.
The young patriot grinned happily.
The problem is: who kissed who and who slapped who?

Learners must work in groups to decide on the original order, then solve the problem. According to Cook (1989: 136), this activity involves a number of discourse and language skills, including:

1. Negotiation of relationships and roles within the group.
2. Turn-taking without control by the teacher.
3. Application of schemata: about trains, tunnels, the Vietnam war.
4. Knowledge of narrative structure.
5. Article use, indicating previous mention or assumed default in schema.
6. Following lexical chains.
7. Assessing hypotheses.
8. Presentation of a group decision to an outsider (the teacher).

9.1.3 Comments on the model

Although Cook's model seemed to have much in common with mine, it has become clear that there are important differences. Firstly, Cook focusses on written English as well as on spoken English – in fact, apart from the section on conversational mechanisms, Cook probably pays greater attention to the written than to the spoken. Secondly, his application of the model is more fragmented and less developed. Thus he offers a good analysis of social relationship, but does not really suggest how it can be exploited; he has some good ideas for making learners aware of shared knowledge, but only in written English; he is not clear on how to approach discourse type in the classroom, though he has some reasonable suggestions for discourse structure and discourse function; in his exploration of conversational mechanisms he outlines several very useful activities, including some that involve negotiation of meaning, but passes up a golden opportunity to link conversational interaction with the other components of his model. And thirdly, when he applies the model as a whole (in the problem-solving activity involving the four people on the train), he appears to switch emphasis, from the process of using the language implied in his previous analyses of discourse to the process of classroom methodology implied in the skill of 'negotiation of relationships and roles within the group'.

This last may seem like a minor point, but is in fact more significant than it appears. The reason is summed up by one of the discourse skills involved, namely 'application of schemata: about trains, tunnels, the Vietnam war': students are mobilizing knowledge *about* schemata, but not knowledge *of* schemata, as I attempt to do in my interactional exercises. Tasks that ask learners to call on their knowledge about schemata are, of course, perfectly valid exercises, but they are no substitute for actually *living* schemata in some sort of role play, no matter how artificial it may be – an objection to a syllabus based on classroom processes, perhaps.

To sum up, while Cook has many valuable insights to offer into the teaching of discourse, his model and the way he applies the model differ in many respects from the process model of discourse and the topical-interactional approach to language teaching and learning that I have outlined, and say little about the meaning negotiation that is central to my enterprise. But if Cook shows less interest in process than might be expected, then Nunan should be keenly aware of process in his discussion of the task-based syllabus, so it is to Nunan that I now turn.

9.2 THE TASK-BASED SYLLABUS AND PROCESS IN LANGUAGE TEACHING

9.2.0 Introduction

Interest in a process approach to syllabus design has been growing in recent years, but much uncertainty remains as to what such a syllabus would be like. One attempt to clear up this uncertainty is the task-based syllabus, of which a leading advocate is the Australian applied linguist David Nunan. I now consider his approach to a task-based syllabus (Nunan 1989) – I will not attempt to summarize the book, which is an extremely detailed account of all the complex factors that bear on the design of a task-based syllabus, but will discuss only those features which seem relevant to my topical-interactional syllabus.

9.2.1 The task-based syllabus

9.2.1.1 Describing a task

What is a task? In his book on designing tasks for the communicative classroom, Nunan (1989: 10) writes:

> In general I will consider the communicative task as a *piece of classroom work which involves learners in comprehending, manipulating, producing or interacting in the target language while their attention is principally focused on meaning rather than form.* The task should also have a sense of completeness, being able to stand alone as a communicative act in its own right.

All tasks, he continues, have some form of input data, either verbal or non-verbal, an activity derived from the input, and a goal and roles for teachers and learners. Thus the final activity in the interactional exercises for each of the four dialogues discussed in Chapter 7 could be characterized as follows:

Goal Understanding how meaning is negotiated.
Input Unfinished dialogue.
Activity

(i) Deciding why one participant in the dialogue does or could misunderstand another participant.
(ii) Deciding ways in which the dialogue could end.
(iii) Role-playing the dialogue.

Teacher role Monitor and facilitator.
Learner role Member of problem-solving group; partner in role play.

9.2.1.2 Origin of the task

The task as a tool in language learning emerged from the same movement – discussed in Chapter 1 – that criticized the functional-notional syllabus and advocated a process approach to language learning. For this movement, says Nunan (1989: 12), language was 'an integrated process rather than a set of discrete learning outcomes', which created considerable difficulties for syllabus designers, since 'processes belong to the domain of methodology' and are therefore somebody else's business. This would seem to imply that specifying tasks is the responsibility not of syllabus designers but of methodologists, and that tasks oriented towards 'discrete learning outcomes' (the learning of structure or functions, for example) are, almost by definition, valueless. Nunan, however, does not adopt so extreme a position, for, he says (1989: 14):

> I take the view that any comprehensive curriculum needs to take account of both means and ends must address both content and process. In the final analysis it does not really matter whether those responsible for specifying learning tasks are called 'syllabus designers' or 'methodologists'. What matters is that both processes and outcomes are taken care of.

9.2.1.3 Tasks and the speaking skill

Before he considers in greater detail the components of a language learning task, Nunan summarizes recent research into the four macro-skills, and it is naturally of interest to us to see what he has to say about speaking. Some of what he says (1989: 26–7) is of limited interest to us: for example, that spoken language consists of short, often fragmentary utterances, with a great deal of repetition, overlap between speakers, fillers like 'well' and 'oh', and non-specific references like 'that thing'. But one researcher he refers to (1989: 30) is more relevant to the present work: Bygate distinguishes between motor-perceptive skills, which are concerned with the sounds and structures of the language, and interactional skills, which include skills in the management of interaction (e.g. when and how to take the floor, when to introduce a topic or change the subject, how to keep a conversation going, when and how to terminate a conversation), and skills in the negotiation of meaning (making sure the person you are speaking to has correctly understood you and that you have correctly understood them).

9.2.1.4 Real-world and pedagogic tasks

It might be inferred from this research that tasks which focus on the speaking skill should reflect the 'real world' (as I suggested in 9.13 above), but in fact this is a matter of some debate, as Nunan (1989: 41) indicates. Obviously there are language courses in which all tasks are specified in real-world terms, in which learners undertake classroom activities which require them to practice real-world activities. (Nunan refers to this as the 'rehearsal' approach.) But there are those who advocate tasks whose rationale is largely pedagogic (the 'psycholinguistic' approach): their argument is that while learners may never be called on to perform these particular tasks in the real world, accomplishment of the tasks will 'provide them with skills for those real-world tasks which are difficult to predict in advance, or which are not feasible to practice in class'. Nunan's position (1989: 44) is that the distinction between real-world and pedagogic tasks is 'more apparent than real', in that pedagogic tasks often have a real-world application – a point that I will return to presently.

9.2.1.5 Components of a task

The first component of a task that Nunan discusses in detail is the goal of a task. Tasks, he says (1989: 49), may have one or more of the following goals: they may be communicative (oriented to establishing and maintaining interpersonal relations); they may be socio-cultural (oriented to promoting understanding of the everyday life patterns of the target language speech community); they may involve 'learning-how-to-learn'; or they may promote awareness of language and culture.

The second component of a task is input, and Nunan suggests a wide variety of sources (1989: 53–4), too many in fact to enumerate. All these sources involve authentic material, which Nunan seems to favour – the reasons he advances for preferring authentic dialogues are of particular interest to us. Basically the argument here (1989: 54–5) is that invented dialogues (as recorded on cassette) differ markedly from authentic conversation in that most speakers in these dialogues have an RP accent; words are enunciated with excessive precision; particular structures or functions appear with abnormal frequency; sentences are short and well formed; one speaker waits until the other has finished; and attention signals like 'uh-uh' and 'mm' are generally missing. I'll return to this apparent criticism of invented dialogues presently.

The third component of a task is the activities specified for the learners. Nunan believes (1989: 59) that there are three general ways of characterizing activities: 'rehearsal for the real world; skills use; and fluency/accuracy'. He also refers (1989: 66) to the three activity types used in the Bangalore project: information-gap activity (familiar to all EFL teachers), reasoning-gap activity (deriving new information from given information through processes of inference, deduction, practical reasoning or perception of relationships or patterns), and opinion-gap activity (identifying and articulating a personal preference, feeling or attitude in response to a given situation). Rather different from these are the seven broad communicative activity types proposed by Clark and listed by Nunan (1989: 67). These include: solving problems through social interaction with others; establishing and maintaining relationships; searching for specific information for some given purpose; and listening to or reading information, processing it and using it in some way.

The fourth component of a task is the learner role, which obviously varies according to teaching approach. Thus in traditional approaches to teaching English the learner, according to Nunan (1989: 80), was a passive recipient of outside stimuli; in the communicative approach, however, the learner is an interactor and negotiator who is capable of giving as well as taking. Parallel to this is the fifth component, teacher role, which, as Nunan points out (1989: 84), is related to the following issues: (1) the types of function teachers are expected to fulfil (e.g. 'practice director, counsellor or model'); (2) the degree of control the teacher has over how learning takes place; (3) the degree to which the teacher is responsible for content; (4) the interactional patterns that develop between teachers and learners.

9.2.1.6 Grading tasks

Nunan looks at a number of ways of grading tasks, but I will refer to only two schemes. The first (1989: 110) is adapted from Bruner and grades tasks according to the cognitive demands they make in the following areas: (1) attending and recognizing (the nature of the input/experience); (2) making sense (of the input); (3) going beyond the input given (e.g. hypothesizing, inferring and making judgements about a text); (4) transferring and generalizing (e.g. skills gained in studying a particular text).

The second way of grading tasks (1989: 111) was developed by Candlin (see his paper 'Towards task-based learning', in Candlin and Murphy 1987) and takes into consideration five factors: (1) cognitive load, which should on no account be confused with (2) communicative stress – in all probability, if one is high the other will be low; (3) particularity and generalizability – tasks which follow some generalized pattern are easier than those which do not; (4) code complexity and interpretive density – if the language is difficult, the questions should be easy, and vice versa; (5) process continuity – learners should be 'encouraged to create their own continuity and sequencing'.

9.2.1.7 Sequencing tasks

In this section Nunan examines various ways of sequencing tasks. One way of doing this is what he calls (1989: 118) the 'psycholinguistic processing approach', which starts with processing (this may require no overt response from the learner, or some sort of physical or verbal response), goes on to productive activities (e.g. repeat utterance, complete drill, answer question), and finishes with interactive activities (e.g. simulation, discussion, problem-solving).

It is also possible to use 'experiential content' (1989: 125) as the basic building blocks in lesson design – this is common in English for Specific Purposes textbooks, or in foreign language 'immersion' programmes in which school students learn maths, science, history, etc., through the target language. A third way of sequence tasks is to use problem situations: as examples of this Nunan cites (1989: 128–9) Scarcella's 'sociodrama', in which learners are presented with a dilemma, then act out various possible resolutions to the conflict entailed by the dilemma; and Di Pietro's 'strategic interaction', in which students, having memorized situations and roles that they are expected to play, act out scenarios – at certain points during the acting out, additional information is 'injected into the scenario, requiring learners to modify their intended role, and to alter the direction of the interaction'.

9.2.2 Tasks and the topical-interactional syllabus

Has a topical-interactional course as sketched in Chapter 7 anything in common with the task-based syllabus? The first feature of a task is that it focuses learner's attention on meaning rather than form, and this certainly applies to the interactional activities, though less so to the topical exercises, which are directed as much to form as to meaning. The second feature of a task is that the emphasis is on process (methodology) rather than product (discrete learning outcomes); however, like Nunan, I believe that a syllabus needs to take account of both 'means and ends', content and process, as the dual orientation of the topical-interactional course makes clear. The third feature of tasks is that they may have either a real-world or a pedagogic rationale – as far as the topical-interactional course is concerned, although the dialogues plainly have a real-world basis, most of the activities (e.g. those tasks which require the learner to explain why a particular misunderstanding may have occurred) have a pedagogic rationale (but do have a real-world application).

Tasks also have a number of components, which I will examine in relation to the topical-interactional course. First there are goals, and I would have to say that the topical-interactional course has three of the goals that Nunan mentions: it has a communicative goal, it has a socio-cultural goal, and it aims to promote awareness of language and culture. The second component is input – Nunan favours authentic material, a point I would normally agree with, but in this particular case I would argue that, given the relative sophistication (and authenticity – see the discussion in Chapter 8 of the unresolved idio-schema) of the activities that the learners have to carry out, an invented (and therefore controlled) dialogue is justifiable. The third component is activities, and the topical-interactional course includes several different types, among which are Prabhu's reasoning gap activities, and the communicative activities of solving problems through social interaction with others, and establishing and maintaining relationships. The fourth and fifth components are learner role – here the learner is an interactor and negotiator who is capable of giving as well as taking – and teacher role (the teacher facilitates the interaction and negotiation).

There is also the question of grading tasks, and here Candlin's scheme is useful in assessing the topical-interactional course. In the dialogues presented, the cognitive load is relatively light, but the communicative stress is high; the interactional tasks appear to be rather particular, though there is more generalizability, perhaps, than at first seems to be the case; and, while the code is not complex, the interpretive density is relatively high. This supports the view that it is at least defensible to use invented dialogues initially, though at a later stage authentic dialogues would seem to be essential. It also indicates that a task like the unresolved idio-schema, which almost certainly imposes a heavier cognitive load than the four dialogues, is a more difficult task than the interactional exercises discussed in Chapter 7. Finally tasks need to be sequenced, and the topical-interactional course uses two of the sequencing methods mentioned by Nunan – experiential content (the topics), and problem situations (the interaction, which in some respects is closer to Di Pietro's strategic interaction than Scarcella's sociodrama).

9.2.3 Process in language teaching

In as much as tasks focus on meaning rather than form, and on methodology rather than discrete learning outcomes, they can clearly be said to be process-oriented. But is the same true of the topical-interactional course? At first glance, the topical-interactional course is process-based only up to a point – for it appears that the topical exercises are overtly directed towards discrete learning outcomes (e.g. grammatical structures), and even the interactional activities are built around apparently discrete linguistic or extra-linguistic phenomena such as thematic systems, role relationships and interaction sequences. But I would argue that appearances here are deceptive. The topical exercises *do* concentrate on grammatical structures and functions (speech acts), but it is my contention (see Chapter 8) that these structures and functions are manifestations of thematic systems which shape/are shaped by the world view of our society at a given moment, knowledge of which is essential to learners of English who need to be socialized into our language and culture. The interactional activities *do* place considerable emphasis on certain discrete linguistic and extra-linguistic forms of behaviour, but only in the belief that they cast light on the process of using a language. Thus the interactional exercises highlight the process of using a language rather than the process of learning a language, though methodology obviously plays an important part in, for example, the problem-solving activities. In short, the topical-interactional course in its way meets the two criteria of a process-oriented course mentioned above: it focuses on meaning rather than form – with the proviso that meaning here is not simply semantic, but rather sociosemantic, cultural – and it focuses not only on the process of learning a language (methodology) but also, crucially, on the process of using a language.

9.3 CONCLUSION

The conclusions I can draw from the discussion in Chapter 9 also form the conclusion to the present work. For I launched this work by claiming that linguistics still has a role to play in communicative syllabus design, and the previous discussion has, if only indirectly, borne out the claim. And when I make this assertion I am not thinking merely of the discussion of Cook's discourse model, where linguistics necessarily has a part to play, but of our explorations of the task-based syllabus as outlined by Nunan. As a result of these explorations, it becomes necessary to determine the extent to which the topical-interactional course focuses on meaning rather than form, and on methodology rather than on discrete learning outcomes. With regard to the balance struck between meaning and form, I submitted that although the topical exercises appear to concentrate on form, they are in fact directed towards sociosemantic patterns that reflect the norms of a particular social group at a particular point in time. As for the concern with methodology rather than discrete learning outcomes, I argued that, in spite of a real concern with methodology, the topical-interactional course does place great emphasis on discrete learning outcomes, but only because an understanding of these 'discrete' learning outcomes – I have used the scare-marks to remind the reader that in reality they usually come in clusters or constellations, and are therefore about as 'discrete' as the element oxygen in the compound water (H_2O) – is, in my view essential to the process of using language.

But it is possible to go a step further. If understanding of so-called discrete learning outcomes such as thematic systems, social relationships and interaction sequences is indeed essential to the process of using language, then it may well form part of the process of learning language. If such were the case, then linguistics would be able to make a contribution to methodology, and to breach the wall the separates the (linguistic) syllabus from (pedagogical) methodology. But in a process linguistics such an outcome should not be surprising.

Bibliography

Abbs, B., and Freebairn, I. (1977), *Starting Strategies,* London, Longman.

____ (1979), *Building Strategies,* London, Longman.

Allen (1984), 'General-purpose language teaching: a variable focus approach', in Brumfit (1984')

Austin, J. L. (1962), *How to do things with words,* Oxford, Clarendon Press.

____ (1979), 'Three ways of spilling ink', in *Philosophical Papers,* London, Oxford University Press.

Bell, J. (1985), *Variety,* Cambridge, Cambridge University Press.

Benson, J. D., and Greaves, W. S. (eds) (1985), *Systemic Perspectives on Discourse,* Norwood, N.J., Ablex.

Birdwhistell, R. L. (1970), *Kinesics and Context,* Philadelphia, Pa., University of Pennsylvania Press.

Breen, M., and Candlin, C. (1980), 'The essentials of a communicative curriculum in language teaching', *Applied Linguistics* 1.2, 89–112.

Brown, G., and Yule, G. (1983), *Discourse Analyusis,* Cambridge, Cambridge Univeristy Press.

Brumfit, C. (1984a), *Communicative Methodology in Language Teaching,* Cambridge, Cambridge, Cambridge University Press.

____ (1984b), 'Function and structure of a State school syllabus for learners of foreign or second languages with heterogeneous needs', in Brumfit (1984c).

____ (ed) (1984c), *General English Syllabus Design,* Oxford, Pergamon.

Candlin, C. (1984), 'Syllabus design as a critical process', in Brumfit (1984c).

Candlin, C., and Murphy, D. (eds) (1987), *Language Learning Tasks,* Englewood Cliffs, N.J., Prentice-Hall.

Chomsky, N. A. (1957), *Syntactic Structures,* The Hague, Mouton.

____ (1965), *Aspects of the Theory of Syntax,* Cambridge, Mass., MIT Press.

Christie, F. (ed.) (1986), *Language and the Social Construction of Experience,* Geelong, Vic., Deakin University.

Clark, R., and McDonough, J. (1982), *Imaginary Crimes,* Oxford, Pergamon.

Cook, G. (1989), *Discourse,* London, Oxford University Press.

Cook, V. J. (1985), 'Language functions, Social factors, and second language learning and teaching', *IRAL* 23.3, 177–98.

Coulthard, M., and Montgomery, M. (eds) (1981), *Studies in Discourse Analysis,* London, Routledge.

Davies, A. (1983), *Report on a Visit to South India, February 1983: Evaluation and the Bangalore/Madras Communicational Teaching Project,* London, British Council.

Derrida, J. (1976), *Of Grammatology,* trans. Gayatri Chakravorty Spivak, Baltimore, Md., Johns Hopkins University Press.

____ (1977), 'Limited Inc abc . . . ', trans. Sam Weber, *Glyph* 2, 162–254

____ (1981), *Positions,* trans. Alan Bass, Chicago, Ill., University of Chicago Press.

____ (1982), *Margins of Philosophy,* trans. Alan Bass, Brighton, Harvester Press.

Fawcett, R. P. (1980), *Cognitive Linguistics and Social Interaction: towards an Integrated Model of a Systemic Functional Grammar and other Components of a Communicating Mind,*

Heidelberg, Julius Groos/Exeter, University of Exeter.

____ (1986), 'Children are choosers: a socio-cognitive framework, using systemic linguistics, for thinking about language in education', in Christie (1986).

Fawcett, R. P., van der Mije, A., and van Wissen, C. (1988), 'Towards a systemic flow chart model for local discourse structure', in Fawcett and Young (1988).

Fawcett, R. P., and Young, D. J. (eds) (1988), *New Developments in Systemic Linguistics* 2, *Theory and Application,* London, Pinter.

Fillmore, C. J. (1968), 'The case for case', in Bach, E., and Harms, R. T. (eds), *Universals in Linguistic Theory,* New York, Holt Rinehart & Winston.

____ (1971), 'Types of lexical information', in Steinberg, D. D., and Jakobovitz, L. A. (eds), *Semantics,* Cambridge, Cambridge University Press.

Firth, J. R. (1957), *Papers in Linguistics, 1934–1951,* London, Oxford University Press.

Foucault, M. (1972), *The Archaeology of Knowledge,* London, Tavistock.

Hall, E. T. (1966), *The Hidden Dimension,* New York, Doubleday.

Halliday, M. A. K. (1966), 'Some notes on deep grammar', *Journal of Linguistics* 2.1, 57–67; also in Kress (1976).

____ (1967–8), 'Notes on transitivity and theme in English' (Parts 1–3), *Journal of Linguistics* 3.1, 37–81; 3.2, 199–244; 4.2 179–215.

____ (1970), 'Functional diversity in language, as seen from a consideration of modality and mood in English', *Foundations of Language* 6.3, 322–61; extract in Kress (1976).

____ (1972), 'Sociological aspects of semantic change', in *Proceedings of the 11th International Congress of Linguists,* Bologna, Società Editrice Il Mulino; also in Halliday (1978).

____ (1973), *Explorations in the Functions of Language,* London, Edward Arnold.

____ (1978), *Language as Social Semiotic,* London, Edward Arnold.

____ (1984), 'Language as code and language as behaviour', in Fawcett, R. P., Halliday, M. A. K., Lamb, S. M., and Makkai, A. (eds), *The Semiotics of Culture and Language* 1, London, Pinter.

____ (1985), *An Introduction to Functional Grammar,* London, Edward Arnold.

Halliday, M. A. K., and Hasan, R. (1976), *Cohesion in English,* London, Longman.

____ (1985), *Language, Context and Text,* Geelong, Vic., Deakin University.

Halliday, M. A. K. McIntosh, A., and Strevens, P. (1964), *The Linguistic Sciences and Language Teaching,* London, Longman.

Hymes, D. (1972a), 'Models of the interaction of language and social life', in Gumperz, J. J., and Hymes, D. (eds), *Directions in Sociolinguistics,* New York, Holt Rinehart & Winston.

____ (1972b), 'On communicative competence', in Pride, J. B., and Holmes, J. (eds), *Sociolinguistics,* Harmondsworth, Penguin.

Kress, G. R. (ed.) (1976), *Halliday: System and Function in Language,* London, Oxford University Press.

Labov, W. (1972), 'The transformation of experience in narrative syntax', in *Language in the Inner City,* Philadelphia, Pa., University of Pennsylvania Press.

Lemke, J. L. (1983), 'Thematic analysis: systems, structures, and strategies', *Semiotic Inquiry* 3.2, 159–87.

____ (1985a), 'Ideology, intertextuality and the notion of register', in Benson and Greaves (1985).

____ (1985b), 'Textual Politics: Heteroglossia, Discourse Analysis and Social Dynamics', unpublished paper given at the International Summer Institute for Structuralist and Semiotic Studies, Bloomington, Ind., University of Indiana.

Levinson, S. C. (1983), *Pragmatics,* Cambridge, Cambridge University Press.

Littlewood, W. (1981), *Communicative Language Teaching,* Cambridge, Cambridge University Press.

Malinowski, B. (1923), 'The problem of meaning in primitive languages', in Ogden, C. K., and Richards, I. A., *The Meaning of Meaning,* London, Kegan Paul.

Martin, J. R. (1984), 'Lexical Cohesion, Field and Genre: Parcelling Experience and Discourse Goals', paper presented at the second Rice Symposium in Linguistics and Semiotics.

Martin, J. R. (1985), 'Process and text: two aspects of human semiosis', in Benson and Greaves (1985).

Matthews, A., and Read, C. (1982), *Themes,* London, Collins.

Metzing, D. (ed.) (1979), *Frame Conceptions and Text Understanding,* Berlin and New York, Walter de Gruyter.

Munby, J. (1978), *Communicative Syllabus Design,* Cambridge, Cambridge University Press.

Nunan, D. (1988a), *The Learner-centred Curriculum,* Cambridge, Cambridge University Press.

—— (1988b), *Syllabus Design,* Oxford, Oxford University Press.

—— (1989), *Designing Tasks for the Communicative Classroom,* Cambridge, Cambridge University Press.

Pennycook, A. (1985), 'Actions speak louder than words: paralanguage, communication and education', *TESOL Quarterly* 19.2, 259–282.

Searle, J. R. (1969), *Speech Acts,* Cambridge, Cambridge University Press.

—— (1977), 'Reiterating the differences: a reply to Derrida', *Glyph* 1, 198–208.

Sinclair, J. McH., and Coulthard, R. M. (1975), *Towards an Analysis of Discourse,* London, Oxford University Press.

Threadgold, T. (1986), 'Semiotics–ideology–language', in Threadgold, T., Gross, E. A., Kress, G., and Halliday, M. A. K. (eds), *Semiotics, Ideology, Language,* Sydney, N.S.W., Sydney Association for Studies in Society and Culture.

van Ek, J. (1975), *The Threshold Level,* Strasbourg, Council of Europe.

Ventola, E. (1979), 'The structure of casual conversation in English', *Journal of Pragmatics* 3, 267–98.

—— (1984), 'Orientation to social semiotics in foreign language teaching,' *Applied Linguistics* 5.3, 275–86.

Wessels, C. (1987), *Drama,* London, Oxford Univerity Press.

Widdowson, H. G. (1978), *Teaching Language as Communication,* London, Oxford University Press.

—— (1984), 'Educational and pedagogic factors in syllabus design', in Brumfit (1984c).

Wilkins, D. A. (1972), 'Grammatical, situational and notional syllabuses', *Proceeding of the Third International Congress of Applied Linguists, Copenhagen, 1972,* Heidelberg, Julius Gross.

—— (1976), *Notional Syllabuses,* London, Oxford University Press.

Yalden, J. (1984), 'Syllabus design in general education: options for ELT', in Brumfit (1984c).

Index